Rural Development in Central America

Also by Ruerd Ruben

*   SUSTAINABLE AGRICULTURE IN CENTRAL AMERICA (*co-editor with Jan P. de Groot*)
*   AGRARIAN POLICIES IN CENTRAL AMERICA (*co-editor with Wim Pelupessy*)
    MAKING COOPERATIVES WORK

*   *From the same publishers*

Rural Development in Central America

Markets, Livelihoods and Local Governance

Edited by

Ruerd Ruben
Senior Lecturer in Development Economics
Wageningen Agricultural University
Netherlands

and

Johan Bastiaensen
Researcher
Centre for Development Studies at UFSIA
University of Antwerp
Belgium

First published in Great Britain 2000 by
MACMILLAN PRESS LTD
Houndmills, Basingstoke, Hampshire RG21 6XS and London
Companies and representatives throughout the world

A catalogue record for this book is available from the British Library.

ISBN 0–333–73972–8

First published in the United States of America 2000 by
ST. MARTIN'S PRESS, INC.,
Scholarly and Reference Division,
175 Fifth Avenue, New York, N.Y. 10010

ISBN 0–312–22659–4

Library of Congress Cataloging-in-Publication Data
Rural development in Central America : markets, livelihoods and local
governance / edited by Ruerd Ruben, Johan Bastiaensen.
p.   cm.
Includes bibliographical references and index.
ISBN 0–312–22659–4 (cloth)
1. Rural development—Central America.   2. Markets—Central
America.   I. Ruben, Ruerd.   II. Bastiaensen, Johan.
HN125.2.C6R87   1999
307.1'412'09728—dc21   99–33853
                                                                    CIP

This book is printed on paper suitable for recycling and made from fully managed and sustained
forest sources.

10   9   8   7   6   5   4   3   2   1
09   08   07   06   05   04   03   02   01   00

Printed and bound in Great Britain by
Antony Rowe Ltd, Chippenham, Wiltshire

Contents

List of Tables   vii

List of Figures   ix

Notes on the Contributors   x

List of Abbreviations   xii

Source of the Book   xiv

1 Introduction   1
   Ruerd Ruben and Johan Bastiaensen

Part 1   Agrarian Commodity Markets

2 Exchange Relations and Food Security: Maize and
   Markets in Honduras   21
   Hazel Johnson

3 Small-Scale Producers and the Sesame Commodity
   Chains under Structural Adjustment   39
   Ner Artola

4 The Hierarchical Legacy in Coffee Commodity Chains   58
   René Mendoza

Part 2   Land Reform and Land Markets

5 Land Reform and Land Transfers in El Salvador   79
   Hans van Heijningen

6 Property Rights, Missing Markets and Agricultural
   Diversification: Consolidation of Agrarian Reform in
   Masaya, Nicaragua   98
   Ben D'Exelle and Johan Bastiaensen

7 Transformation of Cooperative Organizations: Pathways
   of Change for Agricultural Production Cooperatives
   in León-Chinandega, Nicaragua   115
   Jos Vaessen, Orlando Cortéz and Ruerd Ruben

Part 3 Rural Financial Markets

8   Rural Finance and Poverty Alleviation in
    Central America: Evolution and Challenges   141
    Osvaldo Feinstein

9   Institutional Entrepreneurship for Rural Development:
    the Nitlapán Banking Network in Nicaragua   151
    Johan Bastiaensen

10 Credit and Rural Income: Biases in Credit Supply by
    Semi-Formal Financial Institutions in Nueva Guinea,
    Nicaragua   171
    Arie Sanders, Harry Clemens and Eelco Mol

Part 4 Labour Markets and Technological Change

11 Farmers' Selective Participation in Rural Markets:
    Off-Farm Employment in Honduras   189
    Ruerd Ruben and Marrit van den Berg

12 Seasonal Migration and Peasant Livelihood Strategies:
    Migration of Nicaraguan Smallholders to Costa Rica   210
    Giel Ton

13 Low and High External Input Agriculture in the
    Agrarian Frontier   228
    Michiel Bourgondiën

Index   249

List of Tables

2.1 Land, labour, finance and output characteristics of
28 maize farmers by farm size grouping in two
villages in El Paraiso, 1986–7   28
3.1 Evolution of sesame production in Central America,
1979–93   41
3.2 Volume and share of sesame exports, 1992   44
3.3 Main characteristics of the sesame
commodity chains   47
3.4 Margins in the hulled sesame chains, 1996/7   49
3.5 Evolution of the producer price/fob price gap, 1991–5   50
4.1 Composition of average price of 100 gm of coffee, 1996   60
5.1 Results of the Agrarian Reform Programmes
in El Salvador   87
6.1 Typology of peasant producers: resources, income
composition and investments   107
7.1 Production cooperatives in Region II: resources and
membership, 1989–97   122
7.2 Evolution of cooperative characteristics, 1989–97   124
7.3 Internal organization and the cooperative production
system, 1989   126
7.4 Cooperative behaviour and management regimes, 1997   127
7.5 Individual member characteristics, 1997   129
7.6 Contract choice and member characteristics, 1997   131
8.1 Comparison of views on rural finance and poverty
alleviation in Central America   142
8.2 Evolution of outreach, targeting and sustainability
priorities in rural finance and poverty alleviation
programmes, 1970–90   143
8.3 Numerical illustration of trade-offs between outreach
and targeting (TOBOT) in a typical credit project in
Central America   146
10.1 Average gross household income
composition   178
10.2 Definition of variables and descriptive statistics   179
10.3 OLS estimates of household income function   182
10.4 OLS estimates of basic grains income share   184

11.1   Economic activities of farm household members   199
11.2   Market participation and farm and household
       characteristics   199
11.3   Probability of labour market participation by
       economically active adults   201
11.4   Relationships between wage income and other
       income sources   202
11.5   Income sources and capital intensity of agricultural
       production (all households)   203
11.6   Wage income and capital intensity of agricultural
       production (households with wage income)   204
11.7   Income sources and food security
       (all households)   205
11.8   Income sources and food security
       (households with wage income)   206
12.1   Farm size and land use in the Pire area   214
12.2   Average gross value of production for the major
       subsystems, 1995/6   215
12.3   Expenditure from migratory income, 1994/5   217
12.4   Migration patterns of villages   219
12.5   Factors determining the probability of seasonal
       migration   221
12.6   Net migrant income from work in Costa Rica, 1995   223
13.1   Plot size and tenancy status   235
13.1   Labour requirements   236
13.3   Non-labour input costs   237
13.4   Production costs, productivity and returns to
       factors of production   239
13.5   Regression results of three systems of maize
       production   240
13.6   Factors influencing the choice of chemical,
       ecological or traditional maize production systems
       (multinominal logit analysis)   242

List of Figures

7.1   Three pathways of cooperative change   132
8.1   Increasing leakage as disbursements increase   147
9.1   Actors and procedures of the Nitlapán
      banking network   158
10.1 Agricultural production and the supply and
      demand of credit   175
11.1 Analytical framework for the analysis of
      off-farm income   196
11.2 Farm size and income composition in rural
      Honduras, 1993/4   200
12.1 Migration of women by age category   216
12.2 Migration of men by age category   216

Notes on the Contributors

Ner Artola is an agro-economist and researcher at the Nitlapán research and development institute of the Central American University (UCA) in Managua, Nicaragua.

Johan Bastiaensen is a researcher at the Centre for Development Studies at UFSIA, University of Antwerp, Belgium.

Marrit van den Berg is a PhD candidate at the Department of Economics and Management of Wageningen Agricultural University, The Netherlands.

Michiel Bourgondiën is a research assistant at the Department of Economics and Management of Wageningen Agricultural University, The Netherlands.

Orlando Cortéz is a senior researcher at the School of Agricultural Economics of the National University of Nicaragua.

Harry Clemens is coordinator of the Centre for Rural Development Research of Free University Amsterdam, located in San José, Costa Rica.

Ben D'Exelle is an associate researcher involved in field work at the Nitlapán research and development institute of the Central American University (UCA) in Managua, Nicaragua.

Osvaldo Feinstein until recently worked in the Evaluation Section of the International Fund for Agricultural Development (IFAD) in Rome, and is now with the World Bank, Washington, DC.

Hans van Heijningen has a PhD in social sciences from the Catholic University in Nijmegen and currently works with the X-Y Development Foundation in Amsterdam, The Netherlands.

Hazel Johnson is a lecturer in the Development Policy and Practice Discipline in the Centre for Complexity and Change at the Open University, UK.

René Mendoza is director of the research programme of the Nitlapán research and development institute of the Central American University (UCA) in Managua, Nicaragua.

Eelco Mol is an associate expert with the UN food and Agriculture Organization (FAO) located in Honduras.

Ruerd Ruben is a senior lecturer in Development Economics at the Department of Economics and Management of Wageningen Agricultural University, The Netherlands.

Arie Sanders is a researcher with the Centre for Rural Development Research of Free University Amsterdam, located in San José, Costa Rica.

Giel Ton is a development economist with the COOPIBO programme in Condega, Nicaragua, and research fellow of the TLOD Foundation in Wageningen, The Netherlands.

Jos Vaessen is a research assistant at the Department of Economics and Management of Wageningen Agricultural University, The Netherlands.

List of Abbreviations

ACCP	*Asociación Campesina de Condega* (Nicaragua)
APC	Agrarian Production Cooperative
ASERCCA	Association of European Research on Central America and the Caribbean
BANADES	*Banco Nacional de Desarrollo* (Nicaragua)
BANADESA	*Banco Nacional de Desarrollo Agropecuario* (Honduras)
BCN	*Banco Central Nacional*
CAS	*Cooperativa Agricola Sandinista* (Nicaragua)
CEA	*Centro Experimental del Algodón* (Nicaragua)
CEA	*Comisión Especial Agraria* (El Salvador)
CEI	*Centro de Exportaciones e Importaciones* (Nicaragua)
CENTA	*Centro Nacional de Tecnología Agropecuaria* (El Salvador)
CGAP	Consultative Group to Assist the Poorest
COPAZ	*Comisión Nacional para la Consolidacíon de la Paz* (El Salvador)
DGEC	*Dirección General de Estadísticas y Censos*
ECODEPA	*Empresa Cooperativa de Productores Agropecuarios* (Nicaragua)
ENAL	*Empresa Nacional del Algodón* (Nicaragua)
FAO	Food and Agriculture Organization
FINATA	*Financiera Nacional de Tierras Agrícolas* (El Salvador)
FMLN	*Frente Farabundi Marti de Liberación Nacional* (El Salvador)
FUNDE	*Fundación para el Desarrollo* (El Salvador)
GOES	Government of El Salvador
HEIA	High External Input Agriculture
IFAD	International Fund for Agricultural Development
IHMA	*Instituto Hondureño de Mercadeo Agropecuario* (Honduras)
ILO	International Labour Organization
INA	*Instituto Nacional Agrario* (Honduras)
INRA	*Instituto Nacional de Reforma Agraria* (Nicaragua)
INTA	*Instituto Nacional de Technología Agropecuaria* (Nicaragua)
ISTA	*Instituto Salvadoreño de Transformación Agraria* (El Salvador)
LBF	Local Bank Fund
LEIA	Low External Input Agriculture
MAG	*Ministerio de Agricultura y Ganadería*
MFI	Micro Finance Institution
NGO	Non-governmental Organization

ONUSAL	*Organización de Naciones Unidas Misión para El Salvador*
PNUD	*Programa de las Naciones Unidas para el Desarrollo*
PREALC	*Programa Regional del Empleo para América Latina y el Caribe*
PRODES	*Proyecto de Desarrollo Rural Nueva Guinea* (Nicaragua)
PTT	*Programa de Transferencias de Tierras* (El Salvador)
PTT	*Programa de Titulación de Tierras* (Honduras)
SAP	Structural Adjustment Programme
SECPLAN	*Secretaría de Planificación, Coordinación y Presupuesto* (Honduras)
SRN	*Secretaría de Recursos Naturales* (Honduras)
UNAG	*Unión Nacional de Agricultores y Ganaderos* (Nicaragua)
UNDP	United Nations Development Programme
USAID	United States Agency for International Development

Source of the Book

The chapters that follow are substantially based on papers from the 1997 Annual Conference of the Association for European Research on Central America and the Caribbean (ASERCCA) held in 19–21 September 1997 in Portsmouth, England.

1
Introduction

Ruerd Ruben and Johan Bastiaensen

Rural development has been considered for a long time to be almost synonymous with engagement in market exchange. Most debates on Central America's development strategies have focused their attention on the competitive condition on local, regional and international markets, and the conditions required for improving the 'insertion' of the peasantry into market production. Land reform programmes and integrated rural development projects have been launched to enhance access to basic production factors (that is, land, credit and knowledge), and a wide range of initiatives have been taken to provide technical and financial assistance to local peasant organizations to improve marketing networks (that is, trade and transport, storage and processing).

While operational conditions in rural markets could certainly benefit from substantial improvement, far greater limitations are found at the level of the market structure. Central American peasant production is characterized by an already high level of commercialization (partly as a result of the land reform process), but most factor and commodity markets are strongly segmented and dominated by clientelistic relations. Instead of considering market development as the solution, deficient organization of the 'market' is perceived as a major development problem. Therefore, current analyses of the structure and performance of rural markets focus attention on the causes and consequences of frequently occurring market failures. Where high transaction costs (resulting from a lack of information or insecure property rights) inhibit market exchange, local institutional or contractual arrangements tend to replace market transactions.

The contributions included in this book offer a comprehensive review of current discussion on the role and importance of 'markets' in

1

the Central-American rural development process. The book is divided into four parts, each with three chapters, dealing successively with (i) the performance of agrarian commodity markets; (ii) the structure of rural land markets; (iii) rural financial markets; and (iv) the dynamics of rural labour markets. This chapter presents a general analytical framework for a discussion of the relationship between market (under) development, peasant livelihood strategies, and the emergence of local governance structures. Attention is focused on 'real markets' as the relevant interface for different types of exchange relations. Moreover, different economic, socio-cultural, political and institutional dimensions of 'markets' are highlighted. The historical background of the process of commoditization and recent policies towards market liberalization are discussed, to enable a better understanding of the political and economic conditions that influence the evolution of (market and non-market) exchange relations. Finally, we review the decisive impact of prevailing market and institutional failures on farm household decisions regarding production and consumption behaviour and resource allocation, and discuss implications for their livelihood strategies. Different local initiatives for innovative governance structures are identified that could replace traditional hierarchical relations and permit peasant organizations to take better control of the market.

The Central-American commoditization process

The structure and performance of Central-American markets has to be analyzed from the perspective of the historical evolution of the commoditization process. Before the conquest, the northern part of Central America had a substantial population living in highly organized societies that already maintained complex market and non-market relationships (using cocoa as an exchange medium). During the colonial period, local producers were further forced into market exchange within the framework of the *encomienda* system, which demanded compulsory deliveries of commodities and labour services. The traditional social structure was thus replaced by a new hierarchy that took full control of the peasants' livelihoods.

The integration of the peasantry into the markets in Central America is usually related to the establishment of the agroexport economy (initially based on coffee and banana production, but later expanded towards cotton, sugar cane and beef) in the second half of the eighteenth century, accompanied by so-called liberal reforms that established private property rights and created the conditions for infrastructure development and the modernization of banking facilities and trade networks. The export-led growth model essentially relied on the availability of large amounts of seasonal labour that was mobilized through a mixture of coercion and market forces. Access to land was severely restricted to guarantee the supply of sufficient wage labour, and labour costs were controlled by maintaining the peasantry in a subordinate position. While labour organization remained illegal, the peasants' resistance against repression led to frequent upheavals.

The structural limitations of this outward-orientated pattern of economic growth became evident during the 1930s, when prices on the international markets collapsed, subsequently causing rural wages to be reduced heavily. Growing external debt and high public-sector deficits began to demonstrate the fundamental inconsistencies of the export-led model. Neglect of the domestic economy and over-dependence on external commodity and capital markets that are vulnerable to fluctuations, along with state policies that discriminate against the peasantry, led inevitably to a political and economic crisis. In most countries, land reform attempted to reduce some of the pressure, but market conditions and institutional frameworks changed only marginally.

Structural adjustment programs (SAPs) launched during the 1980s focused attention on the reform of price policies, the elimination of subsidies and the reduction of government expenses. Major emphasis is laid on the liberalization of domestic and external markets and the privatization or decentralization of former state services (for example, credit, commerce and extension). Subsequent evaluations of ongoing SAPs indicate a certain macroeconomic recovery of growth rates, but register limited improvements in welfare distribution.

Far less attention has been paid to the implications of structural adjustment for the dynamics of rural social organization. It is generally understood that 'getting prices right' alone is not enough to ensure agrarian change, as long as market and institutional failures prevent farmers from reaping the benefits. Instead, livelihood strategies show an increasing complexity and heterogeneity, since farm households are engaged in a broad number of simultaneous exchange relations on different 'markets', and maintain institutional linkages with several agents. We therefore provide a detailed analysis of the understanding of markets by the peasantry and the important effects of these different exchange relationships on the peasants' livelihood strategies.

Real markets and livelihoods

The general perspective underlying many of the ideas developed in this book is that today's processes of market liberalization and political democratization in Central America and their impact on rural society need to be analyzed from their interaction with the inherited institutional environment. The development of both a market society and a democratic–civic state should not be thought to be just a matter of liberalization policies and constitutional design, but should be understood as a complex process of introducing and transplanting innovative forms of social interaction in not necessarily receptive socio-cultural soils. The main focus in this volume will therefore be on the institutional conditioners of 'real markets': that is, the concrete configurations of both market and non-market exchange forms that constantly shape and reshape people's opportunities and constraints. As will be seen from the various contributions to this volume, people's livelihoods depend critically on the precise nature of these evolving 'real markets'.

Understanding 'markets' as embedded into complex real-world exchange networks opens the way to analyzing apparently contradictory or even 'perverse' responses to the liberalization processes imposed under present-day outward-orientated rural development strategy. It also draws attention to the need for the design and social appropriation of adequate institutional frameworks, to enable more effective exchange and collective action. Additionally, it sheds critical light on all-too-optimistic expectations about across-the-board generic rural development policies. The focus on the complex, real-world exchange networks adds an important new dimension to our understanding of rural differentiation. Not only is the Central-American rural space characterized by a considerable amount of agroecological and infrastructural diversity, but also its institutional and socio-cultural conditions differ greatly from one region to another, and even from one social group to another. The existence or non-existence of markets, the degree of market imperfection, and the relative mix of market and non-market exchange mechanisms, as well as the nature of these mechanisms, vary considerably across geographical regions and household types. Evidently, the same can also be said about the regions' and households' articulation to the diverse expressions of the Central-American states.

We are thus in the presence of region-specific and household-specific market as well as government failures determined by very different and unequal solutions to a diversity of transaction problems. One evident and important constraint on the development of more effectively functioning markets is, of course, the poorly developed physical infrastructure in many regions of rural Central America; much remains to be done to improve rural roads and other communications networks. A similar argument applies to the deficient social infrastructure for education, health and sanitation, which are indispensable for the creation and maintenance of human capital resources. Often markets are very shallow, or simply do not exist, because of prohibitively high transaction costs associated with costly information search as well as the insecurity and practical difficulties of contract enforcement in the rule-deficient rural space. Traditionally, many of these problems have been solved by recurring to non-market exchange mechanisms related to the vertical social governance structures of rural society (such as sharecropping). Interlocked exchange patterns embedded in patron–client dependency relationships very often substitute for otherwise missing markets, and in this way constitute a second-best solution to the problems of exchange and cooperation. However, innovative, modern non-market governance structures, such as the agricultural cooperative, can also find their rationale in their potential savings on overall transaction costs as compared to the market solution of exchange in various factor and product markets. One might even wonder whether, in some cases, the efficiency loss associated with state intervention in exchange would not be preferable to the shallowness of private markets confronted with insurmountable transaction costs. A major challenge in the future development of the region's rural economy will therefore also be the improvement of the rural institutional environment so as to allow for substantial reductions in transaction costs that can make hitherto impossible market transactions viable. Policies and mechanisms to deepen information flows and a substantial improvement in the state's ability to support easier contract enforcement among private parties as well as to play its critical role as the neutral third-party enforcer are important dimensions of this institutional development. Equally important, however, might also be the 'cultural and moral rearticulation' of local societies, especially in those regions hard hit by war and long-lasting social instability.

The latter discussion brings us to considering the role of the state. First of all, both the possibilities and the constraints of the state, in its various expressions, as a development actor, should be reflected upon seriously. There is evidently a social and cultural realm outside the reach of state intervention that might, however, have a decisive impact on development opportunities. In particular, there is the question of whether the state, or any other development agency for that matter, has a real capacity to change inherited institutional environments in the relatively short time periods in which policy debates usually count. The pessimism of Robert Putnam, for whom institutional change has to be counted in decades rather than years, should preserve us from thinking too lightly about the limits of development action. A second tricky problem when considering the role of the Central-American state as a development actor is, of course, its own embeddedness in the inherited authoritarian, clientelistic culture. Far from being a neutral third-party enforcer or an independent actor on behalf of the common good, the state typically serves the particular short-term interests of the restricted social groups represented by the party that happens to be in power. Principles and practices of state action are therefore hardly ever supportive of a more civic, tolerant and nation-building culture. In countries such as Nicaragua it proves impossible even to maintain the bulk of government employees after a shift in government, since the newly-arriving party apparently has to allocate its own clientele to the scarce government jobs. The instalment of regular democratic elections in the Central-American region has not yet engendered much of the kind of nationwide social contracts that should provide the basis for a stable framework of minimally consensuated national structures and policies. In a sense, one has the impression that electoral struggle has become the continuation of war by other, more peaceful, means, and that one of the few pieces of national consensus is precisely about the prohibitive costs of continuing the political struggle by military means. Although these themes about the limitations of the Central-American state as a development policy actor are not dealt with explicitly in the contributions to this volume, it is clear that at least part of the improvement in development policies will depend critically upon a gradual modernization of the state, allowing it to assume its envisaged role effectively. Only in this way might a dynamic synergy between the actions of the state, the entrepreneurial activities in more developed markets and the collective voluntary action of the civil society be created.

Commodity markets

The first section of this book offers three contributions on the functioning and perspectives of commodity markets. Hazel Johnson starts with an analysis of the nature of maize production and maize markets in Honduras and its relationship to the food security of vulnerable sectors of rural society. The theoretical part argues for an integral institutional approach that takes into account the variety of real-world market and non-market exchange mechanisms that determine the concrete conditions of production and access to food. Policy measures, like those under the present-day market liberalization paradigm, can only be evaluated correctly when their effects on the functioning of both markets and non-market exchange mechanisms are studied. Therefore, a plea is made for an actor-orientated approach to institutional change in which the institutional framework is not treated as a given, but as the subject and the result of ongoing social interaction and struggle. Based on data from the Jamastran Valley in the department of El Paraiso, Honduras, a number of issues concerning the relationship between food security and the conditions of maize production and exchange in this region are analyzed. Key problems for the small producers are to secure access to land, the means to resource production, and opportunities to exchange production. Almost always a solution to these problems was found in establishing complex market and non-market relationships, at the minimum comprising a land–labour exchange arrangement with a commercial farmer or landowner. In this way, interlocked transactions substitute for the lack of access to resources and the absence of functioning markets. The chapter puts particular stress on the mixed nature of these exchange configurations. While reference is made to market values, at the same time personal loyalties and social ties come into play, along with their norms and obligations. Together these make up the real-world institutional framework in which maize-related transactions take place. As has already been indicated above, policy measures should be evaluated with respect to their impact on this entire complex of rights and obligations.

In the next chapter, Ner Artola uses the methodology of commodity chain analysis to inquire into the recent evolution of sesame production and trade in Nicaragua. After a brief overview of world sesame markets and the place of Central America and Nicaragua within those markets, an analysis of the impact of recent liberalization policies in Nicaragua is undertaken. An initial component of these policies was the abolition of the state monopoly of sesame procurement, processing and trade, which resulted in the emergence of a limited number of private processors and traders. Another important point was the implementation of national export promotion policies aimed directly at supporting the sesame crop. After this general analysis of liberalization policies, a detailed comparative analysis of the four types of commodity chain presently in use in Nicaragua is undertaken. The types identified are chains governed by (i) processing and trading cooperatives; (ii) decentralized private Nicaraguan traders; (iii) the Guatemalan processing industry and traders; and (iv) Nicaraguan processing plants. Besides providing detailed information about the similarities and differences in the functioning and relative efficiency for producers, processors and traders of the chains, this analysis also sheds light on the reasons for the apparent contradiction that, despite export promotion policies and price premiums, farm-gate prices for sesame have gone down. Structural rigidities as well as changing relative power balances between producers and traders, especially because of the reduction in formal credit supply, go a long way towards explaining this crucial problem. Artola identifies a need as well as many possibilities to improve the level of vertical articulation between the different actors in the chains. He finds that the chains that are best articulated to the world market are the least articulated downwards, and vice versa. Bridging the gap more effectively between the better processor-traders and the producers would enable Nicaragua to reap more benefits from sesame production and achieve greater success in its efforts to promote the crop.

The last contribution on commodity markets refers to coffee. René Mendoza presents an analysis of three coffee commodity chains: a traditional commercial; an alternative 'fair trade'; and an alternative 'fair trade'–biological chain. The inquiry starts with a diagnosis of the structure of value added in the three chains. It is found that an ever-larger share of this value added is generated in the processing and trading stage in the coffee-consuming countries, leaving the smaller coffee producer in particular with only a small part of the final price. Comparing the data of the commercial chain with the alternatives, the latter show a similar, or even worse, structure of value added in terms of what is left for the producing countries and the producers. One of the more striking results is that the clear advantage of the higher absolute fob prices in the 'fair trade' chain is thereby almost completely lost at the farm-gate level. The 'fair trade'–biological chain performs strikingly better in this respect. In search for possibilities of improvement, Mendoza then reflects on the reasons for the poor functioning of the coffee chains. These are related to the prevalence of a 'culture of impotence' that is a consequence of the general institutional environment of rural Nicaragua with its legacy of hierarchical, patron–client dependency relationships and relatively disintegrated local social networks. This culture influences the functioning of the coffee chains by engendering disfunctioning hierarchical organizational forms with self-reinforcing vicious circles of 'mutual distrust–abuse–more mutual distrust'. These circles generate a negative dynamic that does not allow the organizations to create or seize new and better opportunities in terms of output, quality, market niches and so on. This particularly affects the smaller coffee producers, but has a clear overall negative impact. Finally, this contribution reflects on ways to break out of the organizational stalemate in which the coffee commodity chains find themselves. Based on the more positive aspects and results of the 'fair trade'–biological chain a proposal is developed for an alternative organizational design of a commercial chain and ways to develop it. In this design, several countervailing actors participate to secure information flows and mutual control so as to generate and sustain a positive dynamic of cooperation, compliance and trust which will provide the basis on which to create new opportunities and reap more benefits.

Land markets

The second section of the book deals with the dynamics of local land markets after the process of land reform. Since land reforms can be characterized by their 'incomplete' nature, producers who were entitled to land still face major constraints regarding their access to inputs and financial markets, and are subject to less favourable conditions on local commodity markets. Therefore, far fewer changes occurred in land-use patterns and production technologies, especially when the absence of property rights inhibited investment in farms. On the other hand, land reform and subsequent land titling proved to be an important vehicle for reinforcing engagement in market exchange. Meanwhile, agricultural production cooperatives established during land reforms experienced major transformations with respect to their internal organization. While collective production almost disappeared, cooperative members opt for alternative risk-diversification strategies through multiple mechanisms, such as crop diversification and off-farm employment, as well as contractual agreements for joint activities in the sphere of input purchase and marketing.

Hans van Heijningen starts with an analysis of the programme for land transfers in El Salvador that was implemented within the framework of the Peace Treaties. Given the high population density and the absence of an agrarian frontier, available margins for the development of peasant agriculture depend fundamentally on land redistribution. Land reforms in the 1980s contributed to the confiscation (with compensation) of enterprises larger than 500 hectares and their redistribution towards agrarian production cooperatives and the titling of small leasehold plots to individual farmers. The results of these reforms were rather limited in terms of welfare and income distribution, however, since most land-reform beneficiaries were not able to improve land productivity. The small size and low quality of most of the parcels and the restricted access to rural finance inhibit progress in the fields of input intensification and crop diversification. Further reforms are therefore required, and the new land transfer (PTT) programme had to address simultaneously the issues of improving access to land and creating better agrarian production conditions. Innovative aspects of the land transfer programme refer to the market-assisted procedures for the purchase of land. A semi-autonomous land bank was established, which was put in charge of the negotiation over properties and their subsequent assignment to beneficiaries. Declining agricultural prices and limited profitability of agricultural production encouraged traditional landowners to sell their land. However, the PTT programme neglected to attend to the provision of complementary policies regarding access to credit, education and technical training, and membership organization. Therefore, similar problems occurred as were manifest in earlier land reform programmes: land use is strongly concentrated in low-value food crops, reliance on yield-increasing inputs is restricted, and marketing takes place in highly monopolized outlets. Sadly, land market reforms coincided with a structural adjustment programme that marked the disappearance of the Salvadorian state from rural life. Even more serious constraints appear, because political interest in rural development has declined severely, and agriculture is no longer considered to be a fundamental economic sector. Within such an 'exclusive' rural development framework, reliance on markets for the redistribution of land rights is clearly an insufficient measure.

The post-agrarian reform situation in the densely populated department of Masaya, Nicaragua is analyzed by Ben D'Exelle and Johan Bastiaensen. The movement of peasants has been particularly important in this region following a more drastic land redistribution towards landless families during the former Sandinista government. However, access to land remained conditional to membership of cooperative organizations, and the monoculture pattern of land use that relied on the high use of external inputs was generally maintained. But with the introduction of market reforms and the reduction of price and credit subsidies, this production structure proved to be no longer viable. The chapter identifies a number of strategies that land-reform beneficiaries followed as a response to these market reforms. Parcellation of the cooperative and registration of individual land titles are considered to be 'reforms from below' that legitimize ownership rights and offer protection against possible counter-reforms. Major problems arise, however, when farmers intend to consolidate the productive potential of their holdings. Investments in fencing, housing, inputs (seed, fertilizers) and livestock are required for the integration of viable family farms. Diversification of household (farm and non-farm) activities, intensification of arable production, establishment of perennial crops, and the purchase of livestock are generally considered to be major components of this consolidation strategy. Three different cases of farm households are compared, with various levels of investment and diversification of activities with respect to their income potential. It is concluded that the transition towards viable family farms depends critically on access to investment sources.

Different pathways for the transformation of cooperative organizations are analyzed by Jos Vaessen, Orlando Cortéz and Ruerd Ruben in their contribution on the adjustment in agricultural production cooperatives (APCs) in the departments of León and Chinandega in Nicaragua. The decollectivization process is presented as a shift in contract choice that can be understood as a response to changes taking place in the surrounding market and institutional environment. Different patterns of adjustment in cooperative organization are noted, and this diversity can be related to individual characteristics of (former) cooperative members, the types of services provided to members, and the availability of productive resources. The empirical analysis is based on a unique data set that permits the comparison of cooperative contracts over an eight-year period. Three distinct pathways of cooperative change are identified: (i) cooperative enterprises that retain some collective production combined with individual allotment of land; (ii) fully parcelled enterprises that provide productive services to their members (that is, transformation from production to service cooperative); and (iii) complete disintegration and full distribution of collective assets. The first strategy is mainly followed by cooperative enterprises specialized in large-scale production of commercial crops, using machinery and maintaining strict internal controls on labour organization. Transition towards a service cooperative occurs when economies of scope are registered with respect to the purchase of inputs and the use of pastures. Structural adjustment policies have resulted in substantial internal price changes that make basic grains and livestock production relatively more attractive. They also result in the raising of interest costs,

which brings a shift towards more labour-intensive production processes. Both tendencies favour more individualized production, but
constraints in access to markets and information are still considered to
be important reasons for maintaining some cooperative relationships
to encourage risk diversification.

Rural financial markets

The contributions in the third section deal with the issue of capital
markets in the liberalizing context of Central America. Osvaldo
Feinstein places the present-day 'new orthodoxy' in the historical context of changing paradigms on rural finances and poverty alleviation.
This historical overview shows that Central America followed the
world-wide shift of strategy from state-led, unsustainable agricultural
development banking towards an option for more diversified, private
and sustainable rural finances. The author, however, also highlights a
number of challenges to the new approach, indicating that the 'critique
was effective in showing what did not make sense', but was less clear as
to the alternatives. A lot certainly remains to be done in terms of comparison and systematization of experiences. Important topics for further
research and reflection are methodologies to reduce transaction costs,
guidelines for supportive government intervention, and alternative collateral mechanisms. Feinstein also analyzes project-level dynamics concerning the trade-off between targeting and outreach, wherein the
pressure to disburse funds leads to increasing leakage of credit funds
towards non-targeted groups at the end of project cycles. These experiences engender further challenges: the need to develop viable methodologies of targeting, and of estimating realistically credit demand. It is
also noted that the direct role of credit in poverty alleviation is often
overdimensioned, but at the same time evaluations operate with too
narrow a set of indicators. Besides financial indicators, such as disbursements and recovery rates, the income indicator should be
complemented by alternative indicators referring, among others, to the
process of 'social intermediation'. These should be able to capture
social capital formation effects that continue to exist and contribute to
the development of beneficiaries, often long after the termination of
the initial credit project.

The possibility of such social capital effects of financial institution-
building (as well as the influence of the existing endowment in such
capital) on the difficulty of creating a viable rural finance system are
dealt with more in detail in the contribution by Johan Bastiaensen.

First, a number of severe institutional deficiencies are identified which profoundly hamper the realization of a dynamic post-agrarian reform development path in the rural areas of Nicaragua. Following decades of institutional shocks caused by revolution, war and economic regress, much of rural society finds itself in a kind of institutional vacuum between the disintegrated traditional vertical governance structures connected to the previous unequal land property structure and the not-yet-existing horizontal structures that should accommodate the modern agrarian structure. The creation of innovative rural financial systems is then analyzed within the perspective of these institutional inheritances and challenges. First, an historical sketch of rural finance in recent decades indicates the effect of institutional change on finance: from a configuration governed by local patrons over a massive, unsustainable and politicized subsidy system towards present-day liberalization causing the virtual disappearance of formal rural banking that has left large sectors of rural society underfinanced. The experience of Nitlapán with the creation of an innovative rural financial system is discussed in depth and related to the inherited institutional context in which it had to operate. Among other things, attention is directed to the mechanisms which comprise the organizational framework that generates high levels of self-enforcement and reduces transaction costs of information and external enforcement. Nitlapán's experiences, which started with an option for local self-managed banks, also highlight the need for a strong top-down intervention to impose clear and transparent 'rules of the game' that are crucial to guaranteeing sustainability of, and access to, the system. It is argued that this methodology is not only necessary to enable viable financial business to be done, but might also represent an important change in the local institutional environment precisely by creating a neutral and rule-bound organizational realm that is not governed by inherited patron–client relationships.

The last contribution to the section on capital markets is an analysis of credit demand and supply in the municipality of Nueva Guinea. This vast municipality is located in the older agricultural frontier zone of the interior of Nicaragua. After the end of the war against anti-Sandinista guerilla movements in 1990, the region regained its momentum as a colonization area with a high net immigration from other regions. Many production systems are therefore of relatively recent origin, with a prominent share being allocated to staple food products. With accumulation, on the other hand, farmers try rapidly to develop more profitable cattle-raising activities because of its capacity to utilize the abundantly available land with relatively little labour. In this context, Arie Sanders, Harry Clemens and Eelco Mol analyze the interaction between the demand for credit from the various sectors of this local economy and the supply of credit by a relatively abundant number of mainly semi-formal credit institutions. The basis of their analysis is a conceptual model that identifies various household characteristics determining credit demand, such as farm size; the perceived profitability of credit financed activities versus the cost of credit; risk aversion; and the degree of liquidity and savings capacity of the household. The model allows us to distinguish between the total 'demand' for financing, including self-financing, and the borrowing demand that only exists when self-financing capacity falls short of financial needs. Producers are credit-constrained only when supply does not meet their borrowing needs. Based on analysis of an estimated income function for the municipality, it is then concluded that poor, staple grain farmers use substantially more credit than the richer farmers with more cattle-raising activities. Following the model, this can partially be explained by the higher demand among poorer producers, since they face stronger peaks in working capital needs than do the cattle systems, they have less regular income flows, and evidently witness of a lower savings capacity. Since many of the semi-formal financial systems assume at least a part of the high risk of staple production, risk aversion does not deter credit use, but rather reinforces it. However, demand explains only part of the story; supply-side factors also evidently come into play. The semi-formal credit systems clearly target their interventions on the poorer sections, and on staple food producers in particular. The data show a strong correlation between the share of food in total production and the use of credit. At the same time, it is clear that the richer cattle farmers, with little need for short-term credit, show a substantial demand for longer-term investment capital for which no supply exists.

Rural labour markets

In the final section of the book, attention is focused on the functioning of rural labour markets and the different employment possibilities that are available within farm households, through temporary engagement in wage labour or by relying on seasonal migration. Since structural adjustment policies occasion a general rise in interest rates and input costs, agrarian production systems tend to become more labour-intensive. Therefore, internal demands for labour increase, especially when farmers shift towards low-external input agriculture that relies on additional labour for manual land preparation, weeding and crop maintenance activities. Another strategy to maintain the food security of households and to guarantee access to cash resources for the purchase of yield-improving inputs can be found through engagement in the labour market. Local off-farm employment and seasonal migration prove to be important strategies to sustain the livelihoods of farmers living in dryland areas and marginal regions.

The increasing importance of farmers' engagement in off-farm employment is highlighted by Ruerd Ruben and Marrit van den Berg for the rural areas of Honduras. Their contribution is based on an analytical framework that considers selective market failures on land and capital markets. Therefore, income from non-farm employment is required to substitute for credit restrictions. Data from the National Income and Consumption Survey show that almost 70 per cent of farm household members are wholly or partially engaged in wage labour or self-employed non-agricultural activities. This is especially the case for smaller farms, located in marginal agroecological regions, and with a less commercially-orientated production system. Moreover, at the individual level, gender and education strongly influence labour market participation. Further empirical analysis confirm the inverse relationship between wage income and credit use. Households with more wage income generally maintain a significantly lower farm income and rely less on credit. Secondary effects of non-farm income sources on farm production and on household consumptive expenditure could be analyzed with regression techniques. It is shown that access to non-farm income is an important source for the purchase of yield-increasing inputs, and that this aspect provides twice as much as the contribution from credit sources. Moreover, households with non-farm income are also able to maintain a higher level of food security. The latter effect is substantially higher when compared to the contribution from remittances, since these resources are used mainly for the purchase of durable household assets. It may be concluded, therefore, that access to wage labour and non-agricultural activities are important elements for rural livelihood strategies that, far from disintegrating the family farm, could substantially contribute to the consolidation of viable farming units under conditions of market failure in land and capital markets.

A similar analysis of the causes and implications of seasonal migration and the contribution of migratory income to peasants' livelihood strategies is presented by Giel Ton for the case of smallholders living in Condega village, in the semi-arid northern part of Nicaragua, who migrate towards Costa Rica. Migration is motivated by the absence of local employment opportunities during the dry season, and the increasing costs of living in Nicaragua. It is essentially a seasonal phenomenon that is undertaken to supplement their family income, and most migrants have no intention of staying in Costa Rica. Most migrants are young, male members of rural families dedicated to rainfed basic grains production and possessing few animals. They become engaged in wage labour activities on sugar estates and banana plantations in Costa Rica. Income from migration represents about 34 per cent of family income. The extra income is mainly used for the purchase of food, clothing and agricultural inputs. The analysis of the migration process as presented in Ton's contribution clearly demonstrates the supplementary role of migratory income on farmers' livelihoods, as well as the importance of access to information about employment opportunities in neighbouring Costa Rica. Migration proved to be a highly organized process, where labour contractors make all the arrangements for the 'delivery' of migrants on a fixed day and to a defined spot.

   The final contribution directs its attention to the use of labour within farm households and compares the relative efficiency of low and high-external input agricultural systems in the agrarian frontier area of Nueva Guinea, Nicaragua. Michiel Bourgondiën reviews the viability of production systems based on velvet beans as a cover crop that are promoted in this colonization zone as a substitute for chemical fertilizers. The latter have become extremely expensive, and therefore farmers rely on crop rotation or inter-cropping practices with velvet beans to improve the balance of the soil's organic matter. From a survey of 116 plots, farmers using inorganic fertilizers, organic methods and traditional fallow systems to restore soils are compared with respect to their land use, labour requirements and factor productivity. Labour use on ecological plots is on average 28 per cent higher than on chemical plots, while input costs are about 45 per cent higher when chemical methods are used. Velvet beans are used mainly on small plots, while farmers with larger plots are still able to rely on fallow systems. Net returns are, however, not significantly different among the three systems. It can therefore be concluded, that farmers tend to select the most appropriate production technology for their farms, taking into account their resource endowments and market opportunities.

Further perspectives

The different contributions included in this book offer clear illustrations of the wide array of market and institutional failures that peasant households have to face in the Central-American countryside. While structural adjustment programmes only modified relative prices, to a certain extent, there has been a significant change in rural social relations and derived livelihood strategies. Growing interest in local commercial initiatives aimed at improving the position of the peasantry in the commodity chains, dynamic changes in the sphere of cooperative organization, the evolution of popular financial institutions, and strategic engagement by farm households in the labour market, all demonstrate the wide variety of responses to modified exchange conditions.

This particular dynamic of peasants' livelihood strategies has generally been neglected in most macroeconomic appraisals of agrarian change. The attention given to 'real markets' instead of 'prices' enables us to draw some general conclusions regarding the requirements for further reforms. Market liberalization as such cannot bring about sustained rural development when hierarchical social institutions and governance structures remain in force. Unambiguous guarantees to land property rights, equal access to input and commodity markets, and reduced transaction costs on rural financial markets are basic conditions for guaranteeing the participation of the peasantry in rural development. Therefore, local and global initiatives for reinforcing peasants' political and entrepreneurial organization, as well as efforts at building up social capital among the peasantry in order to improve their negotiating power *vis-à-vis* other rural agents and the state, are likely to offer promising perspectives.

Finally, a remark should be made regarding the role of the state. Since the late 1980s, the state apparatus has been reduced substantially, and most governments seem to consider institutional modernization to be almost identical to 'no state'. This demonstrates the fundamental misunderstanding regarding the appropriate role of the state in the development process. Taking into account the historical heritage of high market fragmentation, the establishment of competitive conditions requires fairly active state intervention. Markets suppose that property rights have to be confirmed and protected, but also ask for government investment in rural physical and social infrastructure to reduce transaction costs and informational failures. Moreover, initial access conditions to markets are highly unequally spread and, from a welfare viewpoint, targeted interventions and temporary subsidies are fully warranted.

Part 1
Agrarian Commodity Markets

2
Exchange Relations and Food Security: Maize and Markets in Honduras

Hazel Johnson

Introduction

This chapter uses an institutional framework to reflect back on some research undertaken in the 1980s examining maize production and maize markets, and the vulnerability of small-scale maize farmers to food insecurity in Honduras. The chapter raises some analytical points about market and non-market exchange, and how institutional arrangements and policies to change them might alleviate or reinforce vulnerability to food insecurity. It then looks at some of the market and non-market exchanges in the production and consumption of maize by small producers in Honduras in the 1980s. The chapter argues that unless there is an awareness of the institutional contexts of exchange within which the entitlements of small-scale maize producers are secured or threatened, it will be difficult to develop policies that meet the needs of the small producers, involve them as actors in institutional change, and hence in local governance. Although the chapter is informed by field research carried out in the late 1980s, it attempts to ask questions still pertinent to the future of small-scale producers of food staples.

Markets, entitlements and vulnerability

Two ongoing issues for food policy are (i) the role of market and non-market relationships in the supply of and command over food for and by poor people; and (ii) the effects of interventions in market and non-market relationships on access by poor people to food staples. These issues are even more pertinent to the extent that the market (or enabling the market to work better) is seen as a key to economic development.

To understand the effects on poor people of policies such as liberalization of price controls, the promotion or reinforcement of particular
markets, or the deregulation of food imports and exports, requires
knowing how poor people are linked into markets, which market and
non-market strategies they pursue to meet food and livelihood needs,
and how they affect or respond to market changes.

Current concerns about the role of the market in food security come
from different strands of thought and historical experience. For example, policy debates about the relative roles of the state and market in
enabling those vulnerable to food insecurity either to produce or to
purchase adequate food. Such issues arose in Honduras at the end of
the 1980s, for example, in proposals to reduce the role of the parastatal
grain marketing board, deregulate food prices and target the food-
insecure with food aid (USAID, 1989). Second, the uneven development
of markets, which may affect people's access to food and income. For
example, if access to land involves tied relationships over output and/or
labour use, small producers can effectively be caught in a cycle of debt
which reinforces their vulnerability (see, for example, Bhaduri, 1983;
Bharadwaj, 1985; Bardhan, 1989). Equally, if such ties are broken by
attempts to establish a free market in land, it may have disruptive consequences for non-market forms of social security in the countryside.
Important to such analysis is the role of social differentiation and power
relationships in conditioning the nature and outcomes of exchange.
Third, the focus on the uneven development of markets has also been
concerned with missing or incomplete markets (see the discussion of
Thorbecke, 1993, below) and producers' and consumers' engagement
in non-market exchange. While such non-market exchanges may or
may not involve power relationships, or be more or less beneficial to
people vulnerable to food insecurity, interventions to create or reinforce markets may also have harmful as well as advantageous effects for
the food-insecure. This suggests that it is difficult to develop single or
blanket policies which have beneficial outcomes for all producers.

Reflected in these strands of thought are different concepts of the
market. A useful threefold distinction is made by Mackintosh (1990):
'the market' as an abstract phenomenon (a 'token of ideological
debate' (Ibid., p. 46), such as the role of the market mechanism in ensuring the best or most efficient resources allocation); abstract models of
particular markets, and markets as a 'wide range of different ways of
buying and selling' (Ibid., p. 47), that is, markets as social institutions –
commoditized transactions embedded in different social relationships,
norms and values. The first of these distinctions is the basis of the

policy debates mentioned above. The second two distinctions are more closely linked to the second and third strands detailed above. These analytical distinctions are necessary if policy is not to focus simply on the role of market mechanisms in food security, or on theoretical models of given food markets, but can also take into account institutional forms of markets and non-market exchange: how the buying and selling of goods and services linked to food security (or food insecurity) operates in practice, the extent to which (and reasons why) non-market exchanges occur, and who benefits from them.[1]

Institutional change and institution-building (as norms, values and practices, and as organizations[2]) have become a key focus of development policy. Yet interventions in the name of institutional change can have unintended effects if existing institutional arrangements, the reasons they exist and how they are used or contested, are not well understood. A further issue for food policy is thus about finding ways of understanding the institutional contexts of market and non-market production and exchange of food staples, how they create or alleviate food insecurity, and the role played by different actors in shaping those relationships. Associated with these concerns is their link to local governance[3] and the role of small producers in defining and building rural institutions, including those of market and non-market relationships.

In terms of analyzing the relationship between market and non-market exchange, Thorbecke (1993) suggests that non-market transactions occur when markets are missing (for example, in rural finance or land); when there is incomplete, imperfect or asymmetrical information about markets and prices (as in oligopolies); and when there is a disparity between the distribution of land, labour and capital (for example, a shortage of land and an abundance of labour may limit the development of a wage-labour market). He concludes that such unevenness would result in 'different incentives' responses by agents that 'lead to the choice of essentially non-market configurations [institutions]' (ibid., p. 593). From a food security or livelihood perspective, however, a critical point is not just the extent to which small producers can engage in markets (and under what conditions, and with what effects) but what processes condition the nature of the non-market choices available, how secure they are, and whether they increase or alleviate vulnerability.

A useful perspective is provided by Engberg-Pedersen (1997) who argues that institutional contexts both condition choice and are shaped by participants. He distinguishes actor-orientated and rational choice approaches which, he suggests, can tend to separate actors and action from the institutional contexts that influence behaviour. He states: 'Institutions should not be viewed as external constraints to actors who conceive strategies to maneuver between institutional limitations. By organizing social life, institutions give meaning to action' (ibid., p. 188). In other words, people are at the centre of institutions and influence how institutions function and change. However, people will also have different social positions within institutions, experiencing and giving different meanings to the social relationships that constitute them. This may, in turn, give rise to struggle or contestation (and institutional change). There may also be tensions for actors between the different institutions they straddle; for example, between a demand to provide unpaid family labour in household production, or to undertake paid work on other farms via the labour market. This tension may centre on the economic calculations of particular individuals or of the household. It may also result from a desire for financial independence, or other benefits that can arise from working for a wealthier farmer. Another example might be the tensions for small producers between relying on the favours of a local landowner who offers to provide some land rent-free, and the risks of engaging in loans offered by credit schemes to buy a plot of land. As Engberg-Pedersen suggests, such a choice is not simply about the constraints in operation with either decision, but is also about the meanings given to the relationship with the landowner (which a small producer may wish either to sustain or to break), and those involved in becoming further engaged with markets as new smallholders. Furthermore, such choices and meanings are not merely individualized phenomena or experiences, but have a collective form in the relations between social groups (for example, landowners and tenants, small producers and traders, small producers and government extension workers and so on).

Integral to understanding the processes and effects of institutional arrangements of market and non-market exchange on small producers is how to conceptualize their vulnerability to food insecurity. In earlier analyses (Johnson, 1995, 1997), I have looked at the endowments and entitlements (Sen, 1981) of small-scale maize producers and analyzed under what market and non-market conditions they may or may not be reproduced, and what role is played by commoditization in creating or alleviating production of and access to maize. An interesting extension of the concept of entitlements is developed by Watts and Bohle (1993), who have theorized about what they call the 'space of vulnerability' in relation to actual or potential entitlement loss. Building on Chambers' (1989) view of vulnerability as inadequate capacities to cope with, and slow recovery from, exposure to crises and shocks, Watts and Bohle distinguish: (i) vulnerability as delineated by the degree of people's resilience to market changes and any social security mechanisms (formal and informal) which support them; (ii) vulnerability as a lack of rights (in households, in the workplace, or in the public arena of civil codes); and (iii) vulnerability as 'a structural-historical space which is shaped by the effects of commercialization, proletarianization and marginalization' (Watts and Bohle, 1993, p. 121). These distinctions then form a framework for a causal structure of vulnerability to food insecurity involving the intersection of the lack of three elements: a lack of entitlements (command over food); powerlessness; and forms of appropriation of poor producers through class relations. How these elements interact, and the relative significance of each, will vary. Moreover, such relationships can also provide forms of security as well as be a source of vulnerability (for example, through patron–client relations).

The Watts/Bohle distinctions provide a complex and dynamic view of how vulnerability to food insecurity can be created or reinforced. However, the institutions that structure vulnerability are also mediated by the actions of different social groups within the triangle. Thus, with respect to food security among small-scale maize producers in Honduras, at issue is both how market and non-market relations can reinforce or threaten the endowments and entitlements of small producers, what strategies small producers pursue to sustain production and access to a food staple such as maize, and how they negotiate their relationships with landowners, traders, non-state bodies such as NGOs, and the state (via government policies and programmes).

In the context of small-scale maize producers in Honduras, I have defined vulnerability to food insecurity as: 'the inabilities of many maize farmers [sic] to produce or consume adequate food staples [in this case, maize] without ongoing debt relations and potential or actual entitlement loss' (Johnson, 1995, p. 2). This definition is based on difficulties facing producers in securing means of production and gaining cash income or adequate maize supplies for their own needs from the outputs of cultivation. Although I adopted a boundaried perspective by focusing on the main food staple, maize, studying the mechanisms of reproduction of a particular food crop can help to illuminate other processes (for example, why producers may continue to grow apparently economically unviable crops, why or how one crop might help to subsidize another, the reasons for off-farm employment, the role of remittances from wage-earning or urban-based family members and so on).

Exchanges over maize: models and practices

I now look at some of the institutional arrangements involved in the production and disposal of maize by small producers. At issue are what types of exchange are involved, their market and non-market characteristics, why they take place in these ways (what relations of production are reflected by them), what role is played by state policies and practices, and whether the types of exchange are conducive to food security or to vulnerability to food insecurity via actual or potential entitlement loss.

Maize is the main food staple in Honduras – a source of food when little else is available, and substituted only by sorghum in times of acute need. The way in which maize is produced and marketed is relatively complex, given that there are many types of maize producer, from large commercial farmers (landowners) to very small producers who may only rent or borrow plots of land, the cultivation of which is usually combined with wage work. There are also collectively organized producers – initially landless or land poor – who obtained land in the land reform of the 1970s and 1980s and who farm communal areas as well as household plots. There are many channels for buying and selling maize: small amounts change hands regularly in local communities, maize is sold to established local traders as well as itinerant traders coming from urban centres, and, in the 1980s, some farmers regularly sold maize to the state marketing board, the Instituto Honduríno de Mercadeo Agrícola (IHMA). Some large farmers sell maize directly to industry for processing, while some medium and large farmers are also known to engage in trade or act as intermediaries. In addition, maize is often sold by small farmers on a pre-harvest basis (to wealthier farmers as well as to traders), to finance inputs for production.

The following analysis and commentary reflects back on data gathered during some field research in 1987 in the eastern department of El Paraíso, where I interviewed both individual and collectively-organized maize producers in two villages in the valley of Jamastrán as well as urban-based traders and local officials. I focus on the data gathered from individual small producers because they demonstrate a variety of market and non-market exchange relationships which may possibly be characteristic of other parts of Honduras but which certainly suggest that such relationships are worthy of closer scrutiny in terms of policy development. The valley of Jamastrán is an important agricultural area in El Paraíso where are number of export crops are grown (tobacco, cotton, sugar cane) as well as having extensive pasture land, with coffee being grown in the surrounding mountainous areas. Maize and beans are also grown extensively, by all types of farmer or producer. In general, small-scale maize producers engage in a range of farming activities (maize, beans, some vegetables and small livestock), which may be on quite reduced areas (as small as 0.7 hectare, although that would be more likely to be a single plot of rented or borrowed land for maize and beans). Some small producers may also engage in artisanal activities or petty trading as well as wage work, and individual household members may also obtain work in urban centres and be additional providers. Inevitably, the poorest producers are those who have relatively limited options for income generation.

This brief description raises questions about how to differentiate rural producers. As well as differentiation according to the carrying capacity of land (for example, del Cid, 1977, who distinguished tiny, sub-family, family and multi-family farms), the characterization of producers of food staples, such as maize and beans, has often differentiated between those who apparently produce maize only for their own consumption and those who produce for the market as well as their own needs (for example, see Aguirre and Tablada, 1988). An additional dimension might be the use of own and others' labour in production. In the villages I researched, I found that even the smallest producers (those with 0.7 hectare) sold – and expected to sell – maize, because they needed the cash income for other needs, including repaying debts. Also, many small maize producers hired labour to work for them on their maize plots (including those who worked for others). A summary of some of these and other characteristics of maize producers interviewed in the two villages in El Paraíso is presented in Table 2.1. The groupings in this table are by access to land (including rented or borrowed). However, elsewhere (Johnson, 1995), I have distinguished two types of small-scale maize producer, differentiated partly on the basis of access to land and partly by access to, and use of, labour. I shall call these two types 'partially-proletarianized farmers' and 'petty commodity producers', the first engaging in both farming activities and wage work, and the second only engaging in farming but at a level of simple reproduction.[4] However, even this dichotomy is not adequate in itself to encapsulate the range of exchange relationships that form part of the process of sustaining maize production among small producers. Understanding the mechanisms by which such producers sustain their maize farming, and how their activities in maize farming might be reinforced or threatened requires a deeper analysis of the social relationships involved.[5]

Table 2.1 Land, labour, finance and output characteristics of 28 maize farmers by farm size grouping in two villages in El Paraíso, 1986-7 (based on data from the main harvest [*primera*])

Farm size (ha)	Number	Land tenure			Labour use			Source of finance			Production outcomes		
		Own land	Other sources**	Mixed (own and other)	Used permanent wage labour	Used seasonal wage labour	Did wage work for others	Institutional credit	Personal loans	Pre-harvest sales	Sold maize	Maize deficit to needs after sales***	Neg. net cash income from maize prod.
<1-5	12	2	5	5	0	9	5	4	4	3	12	6	4
5-50	10	5	1	4	0	9	1	9	0	0	10	3	4
50+*	6	6	0	0	6	6	0	6	0	0	6	0	1
Total	**28**	**13**	**6**	**9**	**6**	**24**	**6**	**19**	**4**	**3**	**28**	**9**	**9**

Notes: *These farmers had substantially more than 50 ha. **Rented, borrowed or national (public) land. ***Including pre-harvest sales.

For small-scale producers, there are three key issues with respect to maize: how to obtain land; how to resource production (agricultural inputs and labour); and how to dispose of maize, so that (a) they are not in debt, which results in endowment or entitlement loss; and (b) have enough remaining for their own consumption (household and animals) and small sales to finance other needs. For partially-proletarianized producers, resolution of some of these issues may revolve around a relationship to a commercial, labour-hiring farmer or landowner. While, historically, particularly during the expansion of pasture land, the production of landlessness has also been bound up in these relationships (working for landowners in return for a plot of land, from which workers were often dispossessed after they had cleared it (personal communications from interviews in El Paraíso and Santa Bárbara, 1987–88), carrying out wage work for commercial farmers in return for renting or borrowing land could be a relationship which offered both landowner and tenant some degree of security. For the landowner, the tenant provides a committed source of labour (especially at peak times), while the tenant is able to produce food staples such as maize.

In one of the village sites, this was a well-known phenomenon. Data from a cluster of five such producers in this village revealed that there were a number of key large, commercial farmers (about three in that village, and various others in nearby villages) with whom it was possible to establish this kind of arrangement. However, the type of land–labour arrangement could vary: labour was always paid (at the market rate), while land might be rented for cash (also at the market rate), for sacks of maize at harvest, or it might be borrowed. Equally, such partially-proletarianized producers might borrow agricultural inputs from the landowner (to be repaid at harvest), and might even have rented machines. That is, they could take advantage of the landowner's access to credit for production (which financed the landowner's own supply of agricultural inputs as well as the purchase of machinery) for their own needs. In two cases among this cluster of interviewees, the producers also partly financed their own maize production from pre-harvest sales. Pre-harvest sales might take place with different types of wealthier farmer, from petty commodity producers to large commercial farmers, and were not necessarily associated with the farmer from whom they rented land. According to informants, such loans incurred an interest rate of 100 per cent because the maize (handed over at harvest) was paid for at half the expected market price.

It is important to recognize the appearances and realities of such exchanges: on the one hand, they take place in the knowledge of market prices; and, on the other, personal agreements are arrived at that might modify prices paid, or the terms of repayment, and part of the exchange might be in the character of a gift which, in turn, might give rise to reciprocal obligations, a sense of loyalty and so on. Such personalized exchanges (Johnson, 1995, 1997) are thus part of the market economy – they involve the commoditization of land, labour, finance and agricultural inputs – but they take place on the basis of personal arrangements which have non-market (and non-commoditized) elements. Such exchanges involve norms and values, as well as material processes, which in part reflect the social hierarchies based on relative wealth and status in the village, and the projections of how parties in the exchange wish to portray the relationship. Discussions with informants thus involved contested meanings about, for example, whether Don *X* had rented out (for payment) or merely lent or 'given' such and such a plot to producer *Y*; or whether producer *A* always did wage labour for Don *B*, or perhaps also worked for Don *C* from whom he also hired a machine or to whom he sold maize on a pre-harvest basis etc. While these relationships provided mutual benefits, they were based on social hierarchy rooted in access to land, as well as bank credit (for which land is the collateral).

Why did small producers engage in such – potentially complex or diverse – exchanges to secure inputs for maize production? And why did large commercial farmers or landowners agree to relations based on favours and patronage in a largely commoditized economy? Was it because land and labour markets were missing or incomplete, or that credit for farming inputs was not available? With respect to land and labour, one needs to look at the interdependent – but potentially precarious or changing – relationship between the landowner and tenant farmer. The research data being used here come from an area where beef cattle, tobacco, coffee and cotton were produced – that is, agriculture was extensively commoditized. There were land markets, but these were apparently sluggish in the sense that there was a highly unequal distribution of land and consolidation of land holdings amongst relatively few owners.[6] Large landowners interviewed were generally trying to accumulate more land (particularly through colonization, and often, but not always, for pasture) rather than selling it (although they might have rented land out to other commercial farmers as well as small plots to their own workers). Renting or lending land to tenants could help to secure labour, particularly for peak periods, while those who borrowed or rented land were generally unable to raise the capital to buy it. There were credit markets but, without the collateral of land, such producers could not access credit. In practice, they used the fact that the landowners could obtain credit and therefore provide small quantities of seed and fertilizer to be repaid at harvest, as well as even hiring out machines for ploughing or shelling maize.

The existence of markets is thus not a guarantee that transactions will there take place, even though non-market transactions might be influenced by market trends. While partially-proletarianized maize producers could only access certain markets indirectly via personalized relations with those who had direct access, it also proved useful, certainly for some landowners, to have such relations with at least some of their workers. The effects of this were, on the one hand, a means of security, and on the other, a source of fragility, in that the relations could change if the markets changed, or if some aspect of the personalized relationship failed. For example, interviews with large landowners indicated a concern with labour costs and a tendency or desire to expand cattle pasture, which would require less labour, or to mechanize crop production further, including maize. Such changes would obviously have had effects on their permanent and temporary workers. In addition, the relationship was based on debt, as well as favours, and it could undermine any capacities to increase incomes, at least from maize production alone.

Connected to this last point is the third key issue for small – in this case, partially-proletarianized – producers: the disposal of maize from production. Returning to the cluster of five partially-proletarianized producers in one of the villages – from their 1987 harvests, four were found to have a consumption deficit from their own output in terms of their calculated needs, and two of them also had a net income deficit from maize production after they had made their post-harvest sales (Johnson, 1995, p. 246). While these data may have been unusual because of high maize losses experienced that year caused by a fungus that had become widespread[7], they still serve to show the fragility or precariousness of sustaining maize crops for these producers. On the one hand, their conditions of production made them highly vulnerable to food and income deficits from maize. On the other hand, their non-market relationships with other farmers enabled them to continue producing maize as well as provided them with other sources of income.

While these small producers would probably have been characterized as subsistence producers providing maize for their own consumption, in practice their maize 'provision' was bound up in market as well as non-market relationships, and different circuits of indebtedness, obligation and cash flows. While maize production might have been seen largely as a food source, a considerable proportion of maize was sold at harvest (if not before) to pay back debts and cover other needs for which cash was required. Among producers with less than 5 hectares of land interviewed in this village, an average of over 70 per cent of the 1987 main crop output was sold at harvest (Johnson, 1995, p. 213). This is when market prices tend to be at their lowest. Thus, while maize was a means of paying for other goods as well as a source of food, cash income from other activities such as wage work, or sales of vegetables, was an important means of buying maize at a later date (and at a higher price).

So far I have looked at some of the dynamics that might take place in exchanges between different types of maize producer. The institutional context of producing, buying and selling maize takes on yet another dimension once government policies directed towards improving maize farming and increasing national maize supplies are brought into the picture. It is particularly instructive to look at the relationship between financial and output markets. In the 1980s, credit provision was seen as a means of improving productivity and increasing marketed output (while price stabilization policies pursued by the state marketing board were expected to provide price incentives to farmers and regulate prices to consumers). In effect, providing credit for purchasing seeds, fertilizers and other technologies was not only a way of trying to improve productivity and output but also a means of commoditizing production processes. In theory, the loans required to do this would be repaid from the sales of maize surplus to consumption needs arising from the increased yields.

Incorporating maize production further into markets via commoditization of inputs and outputs can have contradictory effects. As already mentioned, bank credit tended to be restricted to farmers with collateral (chiefly in land). However, in El Paraíso, as in other parts of Honduras, there was an integrated rural development programme that included the provision of credit to those categorized as small and medium producers (up to about 14-hectare farms) (SRN *et al.*, 1984). In this case, collateral was the expected harvest and the anticipated cash income from maize sales. Those participating in the programme were primarily petty commodity producers of maize (and other crops, such as beans, fruit and vegetables). The financial models being used to develop farmers' applications for credit were based on the purchase of all inputs, including labour, which meant that cash loans were often high compared to farmers' actual cash income from maize sales. Several participant producers interviewed in the two villages had experienced entitlement loss because they had difficulty in repaying loans and were left either with a deficit of maize for direct consumption or a negative net cash income. At the time of interview, of thirteen producers from both the villages that had participated in the programme, it was estimated that four had both a consumption and a net cash income deficit from maize production from the previous harvest, one had a net cash income deficit only, and another had a consumption deficit (Johnson, 1995, p. 246). Some astute farmers were thus learning rapidly to reduce the size of their loans and to target them to specific cash outlays such as pieces of equipment.

Paradoxically, the financial models for maize production for different farm categories suggested that, with the extent of cash outlay proposed, net cash income from maize farming would be minimal, even when the total harvest was sold (SRN *et al.*, 1984). One conclusion from this model was that other, higher-value crops, such as beans and vegetables, were expected to provide cash income or even subsidize maize production. However, such a diversifying strategy requires a good understanding of the exchange relations of which producers may already be part and which may be defined by more personalized transactions, debts and obligations between members of households as well as with other producers and traders. For example, two of the deficit producers mentioned above also carried out wage work for landowners but had aspirations to transcend the situation and become 'independent' producers. Another producer, not in the credit programme, also conveyed his desire to become independent and stop doing wage work for his brother (the money from which he used to finance his own maize production) through participating in the scheme. However, implanting an ideal financial model in such circumstances may induce farmers to produce and to sell more maize, but with a possible reduction in entitlements in other ways.

Some conclusions from these experiences suggest that, on the one hand, there was considerable vulnerability among partially-proletarianized and even some petty commodity producers in relation to markets involved in producing and selling maize; but, on the other hand, partially-proletarianized farmers showed forms of resilience that relied on non-market and personalized mechanisms of securing inputs and 'managing' production. Even though these processes were based on debt relations, their personalized dimension allowed them to continue from one season to the next in ways that were more difficult to sustain within externally-funded formal credit programmes. This is not an argument for maintaining landowner–tenant patronage – the power relations and poverty on which this is based is a denial of broader entitlements as human capabilities (Drèze and Sen, 1989) and as human rights (Gaay Fortman, 1990). However, it does suggest that careful consideration needs to be given to what needs to be changed, and how.

Exchange relations and local governance

To the extent that the above relationships are more or less widespread and continue to exist in the 1990s, the prospect of institutional change and market reinforcement raises wider concerns. I reflect briefly on two areas for further consideration.

The first is the relationship between access to land and resourcing production. If access to land and inputs depends partly on relations with landowners who receive bank credit, and if the production of food staples such as maize on a small scale is not in itself an adequate means of financing further production, what has to change? Thorbecke's (1993) analysis of rural market and non-market 'configurations' concludes by endorsing the creation or reinforcement of property rights in land and a role for voluntary organizations in cushioning credit–debt relations among small producers by assuming joint liability. Schemes such as land banks and micro-credit programmes based on the Grameen Bank are also at the forefront of many development initiatives in the 1990s, with a range of results and experiences (see, for example, Hulme and Mosley, 1996). Without elevating such experiences to blueprints and making unrealistic claims for their success, can such forms of rural finance in practice help to reduce the vulnerability of small-scale food staple producers in Honduras by assisting them to resource production and/or by providing credit to help develop other forms of income generation?

The current preoccupation with the role of the market in development has led to concerns with the institutional framework required for effective and efficient markets. The World Bank, in particular, has strongly associated the need for 'good governance' with a competitive market economy (World Bank, 1992). More recently, this view has not only called for a more capable and effective state (World Bank, 1997, p. 1) but for a strong role for civil society or 'social capital': 'the informal rules, norms, and long-term relationships that facilitate coordinated action and enable people to undertake cooperative ventures for mutual advantage' (ibid., p. 114). In Honduras, there have been some quite specific experiences of 'cooperative ventures' in the collective organization of small-scale producers resulting from the land reform processes of the 1970s and 1980s. Elsewhere I have argued that such units improved on the position of partially-proletarianized producers because '(i) they had more or less assured access to land; (ii) access to land was independent of exchanges agreed with local landowners; (iii) groups had political or ideological principles which guided internal organization and distribution of resources and output as well as social relations with outside individuals and agents; (iv) collective organization also provided internal solidarity and cohesion; (v) groups could take joint action in relation to external forces and pressures' (Johnson, 1997). However, such collective units have also experienced problems of economic viability, and difficulties in maintaining their organizational cohesion under financial and other pressures (Goud, 1986; World Bank, 1983). A recent critical analysis from Eastern Europe of the relative efficiencies of collective units as opposed to individual farms supported by service cooperatives advocated the latter as a way forward (Deininger, 1995). It may be that the creation of more supporting institutions and/or 'cooperative ventures for mutual advantage' is a way forward for at least some of Honduras's small-scale maize producers, and would give them a greater role in local governance.

Notes

1. Gasper and Apthorpe (1996) also make a useful distinction between market mechanism (the forces of supply and demand) and markets as institutions that involve non-economic processes (such as the establishment of rules and shared meanings attached to exchange). Gasper and Apthorpe argue against using one meaning to the exclusion of the other: the first makes 'a machine of the ghost'; the second 'makes a ghost of the machine' (ibid., p. 7).
2. 'Institutions are complexes of norms, rules, and behaviors that serve a collective purpose. Organizations are a structure of roles. While many institutions are organizations (e.g., households, firms, cooperatives), many institutions are not organizations (e.g., money, the law ...) and many organizations are not institutions (e.g., a particular grassroots organization). The distinction is, however, a matter of degree' (de Janvry *et al.*, 1993, p. 566).
3. There is considerable discussion about the concept (and practices) of governance which cannot be detailed in this chapter. The perspective informing the chapter can be encapsulated in the following quotation: 'Governance is ... a process of managing society and facilitating/ensuring the delivery of goods and services through the management of social and power relations. Governance is a means to maintain social stability and well-being through deepening democracy, structuring social relationships and conflicts and ensuring responsive delivery' (Wooldridge and Cranko, 1995, pp. 343–4).

4. 'Partial proletarianization' is an unsatisfactory term; however, it is difficult to find appropriate concepts which encapsulate the two main relations of such producers: cultivating own (or rented/borrowed land) and carrying out wage work. A more technically-appropriate formulation might be 'land-poor peasant households with a labour surplus'. However, this begs questions about (i) the definition (and underlying debate) about the term 'peasant'; (ii) differentiation and use of labour within households; and (iii) which social relations are involved in the way the labour surplus is used. Equally, there has been considerable debate around the concept of petty commodity producers. Again, a more technically-appropriate term might be 'peasant households with a land/labour balance'. However, I think the term 'balance' is probably somewhat contrary to the conditions of many such producers: they may make an adequate living from the land and may not have to work for others, but conditions are often more precarious than the self-sufficiency implied by this phrase.

5. The spectrum of social relations of production and exchange for the household as a whole (and how they are reproduced) is an even wider issue, of course, and not necessarily open to simple classification once all members of the household are taken into account.

6. The Gini coefficient for land distribution in 1974 (the date of the agricultural census previous to the fieldwork on which these reflections are based) was 0.78 (Howard Ballard, 1987, p. 470). Between this census and that of 1952, there had been considerable growth in the number of farms of under 10 hectares, while the growth in land in farms was principally, in those of 50 hectares and above (Johnson, 1995, pp. 139–40). Although there had been some claims on land via the land reform of the 1970s in the area, it was unclear that this had a radical effect on the general pattern of distribution.

7. It was estimated that they lost between 30 per cent and 50 per cent of their harvests (Johnson, 1995, p. 215). Extensionists associated the fungus with the spread of improved seeds and increasing homogeneity of maize types [personal communications].

Bibliography

Aguirre, J. A. and Tablada, G. (1988) *Macro Análisis de la Producción de Granos Básicos en Honduras 1976–87*, Tegucigalpa: Instituto Interamericano de Cooperación para la Agricultura (IICA), December.

Bardhan, P. (1989) 'Alternative Approaches to the Theory of Institutions in Economic Development', in P. Bardhan (ed.), *The Economic Theory of Agrarian Institutions*, Oxford: Clarendon Press.

Bhaduri, A. (1983) *The Economic Structure of Backward Agriculture*, London and New York: Academic Press.

Bharadwaj, K. (1985) 'A View on Commercialization in Indian Agriculture and the Development of Capitalism', *Journal of Peasant Studies*, vol. 12, no. 4, pp. 7–25.

del Cid, R. (1977) *Reforma Agraria y Capitalismo Dependiente*, Tegucigalpa: Editorial Universitaria.

Chambers, R. (1989) 'Vulnerability, Coping and Policy', *IDS Bulletin*, vol. 20, no. 2, pp. 1–7.

Deininger, K. (1995) 'Collective Agricultural Production: A Solution for Transition Economies?', *World Development*, vol. 23, no. 8, pp. 1317–34.

Drèze, J. and Sen, A. (1989) *Hunger and Public Action*, Oxford: Clarendon Press.

Engberg-Pedersen, L. (1997) 'Institutional Contradictions in Rural Development', *European Journal of Development Research*, vol. 9, no. 1, pp. 183–208.

Gaay Fortman, B. de (1990) *'Entitlement and Development. An Institutional Approach to the Acquirement Problem*, Working Paper No. 87, The Hague: Institute of Social Studies.

Gasper, D. and Apthorpe, R. (1996) 'Introduction: Discourse Analysis and Policy Discourse', in R. Apthorpe and D. Gasper, *Arguing Development Policy: Frames and Discourses*, London: Frank Cass/EADI.

Goud, B. (1986) *Empresas Campesinas en Honduras: El Modelo y La Realidad*, Instituto Interamericano de Cooperación para la Agricultura, Fortalecimiento de la Capacidad Gerencial de Empresas Campesinas de Producción Agropecuaria (Proyecto Forge), Tegucigalpa: CEE/FRANCIA/IICA/INA.

Howard Ballard, P. L. (1987) *From Banana Republic to Cattle Republic: Agrarian Roots of the Crisis in Honduras*, PhD dissertation, Madison, Wisc.: University of Wisconsin.

Hulme, D. and Mosley, P. (1996) *Finance Against Poverty*, vols 1 and 2, London and New York: Routledge.

de Janvry, A., Sadoulet, E. and Thorbecke, E. (1993) 'Introduction' in 'State, Market, and Civil Organizations: New Theories, New Practices, and their Implications for Rural Development', *World Development*, vol. 21, no. 4, pp. 565–75.

Johnson, H. (1995) *Reproduction, Exchange Relations and Food Insecurity: Maize Production and Maize Markets in Honduras*, PhD dissertation, Milton Keynes: The Open University.

Johnson, H. (1997) 'Food Insecurity as a Sustainability Issue: Lessons from Honduran Maize Farming', in J. de Groot and R. Ruben (eds), *Sustainable Agriculture in Central America*, London: Macmillan.

Mackintosh, M. (1990) 'Abstract Markets and Real Needs', in H. Bernstein, B. Crow, M. Mackintosh and C. Martin, *The Food Question: Profits versus People?*, London: Earthscan.

Sen, A. (1981) *Poverty and Famines. An Essay on Entitlement and Deprivation*, Oxford: Clarendon Press.

SRN/DARCO, Fondo Europeo para el Desarrollo/CEE, BOOM, Asesores para el Desarrollo (1984) *Reforzamiento a la Reforma Agraria y Desarrollo Rural Integrado de la Región Centro Oriental de Honduras – Formulación del proyecto – NA-82/14*, mimeo, Tegucigalpa, November.

Thorbecke, E. (1993) 'Impact of State and Civil Institutions on the Operation of Rural Market and Nonmarket Configurations', *World Development*, vol. 21, no. 4, pp. 591–606.

USAID (1989) *A Strategy Paper for the Agricultural Sector in Honduras*, draft, Tegucigalpa: USAID, Office for Agriculture and Rural Development, October.

Watts, M. J. and Bohle, H. G. (1993) 'Hunger, Famine and the Space of Vulnerability', *GeoJournal*, vol. 30, no. 2, pp. 117–25.

Wooldridge, D. and Cranko, P. (1995) 'Transforming Public Sector Institutions', in P. FitzGerald, A. McLennan and B. Munslow (eds), *Managing Sustainable Development in South Africa*, Cape Town: Oxford University Press.

World Bank (1983) *Honduras: An Inquiry into Rural Population, Small Farmers and Agrarian Reform*, Country Programs Department 1, Latin America and the Caribbean.

World Bank (1992) *Governance and Development*, Washington: World Bank.

World Bank (1997) *World Development Report 1997. The State in a Changing World*, New York: Oxford University Press and World Bank.

3
Small-Scale Producers and Sesame Commodity Chains under Structural Adjustment

Ner Artola

Introduction

With the initiation of adjustment policies in 1988, the north-western region of Nicaragua (León and Chinandega) entered a deep economic crisis. This crisis was engendered by the disappearance of cotton production which historically had been the key economic activity in the region. Given the context of this regional crisis, this chapter inquires into the perspectives for sesame production, a crop that could be an alternative for the region. In particular, the net generation of foreign exchange of the sesame crop is quite high, since it uses hardly any imported inputs (Bastiaensen, 1991). Another advantage of the crop, compared to other non-traditional export crops, is that it does not require any sophisticated new technology (Kaimowitz, 1992). Many peasant producers in the area have historically cultivated the crop. The belief in the sesame crop as a development alternative is shared by the Nicaraguan government, which has developed policies to stimulate the production and export of sesame, including a direct price subsidy in the form of an export premium.

Under post-adjustment conditions, sesame production experienced a substantial increase in output starting from historically low levels. The area of sesame harvested rose from an average of 11 500 hectares in the period 1980–8 to an average of 25 500 hectares in the period 1989–95. The average value of sesame production rose from US$2.92 million in the period 1986–9 to US$7.6 million in the period 1990–5 (BCN, 1997). Nearly all types of producer, seeking alternatives for the cotton crisis, have been involved in the expansion of sesame production, including some large-scale enterprises. Nevertheless, the largest part of the increase was realized by small-scale producers.[1] However, even where

39

sesame production has expanded, it is important to notice that the observed advance in sesame output still falls substantially short of realizing the full potential of the crop in the region.

In the present analysis we try to find some of the reasons that might explain why sesame production has not reacted as might have been expected. As we shall indicate, one of the fundamental problems relates to the deficient transmission of price signals from the macro to the micro level. In order to shed light on the issues involved in this macro–micro transmission process, we shall analyze the dominant sesame production – marketing chains in Nicaragua. We start our analysis with a brief overview of the principal characteristics of the world market for sesame, and the role of Central America in world production of, and trade in, the crop. The recent history of the sesame trade in Nicaragua will also be reviewed briefly.

Central America in the international sesame market

The world's largest sesame producers are India, China, Myanmar, Sudan, Mexico and Bangladesh. Together they accounted for around 75 per cent of the world supply in 1993 (FAO, 1994). Compared to these players, the Central American region represents only a small force with little influence on the world market, its share of the world supply being scarcely 2 per cent. Within Central America, Guatemala is responsible for 50 per cent of production, and El Salvador and Nicaragua for most of the rest (ibid). The majority of the production is destined for export, as the domestic sesame market in Central America is minute.

Since the end of the 1980s, sesame has shown positive signs of economic reactivation in those Central American countries with the greatest production, thus confirming the relative profitability of the crop under market liberalization. Table 3.1 shows that Guatemala and Nicaragua registered the highest production growth rates, with 69 per cent and 57 per cent, respectively.

The region's sesame production is exported exclusively in seed form. There are two basic varieties: dark (for example, red china) and light (ICTA-R). The latter is larger and contains more protein. The main advantage of the darker variety is that it contains a greater amount of oil. Through a process of hulling, both varieties can be turned into hulled seeds. Good-quality seed is highly valued on the world market. Quality criteria are purity (lack of dirt); uniformity (a homogeneous product without the addition of different varieties); colour/size (for

Table 3.1 Evolution of sesame production in Central America, 1979–93 (1000s of metric tons)

	1979–81	**1991**	**1992**	**1993**	**Difference 1979–81/1991–3**
El Salvador	10	12	10	13	+20 per cent
Guatemala	13	23	23	22	+69 per cent
Nicaragua	7	13	10	11	+57 per cent
Honduras	3	1	1	2	−56 per cent
Total	**33**	**49**	**44**	**48**	**+42 per cent**

Source: Based on the FAO, 1994.

hulled seeds, white and big is preferred to dark and small); and degree of humidity (the lower the better, with a maximum of 5 per cent).

The food industry has developed various consumer goods from sesame seed: oils are used in cosmetics, essential oils, sweets, sauces, butter, flour and so on. In Central America, there has been little development of post-hulling industrial processing. This generally takes place in the importing countries. However, some industrialization initiatives are beginning to emerge. Sesame sweet factories have been set up in Guatemala, and very recently factories have opened in Nicaragua to produce essential oils and sesame flour. There are also some local experiments in Nicaragua with the small-scale processing of sesame oil. However, these initiatives have not altered the fact that 100 per cent of the country's sesame exports are still in seed form, whether natural or hulled.

Three blocks of industrialized countries, where most of the processing capacity and final demand is concentrated, account for most of the demand in the world sesame market. The market in each of these industrial blocks has its own particular requirements and opportunities. In Japan, the market is divided into two areas. The first market segment demands a low-quality, low priced natural seed for use in the oil industry, and China and India are the main suppliers. The second segment is a market for high-quality, high-priced natural seed (the ICTA-R variety). This 'market niche' is highly demanding in terms of quality, and therefore difficult to access. In the Central America region, only Guatemala has made significant advances in technical productive development and the export of this high-quality variety with a substantial price advantage. The market in the USA is predominantly for hulled seed for use in bread and hamburgers. It is a relatively big market (McDonalds, Burger King and bakeries) and demands a high quality of hulling. In 1994, Guatemala and Mexico dominated this market, with 36 per cent and 34 per cent of the market share, respectively. The rest of the market was divided between India, Nicaragua and El Salvador (Centro de Exportaciones e Importaciones, 1996). The last block is the European market for both natural and hulled seed, which is slightly less demanding in terms of quality than the US market. Most of the European demand comes from the German, Dutch and English food industries. Finally, the new 'alternative market' niche should be mentioned, which is found particularly in the US and European markets. Its prices are substantially higher than those of the conventional market because of the attributes 'ecological soundness' and 'social fairness' attached to the products in the alternative circuit. This market, however, shows only a limited demand, although it has the capacity to expand, particularly in the 'organic' segment, as consumers are tending towards attaching a higher value to a healthier and 'more natural' diet.

International sesame prices reached higher levels in the pre-adjustment period (1980–7) than in the crop reactivation period (1988–95). This was because of an increase in world exports within the context of adjustment and export promotion processes. In the 1990s there has also been a greater variation in prices in the region. Among other factors, the 'tequila effect' of 1994 provoked a temporary rise in sesame prices in 1995 caused by the fall in exports from Mexico to the USA, which, because of its proximity, is one of the region's main markets. Also, since sesame most often accounts for only a small share of the cost of the final product (breads) and probably has a very inelastic demand, variations in the supply have a strong impact on the price of the product; this also plays a part in the evolution of sesame prices.

The world sesame market is worth approximately US$100 million,[2] which is relatively small compared to the US$8.4 billion coffee market (Baumeister, 1991). Information is not readily available on this market, which implies that the actors do not know exactly what the market price is, and thus act according to the price range of their competitors. Two factors explain this lack of information. First, there is no public price-setting exchange such as that for coffee, which is subject to the price fluctuations of the 'New York Coffee Contract'. In the case of sesame seed there is a predominance of almost personalized relationships between the main market actors (between the exporters themselves or between exporters and buyers), which play a decisive role when it comes to obtaining information and good commercial contacts.

Organization of the sesame market in Nicaragua

Transition: from state monopoly to private oligopoly

During the Sandinista government, two big state enterprises controlled foreign and domestic trade in sesame. The state cotton enterprise (ENAL) had a monopoly on the export of sesame, while Arlen Siu dominated the storage and processing (hulling) of the product. The main export markets for these enterprises were Germany and Japan; the product was low quality seed. In 1991, trading in sesame was liberalized through decrees 5–91 (which authorizes the issue of export licences) and 6–91 (which authorizes the suppression of taxes on the licences). It was expected that this liberalization policy would see the state's role in foreign and domestic sesame trading taken over by a private sector operating efficiently under the pressures of market competition.

The liberalization and privatization of the state enterprises left the market wide open to new private national and international agents. Following privatization, ENAL continued to operate under the same name as a major export intermediary. Arlen Siu was heavily indebted and subsequently closed down, leaving the storage, processing and marketing tasks to the new participants. The network of peasant stores, constituted as service cooperatives linked to the ECODEPA enterprise, first ventured into procurement and export, and later also into processing. Former sesame hulling plants which had been involved in the processing and marketing of sesame prior to 1979, were also reactivated, and businesses linked to the cotton sector (ANSCA) ventured into husking and marketing activities. Finally, foreign companies, first Salvadoran and later Guatemalan, started operating through national intermediaries. The commercial opening-up thus clearly created a national sesame market with a greater, if still limited, variety of private competitors.

At the beginning of the liberalization process, many different sectors were keen to get involved in the sesame business. However, of the 35 and 40 export licences issued by the Ministry of Economy in 1991 and 1992, respectively, only 11 and 16 agents, respectively, in fact carried out export operations. Many of the licensed companies could not compete because of a lack of access to capital or contacts or a too limited knowledge of the sector. Out of all the businesses that participated in 1992, just four dominated the sesame market, accounting for 70 per cent of the volume of exports (see Table 3.2).

Table 3.2   Volume and share of sesame exports, 1992 (cwt)

Business/product	Natural	Hulled	Total*	Percentage
ENAL		57 879.5	57 879.5	25.7
ECODEPA	78 734.8		55 114.4	24.5
Oleoexport		28 730.2	28 730.2	13.0
INA		13 240.0	13 240.6	6.0
Inversiones Alpha	4 166.3	19 682.6	22 599.0	10.0
AGRONIK S.A.	16 929.2		11 850.3	5.0
PROEXA	9 389.4		6 572.6	2.9
Others	30 503.5	7 802.9	29 155.4	12.9
Total	**139 723.2**	**127 335.8**	**225 142.0**	**100.0**

Note: *The total is hulled; the conversion of natural sesame to hulled sesame is calculated on the basis of 130 lb natural = 1 cwt of hulled.
Source: Based on data from Canales (1993).

The policy of promoting the sesame subsector in the context of the adjustment

Faced with the stagnation and relative lack of profitability of traditional agricultural exports, particularly cotton and sugar, sectoral policies were implemented to encourage non-traditional exports in Nicaragua, as in other countries in the region. Although sesame is historically a Nicaraguan export crop, it was classified as non-traditional and was therefore promoted. In particular, sesame benefited from the reform of the exports promotion law in March 1992 which exonerated non-traditional products from income tax and extended the Tax Benefit Certificate (CBT) for a period of six years. The latter is a subsidy proportional to the fob value and degressive over time. In theory, this subsidy is the equivalent of an increase in the fob export price (Helpman and Krugman, 1992). The assumption behind the policy is that those exporters who receive the CBT are going to pass on the benefits to the producers by paying better prices for the produce they buy.

Another of the promotion measures was the strengthening of the hulling agroindustry. Important flows of monetary resources from foreign donors were channelled through the Nicaraguan Investment Fund (FNI) under soft payment conditions (7 per cent interest rates, 5 years grace period). These funds were aimed at creating new physical capital (for example, plants, warehouses and silos). Relatively little went into renewing the existing, obsolete infrastructure. Three new plants were created: the ECODEPA plant (now known as SIRAMA), linked to the UNAG business sector; ANSCA, belonging to the cotton business

sector; and Inversiones ALPHA, a business owned by private sharehold-
ers. Despite these investments, nearly 50 per cent of the total production exported is still sold abroad without being hulled in Nicaragua
(CETREX, 1996). Apart from the hulling process, there is virtually no
other agroindustrial processing of sesame, so the total contribution of
the sesame subsector to the national economy's value added is low and
follows the same pattern as the traditional export crops. Currently,
sesame fits within the traditional pattern of the integration of the
periphery in the international division of labour: export of semi-
processed raw materials and import of manufactured capital and consumer goods.

Another problem in Nicaragua is that the most widely grown red
china variety has lost popularity on the foreign market. However, assistance and research institutions have not actively promoted or adapted
new genetic material. The privatization of the Cotton Experiment
Centre (CEA), where experiments were also carried out with sesame
seeds, was a failure. For the private sector, experimenting and disseminating new genetic material is unlikely to be profitable in the short
term. Therefore, the present government has had to renationalize the
CEA with the aim of turning it into a dynamic centre for research on
oleaginous seeds (soy, groundnuts, sesame and cotton). The National
Institute for Agricultural Technology (INTA) has also played a rather
weak role in dissemination and extension work.

An important factor is also that with the reform in the state and
private banking sectors, small-scale rural producers have largely
stopped receiving official credit. Not only was credit supply limited
because of monetary programming under economic stabilization,
but also the share of productive credit in total credit fell drastically:
from 30 per cent to 15 per cent between 1991 and 1996, while in the
trade sector it rose from 15 per cent to 41 per cent (Dauner and Ruiz,
1997). As a consequence, the dependency of sesame producers on
unfavourable forms of financing tied to commitments to sell to certain
traders has substantially increased. In 1995/6, approximately 70 per cent
of the total financing provided to the sesame subsector was distributed
via the commodity chain (Artola, 1997, Vermeer and Duarte, 1996).
Although the objective of general policy was to promote the sesame
crop, the impact of this change in credit availability and conditions
influenced quite negatively the real price evolution of the crop for the
producers. When credit took the form of a forward sale, the negative
impact on the price received was in the order of 25 per cent (data from
1996/7).

Analysis of sesame commodity chains in Nicaragua

To obtain a more detailed vision of the problems and opportunities facing the sesame subsector in Nicaragua, we shall now undertake a tentative comparative analysis of different sesame production–marketing
chains. The methodology is based on the methodologies of subsectoral
analysis (Boomgard *et al.*, 1992) and the commodity chain perspective
(Gereffi and Korzeniewicz, 1994). These methodologies are based on
the idea that 'real markets' for products form separate articulated
chains, each with particular characteristics. Each chain is conceived as
'a series of linked activities that run from the first stage, production,
passing through the processing of the product and marketing, before
finally reaching the consumer' (Wallerstein and Hopkins, 1994). So, in
order to reach the consumers of Japan, Europe and the USA, sesame
passes through different arrangements made between producers–
processors and traders–distributors–consumers, and the nature and
content of these arrangements are what gives each chain its particular
character. The chains have a global character, each one having its own
internal governance structures which determine, for better or worse,
how they function and the level of success achieved by the actors in
the market framework. Gereffi and Korzeniewicz (1994) distinguish
between producer-driven and consumer-driven chains. In the latter,
which clearly corresponds to the sesame sector, competitive pressure
determines the environment of the producers who have little capacity
to shape their own participation in the market. As we shall see in
the following analysis of the sesame chains, commodity chains are also
characterized by the degree of vertical integration between their different phases.

The structure of the chains

It is possible to identify four alternative chains, or four different institutional ways of transferring the sesame seed from the farm to the consumer in the foreign markets (see Table 3.3). The first two organize
the procurement and marketing through local networks of buyers
linked to cooperatives and cooperative unions (the 'cooperative' chain),
or through private local traders linked to private companies (the
'private' chain). In both cases, agroindustrial plants are paid to provide
the processing service, while some actors in the chain export directly
without processing. The product is sold, in natural form or hulled,
to national processing plants, regional enterprises (predominantly
Guatemalan) or international brokers. The 'cooperative' chain is

Tabel 3.3 Main characteristics of the sesame commodity chains

Item	Cooperative	Private	Guatemala	Plants
Size				
No. of producers	4833	9000	1526	1518
No. of companies	4	4	2	7 (4 active)
Volume stored (cwt)	58000	162000	38000	63000
Organization of procurement	Local network, linked to credit	Local, mobile network, linked to financing	Mobile and in warehouse, competes via prices procurement agents	Mobile and in plant, pays good commission to
Relationship with producers	Sales contract, pre-harvest buying	Sales contract, pre-harvest buying	Buying of raw materials previously bought raw materials and sold seed	Buying of raw materials,
Relationship with agro-industry	Buys services, previously part of agroindustry	Buys services	Carries out own seed processing	Carries out own seed processing
Level of processing	Natural/hulled	Natural/hulled	Hulled, high quality natural, and sweets	Hulled
Marketing	Sold to broker and alternative market	Sold to broker	Sold to distributor	Sold to broker and distributor

Source: Field interviews, 1997.

relatively more integrated, since a single company consisting of base-level cooperatives and second-degree cooperative unions integrates operations. The 'private' chain is less integrated, with coordination between procurement agents and trading companies running mainly through the market.

In the last two chains, one linked to the Guatemalan agroindustry ('Guatemala') and the other to the Nicaraguan agroindustry ('plants'), the whole procurement, storage, processing and export process is organized by the agroindustry. Both are vertically integrated beyond the procurement stage, which is organized by private agents acting on behalf of the agroindustry. A crucial difference between the two lies in the quality of processing and insertion into the foreign market. 'Guatemala' is building up its reputation for greater variety and better quality of products (natural and hulled ICTA-R seeds and sweets). It has also found a niche in the best markets (Japan and the USA), and is generally much better-connected to profitable markets, while the national plants sell principally to international brokers and to a lesser extent to distributors without enjoying, up to the time of writing, particular benefits from specific markets niches, reputation or quality.

In the procurement process, there is an evident difference between the 'cooperative/private' and the 'Guatemala/plants' chains. Given the greater operating capital of the latter two chains, they contract private procurement agents who travel around collecting the seed during harvest and buy at 'market' prices. 'Guatemala' competes with the rest by paying higher prices, or by accepting lower quality seed for similar prices.

Relative profitability and efficiency of the chains

In order to compare the different chains we calculate two tentative indicators: profitability and efficiency. Profitability will be measured by the profit margin of the chains. Efficiency is approximated by the price gap: the difference between the price paid to the producer and the fob price, including the CBT. The chains with the widest price gaps are the most inefficient ones. Note that in 1996/7 profitability was low in nearly all the chains, because fob prices went down from US$68–70 per cwt in 1995/6 to US$43–45.

From Table 3.4 we derive that the profit margin is lower in the 'cooperative' and the 'Guatemala' chains (8.9 and 8 US$/cwt) than in the 'plants' and 'private' chains (10.5 and 13.3 US$/cwt). The beneficial result of the 'private' chain is mainly because of its lower purchasing price (US$18 compared to US$22–25) and its lower procurement cost (US$2 compared to US$4–6 in plants and 'Guatemala'). Note also that the 'cooperative' chain has higher administrative, but lower financial, costs – the latter resulting from its access to concessional loans.

In terms of the price gap, the 'private' chain is the least efficient. Their local traders buy at the lowest prices, mainly because sesame market transactions are interlinked with other local transactions (for example, provision of credit for sesame or consumption needs or provision of

Table 3.4   Margins in the hulled sesame chains, 1996/7 (US$)

Item	Cooperative	Private	Guatemala	Plants
FOB sale price	43	43	47	45
Sale price + CBT (10% CBT)	47.3	47.3	51.7	49.5
Price paid to producer	22	18	25	22
Price gap (incl. CBT)	28.3	29.3	26.7	27.5
Procurement cost	2	2	6	4
Cost of processing	8.5	8.5	7.5	7.5
Cost of exportation	2	2	2	2
Cost of financing	0.84	1.5	1.5	1.5
Cost of administration	3	2	2	2
Margin before CBT	4.6	9	3	6
Margin + CBT	8.9	13.3	8	10.5

Source: Field interviews, February 1997.

market goods). The traders of the 'private' chain are local patrons with a dominant position in their communities and on whom many of the poorer peasants depend critically for easing their survival strategies. The lower sesame price indicates the premium producers are prepared to pay in order to benefit from the interlocked package of transactions. Expansion of procurement through this chain indicates total transaction costs advantages of the chain at the local level. The arrangement evidently has its efficiency and equity cost.

The 'cooperative' chain is almost as inefficient as the private one, but it pays a better price. In addition to providing intermediary credit in the form of inputs (seeds, urea), or cash when available, the cooperatives offer the producers technical assistance (technical support for production). The credit interest rate is implicit in the overpricing of inputs or the underpricing of the crop delivered. Not all of the costs (of technical assistance in particular) are transferred to the producers, since some are paid for by foreign development assistance. The chain is less flexible than the private system in the sense that it is more strictly tied to the sesame trade. Also, the transaction has relied less on personalized relationships than on formal contracts and supervision (for example, sales contracts or supervision from technicians). The commercial activities involved have nevertheless become increasingly similar to those of the 'private' chain, with the cooperatives supplying medium-scale producers with inputs, and even money, for procurement. The medium-scale producers, in turn, finance the small-scale producers, using almost the same procedures as the local traders.

Both the 'Guatemala' and the 'plants' chains buy straight from the farm or from the warehouses/plants. In contrast to the other chains, they do not offer any services because of the limited nature of their local contacts. Thus, in order to guarantee supply, they need to pay a better price to the producers. The difference between these two chains lies in the fact that 'Guatemala' buys and sells at higher prices than the 'plants', even at the expense of low profits in 1996/7. The chain probably accepted lower profit margins in order to secure its presence in Nicaragua and thus meet commercial obligations with overseas buyers.

Overall, the sesame business has been a profitable one. The most profitable and expanding 'private' chain is, however, the least efficient in terms of the price gap, which implies that it transfers the macro price signals the least effectively to the producers. In this context, it is also worth noting that, despite the sesame promotion policies, the terms of participation of the small-scale producers in all the chains has evolved unfavourably. According to our estimates (see Table 3.5), there was a tendency for the price gap to widen. This indicates that sesame promotion policies at the macro level were blurred by inefficient transmission of price signals through highly imperfect markets to the local producers.

The extension of unfavourable forms of financing following the withdrawal of BANADES in 1992 is undoubtedly an important factor in explaining this tendency. In the 1995/6 cycle, only 36 per cent of the sesame was grown supported by bank financing (BCN, 1997). Also, it is obvious that the incentive provided by the CBT is not being passed on

Table 3.5   Evolution of the producer price/fob price gap, 1991–5

Item	1991/2	1992/3	1993/4	1994/5
Producer price C$*	unavailable	unavailable	135	205
Exchange rate C$/US$**	5	5	6.32	7.08
Producer price US$	22.75	17.4	21.4	28.95
Fob price	34.6	38	35	42.62
Fob price + per cent CBT	34.6	43.7	40.25	49.1
Gap US$	11.85	26.3	18.85	20.15

Notes:
  * Average price paid to producers for 1991/2 in US$ by four large companies; 1992/3, price in C$: source Canales, 1993. The average price for 1993/4 is based on Dauner, 1994, and the price for 1994/5, from Greene *et al.*, 1995.
  ** For the official exchange rate for the 1993/4 and 1994/5 cycles we took the average rate during 1994 and 1995.
Source: Based on BCN indicators for 1994 and 1996, and INCAE indicators for 1992.

to the producers. In the first year of its application, the price paid to producers fell despite a higher export and CBT price.

Prospects for sesame producers' participation in the chains

What are the possibilities for improving the 'real market' of sesame, and especially for enhancing the articulation of peasant producers to the chains? In the following we shall focus particularly on whether improved vertical articulation of the chains could improve perspectives for the sesame trade, as well as peasant participation in the activity. According to the framework of analysis by Williamson (1991), the optimality of market versus hierarchical governance structures depend on the relative presence of certain attributes. In the case of the sesame trade, we believe that there could be at least two factors that indicate efficiency benefits incurred with higher degrees of deliberate hierarchical coordination and cooperation. The first is the presence of asset specificity, which is the degree of specificity of an investment made by an enterprise in order to carry out a specific transaction (Williamson, 1991). In the case of sesame, these are mainly the investments in processing capacity and commercial contacts. The second is the high incidence of 'non-economic factors such as confidence and reputation … which are decisive in terms of economic efficiency' as they create 'mutual and on-going learning effects' between the actors (Bonus, 1991). In the disarticulated and distrustful environment of rural Nicaragua this could be particularly relevant.

First, we see that the 'Guatemala' and 'plants' chains tend to be more vertically integrated after the procurement phase. In terms of upward integration, 'Guatemala' in particular has better access to the international market. The product offered is superior because of its capacity to guarantee the appropriate quality to meet different demands. The ICTA-R variety developed in Guatemala has its best market for natural, high-quality seed in Japan. Meanwhile, the quality of seed hulling is well-recognized by buyers who visit the plants and observe first-hand the different processing stages (drying techniques, control of foreign matter, treatment for salmonella, quality grading and so on). Because of this, Guatemalan sesame has achieved greater prestige and fame than its Nicaraguan equivalent, which sells for US$2–3 less (Hosking, 1994). However, several companies that operate in the 'plants' chain are similar to 'Guatemala', with an acceptable penetration into the North American market (direct sale to distributors) and good contacts and market information.

In both chains, installed processing and commercial capacity is evidently specific to the sesame trade. Profitability depends critically on capacity utilization such that processors and traders are dependent on the producers' 'willingness' to supply sesame seeds. Capacity utilization in Nicaragua is, however, only 48.5 per cent (Parrilli, 1997), indicating problems in the linking of plants with producers. The 'Guatemala' chain also tried to involve Nicaragua in the production of the ICTA-R variety, but failed because of lack of appropriate articulation with producers, both with respect to the diffusion of technology and the compliance of commercial contracts (credit).

Typical for both chains is that the link with the producers operates through a relatively anonymous market. Technical assistance or other services are rarely offered. Contracted procurement agents are responsible for buying and selling the seed, using quality parameters and a buying price set by the companies, although they do have some leeway during negotiations. The company pays the agents a commission for each hundredweight gathered. In practice, the agents first negotiate the price according to the parameters set by the company, but then tend to manipulate the weight and quality of the seed in their own favour, applying fines of 3–4 per cent (equivalent to US$0.40–0.50 per cwt). These abuses prevail more among small-scale producers. Impersonal relations and abuses affect the relative attractiveness of the chains, especially for smaller producers, and thereby contribute to the underutilization of capacity.

In the 'plants' chain, previous efforts to build up a broader relationship with the producers did not work because the conditions were not conducive to an efficient exchange and because of a lack of a long-term perspective. There are two important factors here. First, the policy of providing credit to producers failed because of severe repayment problems caused by a lack of governance structures that might have ensured compliance with contractual commitments. Second, the introduction of new technology (varieties with greater potential) by companies which sold imported 'improved seed' at US$40–50 per cwt was not widely accepted by the producers. They felt cheated paying high prices (US$90–100 per cwt) for genetic material which was of a low quality because it had not been adapted to the local conditions. Thus the company made good profits in the short term, but the producers became increasingly distrustful and the possibility of establishing lasting relations vanished.

The 'cooperative' and 'private' chains are less vertically integrated, although the former tends to have closer links to the plants. Here, production and trade are mainly orientated towards the less profitable areas of the sesame market (low quality, 'mass market'), and so the capacity of the chains is mainly orientated towards producing greater volumes. Both chains have local patterns connected to a supralocal structure (unions of cooperatives, export companies, for example), but have weak links with the international market.

The cooperatives, which were originally ECODEPA distribution and procurement agents, are part of a network consisting of unions of cooperatives. Access to technical information (new varieties, crop handling and so on) and to resources (credit, input and seeds) can help small-scale producer members incorporate technology and increase other market options at the local level. However, credit in the form of inputs and technical assistance does not always respond to people's needs. In this sense, the organic relationship between cooperative companies and their members has grown weaker. The number of members has fallen and the cooperatives have done little to attract new members. Two reasons explain this. The first is confusion over the 'cooperative nature' of the project. While a significant number of the members remarked during interviews that surplus should be distributed in relation to the amount bought or sold by each member, the cooperatives' marketing mechanisms do not allow for the idea of sharing profits (Lewin *et al.*, 1993). Second, the local power structure (dominated by a small rural elite) is largely run by a coordinator who is not accountable to the members and is elected by representatives in the top leadership, who have a better social position (including, for example, a better education, access to training, information and foreign contacts) than the vast majority of members (Lewin *et al.*, 1993). This contributes greatly to the continuation of a hierarchical structure depending on favouritism which channels 'favours' to the local clients through loyal intermediaries (Marchetti, 1994). This type of structure does not allow 'a permanent renegotiation of the terms and prices of a commercial relation' (Bonus, 1991) for the vast majority of small-scale producers.

The 'private' chain has been growing stronger as a result of the lack of liquid resources in rural areas. This chain's governance structure is based on strong ties between local traders and producers. The relationship involves not only buying sesame seeds but also exchanging basic consumer goods used by rural families, and inputs for agricultural production. There is also a close personalized relationship which allows the traders to control the transaction costs because of their access to a local information pool, which provides information on their clients' strengths and weaknesses. The small-scale producers have the advantage of being integrated into a diverse and flexible system which corresponds to their needs, but which is also semi-exploitative, provides limited economic benefits and does not promote horizontal relationships that would lead to mutual learning.

Conclusions

This analysis reveals two fundamental problems in the sesame 'real market'. First, the liberalization policies and incentives aimed at non-traditional exports have run up against a weak downward linkage that does not allow the 'macro' prices to be passed on to the producers, or an improvement in the use of the installed industrial capacity. Second, the existing form of linkage does not generate sufficient vertical collaboration between the actors to improve access to the international market through greater recognition or a greater capacity to guarantee the appropriate quality for the demands of specific, more profitable markets.

The importance of vertical integration for areas with more opportunities poses the question of how to reorganize the 'real market' more efficiently. On the one hand, the linkage of the 'Guatemala' and 'plants' chains is inefficient in its downward vertical integration, both in terms of the high transaction costs and mutual opportunism involved, and in terms of the limited possibilities of collaborating and building confidence with the producers. However, 'Guatemala' does have a relatively better upward integration. On the other hand, while the 'cooperative' and 'private' chains have advantages in their downward integration, they are not very well upwardly integrated. The former is promising in that it provides access to information and resources, but is inefficient and hierarchical, partially reproducing the private scheme of linkage which does not generate the kind of horizontal possibilities that encourage mutual, ongoing learning. The 'private' chain maintains good control over transaction costs, but is semi-exploitative and does not transfer signals/benefits to the producers.

Attempts should be made to improve the vertical integration of the existing chains, based on their particular opportunities and limitations. This could be achieved by increasing the efficiency of the chains and encouraging the producers through price/quality, creating negotiation mechanisms for varieties, production plans, the flow of information and the definition of standards and quality norms. The linkage between the best-organized sesame producers and those chains with access to more profitable areas of the market could be improved, implementing a kind of long-term 'contract farming' which benefits both parties and is governed by more democratic and horizontal relationships. The cooperatives could play an important role in strengthening this link in two directions: (a) in terms of regional integration, the cooperatives could export good quality natural sesame to the Japanese market through Guatemalan companies; and (b) a better internal vertical collaboration would make it possible to sell sesame to the US market through the best hulling plants and Nicaraguan export companies.

Outside intervention could also be helpful in reorganizing the chains. Both the state and civil society could make a contribution. NGOs could act as social intermediaries between the producers and the chain. With the support of technical advice, they could focus on the construction of clear and attainable mechanisms for vertical coordination. The government, for its part, could improve the coordination of the plants with the producers and buyers. This could be done in a backward direction by defining with the cooperatives the quantity and quality of the product flows (seed standards and quality norms, and prices for the different product categories). This will be possible if the measure is accompanied by technical and market research which facilitates the introduction of new production and processing technology adapted to the country's agricultural and industrial structure and the demands of world trade. In a forward direction, they could help to increase contacts (participation by industrialists/exporters in international fairs), and distribute publicly recent information (prices and possible buyers, market niches, for example). In this respect, the diplomatic missions in the main consumer countries and international NGOs interested in fairer north–south trade would be a good source of information and contacts. There is also a need to promote a more diversified industrial structure adapted to local conditions, but which has a greater capacity to respond to a more differentiated demand. New export products based on sesame could be developed. Studies could be carried out on recent experiences in local, small-scale oil extraction and the production of flour and essential oil in the León and Chinandega areas.

Notes

1. The need to harvest the crop at exactly the right moment makes it very difficult to organize the labour process on a larger scale. This is the main reason why it is historically a peasant crop.
2. Baumeister, 1991. The two big consumers (the USA and Japan) total US$62 million between them, and it is estimated that the most important

consumers in Europe (Germany, the United Kingdom and the Netherlands) total around US$40 million.

Bibliography

Artola, N. (1997) *El subsector ajonjolí en Nicaragua*, Managua: Nitlapán-UCA.

BCN (Banco Central de Nicaragua) (1997) 'Indicadores económicos', *Gerencia de Estudios Económicos*, vol. III, no. 3, Managua.

Baumeister, E. (1991) in R. Ruben and G. van Oord (eds), *Más allá del Ajuste*, San José: Costa Rica.

Bastiaensen, J. (1991) *Peasants and Economic Development: A Case-study on Nicaragua*, Antwerp, PhD thesis: UFSIA.

Boomgard, J., Davies, S. P., Haggblade, S. J. and Weed, D. C. (1992) 'A Subsector Approach to Small Enterprise Promotion and Research', *World Development*, vol. 20, no. 2, pp. 199–212.

Bonus, H. (1991) 'The Cooperative Association as a Business Enterprise. A study in the Economics of Transactions', in E. Furubotn and R. Richter, *Journal of Theoretical and Institutional Economics* (JITE), Texas: A & M University Press.

Canales, R. (1993) *Impacto de la desregulación en el mercado del ajonjolí*, Managua: ESECA.

CEI (Centro de Exportaciones e Importaciones) (1996) *Nicaragua reporta crecimiento en sus exportaciones de ajonjolí*, Managua: CEI.

CETREX (Centro de Trámites de Exportaciones) (1996) *Memorias de tramites de exportaciones*, Managua: CETREX.

Dauner, I. (1994) *Chinandega Norte: Caracterización del territorio y tipología de productores*, Managua: Nitlapán-UCA.

Dauner, I. and Ruiz, A. (1997) *Estrategia de financiamiento rural*, Managua: Nitlapán-UCA.

Food and Agriculture Organization (FAO) (1994) *Agricultural Production Year book*, Rome: FAO.

Gereffi, G. and Korzeniewicz, Y. (1994) *Commodity Chains and Global Capitalism*, New York: Praeger.

Greene, D., Espinoza, M. A., Quintanilla N. V. and Garcia, C. (1995) 'Analisis de la proteccion de los productos oleaginosos', Borrador de Discusion, Programa Agricola CONAGRO/BID/PNUD. Ministerio de Agricultura y Ganaderia, MAG. Managua, Nicaragua.

Helpman, E. and Krugman, P. (1992) *Trade Policy and Market Structure*, Cambridge, Mass: MIT Press.

Hosking, N. (1994) *La Cadena Agroexportadora*, Unpublished document.

Kaimowitz, D. (1992) *El apoyo tecnológico necesario para promover las exportaciones agrícolas no tradicionales*, San José, Costa Rica: IICA.

Lewin, E., Hernández, J. R., Lolheme, H. L., Wattel, C. J. (1993) *Apostando a la comercialización cooperativa. ECODEPA y las tiendas Campesinas en la Nicaragua de los noventa*. ASDI/DGIS, Managua, Nicaragua.

Marchetti, P. (1994) *Experimentación con nuevas modalidades de la educación popular para el desarrollo local*, Managua: Nitlapán-UCA.

Maldidier, C. and Marchetti, P. (1996) *El Campesino-Finquero y el potencial económico del campesinado nicaragüense*, Managua: Nitlapán-UCA.

Parilli, D. (1997) *Diagnóstico y propuesta para una estrategia de desarrollo agroindustrial en Nicaragua*, Managua: Nitlapán.

Vermeer, R. and Duarte, R. (1996) 'Investigacion Aplicada: Posibles Mecanismos de Vinculacion entre la Banca Comercial e Intermediarias Financieras'. Banco del Campo, SNV, Nitlapan/Bilance. Managua: Nicaragua.

Wallerstein, I. and Hopkins, T. K. (1994) in G. Gereffi and Y. Korzeniewicz (eds), *Commodity Chains and Global Capitalism*, New York: Praeger Publishers.

Williamson, O. (1991) 'The Economics of Governance: Framework and Implications', in E. Furubotn and R. Richter (eds), *Journal of Theoretical and Institutional Economics* (JITE), Texas A & M University Press.

4
The Hierarchical Legacy in Coffee Commodity Chains

René Mendoza

'Small producers are not poor because they're small, but because they're alone.'

Introduction

In the late 1990s, Nicaragua has gradually started to recover from a prolonged and profound economic crisis and the country faces the challenge of confronting the problem of massive poverty. At the time of writing, over half the population is living below the poverty line, and in rural areas this proportion is even higher (Martínez, 1997). A cause for concern is also that, under current economic recovery, poverty, – especially in the rural areas – is not declining. In this context, this study of the coffee sector investigates some of the reasons why rural poverty seems to persist. Coffee constitutes the most important rural activity and has already played an important role in economic recovery.[1]

Our analysis is inspired by Boomgard *et al*'s 'subsector analysis' (1992) and Gereffi's 'global commodity chain' approach (1994). Within this framework, we shall identify three broad coffee chains: a traditional chain dominated by private national and transnational processing enterprises and accounting for 90 per cent of the market; an alternative chain covering 4 per cent of the market and exporting to European 'fair trade' organizations, and finally, a small organic chain which exports organic coffee and accounts for less than 1 per cent of total exports. In our study we shall focus on the Nicaraguan side of the chains, and particularly on the participation of the poorer small-scale producers.

First, we shall present a brief interpretation of the relative efficiency and the structure of value added of the chains. This provides the starting point for an analysis of the underlying social and institutional reality of the chains, which in turn explains their relative results. In the final section, we develop an approach to tackle the institutional deficiencies that have been encountered.

Coffee chains and the social structures

International coffee prices are quite volatile and show a clear historical downward trend. Both these factors have had negative effects on the production conditions of the crop. Prices to final consumers have not been variable in the same way, since the large multinational corporations, such as General Food and Nestlé, have the capacity to absorb price fluctuations into their profit margins (Clairmonte and Cavenagh, 1988). Oligopolistic control of trade, processing and the final consumer market by these corporations also reduces perspectives for a more advantageous entry into the consumer market by the producing countries. A number of tariff and non-tariff barriers impede the entry of coffee in a form other than as green beans.

The estimates for the three coffee chains in our research (see Table 4.1) indicate that most of the value added of the final coffee product is generated in the industrialized, consumer countries. Both the share of the producer countries and that of the local producers in total value added has decreased dramatically over the years. The Nicaraguan price still represented 50 per cent of value added at the end of the 1970s (Clairmonte and Cavenagh, 1988), but in the late 1990s it accounts for only about 25 per cent (own data), and the producers' share of value added has fallen even more: from 33 per cent in the 1940s (Wickizer, 1943) to between 10 per cent and 20 per cent in the 1990s. It is also interesting to note from our data that the basic structure of value added does not differentiate between the three chains, despite the differences in technology, markets and organization (see below). The fair trade chains do, however, pay higher absolute prices. They can do so since both chains serve specific market niches with their particular types of coffee: a 'fair trade' product produced by poor producers and – in the organic case – also produced without any chemical input. At the same time, however, we see that the distribution of costs and margins is similar (organic) or worse (alternative) in the fair trade chains. For the organic chain, this implies that the producers receive substantially higher farm-gate prices which, coupled to their cheaper technology, results in substantially improved producer incomes. However, in the case study of our alternative chain, much of the absolute advantage is lost through inefficiency in processing and

Table 4.1   Composition of average price of 100 gm of coffee, 1996

| | Instant coffee[+] | | | | Roasted coffee[++] | |
| | Traditional market | | Alternative market | | Organic market | |
	US$	%	US$	%	US$	%[+]
Consumer's price	2.77	100	3.70	100	1.50	100
Wholesale and retail distribution	0.69	25	1.03	28	0.35	23*
Marketing licensing	0	0	0.07	2	–	–
Commercial advertising	0.168	6	0.48	13	0.015	1
Roasting, storage, transport, financing, import	1.24	44.7	1.34	36.34	0.41	27.5
Taxes	0	0	0	0	0.33	22
FOB price	0.69	24.9	0.76	20.5	0.40	26.5
Export taxes and other fees	0.04	1.5	0.05	1.4	0.02	1.3
Processing, financing, transport, bags and other export costs	0.14	5.1	0.15	4.1	0.08	5.2
Producer's price	0.51	18.4	0.53	14.30	0.30	20

Notes: [+]Instant coffee traded with Great Britain. [++]Roasted organic coffee traded with Germany.
*13 per cent of this margin is used to finance development projects.
Source: Mendoza (1996).

marketing. Note that the 33 per cent mark-up on the final consumer price translates into only a 10 per cent higher border price and into a poor 4 per cent higher farm-gate price to the producer.

Although it is clear that the general distribution of value added in the coffee chains and its historical evolution are not favourable to the country, and even less so to the producers, the point of departure of our further analysis is the conviction that there is still a considerable possibility of improving poor producers' participation in coffee activity. In general, efforts can be made to reduce transaction costs, higher quality coffee could be produced and access to international markets could be improved; in particular, specific market niches that are promising for the poor producers – such as the organic and fair trade markets – could be better served. It should, of course, be noted that more could be achieved by reducing costs on the international side of the chains. In the so-called 'fair trade' chains, a relatively larger part of total added value is appropriated by the developed countries. However, we have limited our analysis here to the Nicaraguan side of the chain.

We present a diagnosis of the institutional quality of the different coffee commodity chains and try to relate this to the scope and possibilities for improving their performance. The hypothesis is that the rigidity of the institutional structure of the chains to a large extent determines the poor producers' disadvantageous articulation to the coffee trade, causing both poverty and suboptimal productive efficiency. We believe that the specific situation of the 'real market' for coffee shaped by the coffee commodity chains cannot be understood without reference to the general institutional environment of rural Nicaragua. In fact, we believe that the problems with coffee only illustrate the consequences of the broader rural institutional crisis. In this way, the study of the coffee chains provides us with a better understanding of the broader issues of rural poverty and underdevelopment.

Coffee chains and participation of small-scale coffee growers

A crucial dimension of the institutional environment is the hierarchical–authoritarian culture of rural society. This culture profoundly influences the (lack of) integration in the chains, and consequently their efficiency and effectiveness. We start our analysis with a few observations on this cultural legacy and its influence on rural social organization.

The legacy of the hierarchical culture

Putnam (1993) identified pervasive hierarchical relationships, which he called a 'second best' solution for economic organization, as a main cause of the relative underdevelopment of southern Italy. Following this perspective, it is relevant that in Nicaragua there exist similar social patterns, characterized by: (i) dependency relationships around families that have formed authoritarian and despotic concentrations of local power, and monopolize and control local as well as outside material and relational resources; (ii) the prevalence of ambiguous attitudes shown by the local population towards outsiders (for example, the government, enterprises, merchants and NGOs), involving both apparent submission as well as often passive resistance, attitudes that have been accentuated by marginalization and the need for survival under colonialism and subsequent military dictatorships – including the Sandinista revolution (see Mendoza, 1990); (iii) the predominance of opportunistic and selfish interests over longer-term cooperative and mutually beneficial relationships; (iv) the existence of a social structure in which legitimacy and local and national connections are rooted in patron–client relationships and a culture of bribery.

Over time, the predominance of such relationships has provoked a loss of social cohesion. Families trust ever-smaller numbers of people in their community, rumours and nicknames spread, loyalty is placed with those who have the greatest economic resources, and there is more verbal (if not actual) acceptance of technological and organizational 'packages' imposed by external agents and institutions. A feeling of frustration and impotence about the possibility of evolving alternative forms of organization, of being heard by the government, and of developing endogenous capacity has been emerging. The poor no longer believe in themselves, only in the hierarchical structure in which they grew up and in which they found meaning and security, despite the fact that the system does not fully recognize them. In this sense, the poor producers 'are alone'.

Following North (1990), we can say that these historical social relationships became institutionalized and evolved into generally accepted ways of structuring social interaction. Because of this path of dependency, the families move in a vicious circle of dependency relationships, submission or resistance, and opportunistic behaviour from which it is difficult to escape. Even the perception of an alternative is not evident. In fact, any fundamental change in the underlying structures would require the transfer to another institutional structure. Such a transition will be deemed to be too risky, costly and practically impossible unless external intervention is able to provide a 'system shock'.

The greatest problem with a vertical institutional heritage lies in its consequences for development and poverty. Within this structure of social interaction, it becomes impossible to reduce poverty, because the structure itself generates an unequal distribution of surplus and a lack of accountability, foments a spirit of fragmentation, and discourages cooperation and civic behaviour. Because of its high levels of distrust and mutual deceit, the vertical structure entails substantial additional transaction costs that often make the transactions barely feasible. It also prevents new organizations from becoming more efficient and democratic, since information is concealed and opportunistic behaviour prevails. Families are obliged to stick to traditional patrons because of their lack of access to material (capital or land, for example) and non-material resources (information, contacts with the outside, technology and so on). This dependency, in turn, induces them to reject other local people who may have a clearer vision of the common interest.

It also tends to transform peasant leaders into corrupt administrators in the absence of accountability procedures and controls. Finally, it undermines policies and programmes implemented by state institutions and/or encouraged by NGOs because of the domination of the local power-holders and the absence of real counterparts.

In short, this structure means that *any* government or non-government development action will tend to exclude the poorer groups and thus widen the gap between rich and poor, whatever good intentions might exist. In line with the intuitions of Putnam *et al.* (1993), we believe that the fundamental development problem might be strongly correlated to the deficiencies of the hierarchical social organization as described. As a consequence, the story of development is all too often like that of choosing a desired romantic song (reduce poverty) in a jukebox, putting in a coin (policy measures) and having to cover one's ears because hard rock comes out of the machine instead (poverty increases). In other words, without a change in the institutional structures that sustain poverty and exclusion, it will be difficult to produce more positive results.

The incapacity to overcome the legacy of hierarchical organization to a large extent explains why the country has not been able to take advantage of its existing economic potential, particularly that of the small and medium-sized peasant producers (Marchetti and Maldidier, 1996). This same incapacity also prevents the development of the almost clandestine intra- and inter-family cooperation relationships that could renovate the social fabric and source economic activity. These relationships of cooperation at present serve to resist to the dominant hierarchical structures rather than to serve any positive endogenous development project.

Deficiencies in the coffee chains as a result of the hierarchical legacy

We now turn to the analysis of case studies in the coffee chains in order to identify the impact of this general environment on the particular organization of the coffee trade.

The traditional chain

The traditional chain is poorly integrated, with compartmentalized relationships, mutual deceit between the different phases (production, processing and marketing), a hierarchical organization of intermediaries, and mutual distrust. It is a chain controlled by commercial enterprises which manipulate crucial information. The processors–traders generally underestimate the quality of the products traded in order to pay, on average, lower than adequate prices to the producers. Neither do the marketing enterprises ever disclose information on real costs, while they constantly invoke cost increases to justify the widening gap between the fob and the producer price. Also, for tax reasons, it is common to practice double book-keeping. According to the official data, hardly any profits are made and therefore producer prices cannot be increased.

A second characteristic of the chain is related to product quality and its remuneration. The quality of the coffee grain (grain size, cleanliness and aroma) determines what proportion is exportable and its quality grade (resulting in additional quality premiums from 1 to 4 US\$ per bag). Besides the variety and geographical origin, the relative humidity of the green bean is a crucial variable in determining *ex post* quality. High humidity not only means lower final volume, but also has a negative effect on aroma. Cheating during the process of assessing average humidity is a common practice in the chain, especially when dealing with poorer coffee producers. In some cases, the machine that estimates humidity is manipulated, and in many others, humidity is 'estimated' by the merchants on sight inspection of a small sample. Sometimes quality is determined *ex post* after drying, but clear mechanisms of control are absent.[2] The producers suffering under these generalized malpractices then tend to reciprocate by shirking on product quality, by giving false information on the geographical origin of the crop; selling humid coffee to gain in weight; adding low-quality beans, stones and dirt; doctoring the sample taken for determining average quality and so on. The combination of actions on both sides results in a classical adverse selection dynamic reducing the average quality of market supply substantially as well as reducing the farm-gate price to the poor peasants.

The coffee is procured through an elaborate network of commercial intermediaries, situated between the producers and the marketing enterprises. They operate with capital from the enterprises, which is often distributed as credit tied to the coffee crop. There are three main types of intermediary: those who buy coffee in advance; those who buy and provide credit before or during the harvest; and those who buy on the spot. Some combine all three forms. Pre-harvest sales are most common in regions with poorer access to the market. This is also where more 'intermediaries of intermediaries' can be found, adding up to five levels of intermediary. At the top of the pyramid are people who receive credit from a marketing enterprise. They distribute it to several intermediaries, who travel to the principal market centres and distribute their capital to other local intermediaries. These, in turn, have means of transportation and/or small shops that allow them to transfer working capital to local intermediaries, who are paid commission on the quantities procured. These local intermediaries go from community to community, and from farm to farm, making the respective arrangements. The more 'intermediaries of intermediaries' there are, the greater the margin deducted from the producer's price. When there are more local intermediaries present at the local level, prices tend to be slightly better because of local competition. Quite often, however, the producers only know one single intermediary among the intermediaries upon whom they are entirely dependent. They lack information and the means to gain any other type of access to the market.

Within this traditional form of articulation, mutual distrust is on the rise and transaction costs increasing. Coffee buyers distrust the producers, so they increase their levels of control. The processors distrust the producers, so they invest in more labour in order to detect the problems in the drying yard; and the producers distrust the others and look for ways to avoid the controls. So a circular game of cat (buyers) and mouse (producers) goes on, the former coming up with new forms of control, and the latter with new ways to avoid them. In the end, none of the actors recognizes their responsibility in determining the quality of the product, and they all believe that the others are to blame and are the ones who are stealing. The distrust turns into rumours and gossip, and into frustration and impotence in the case of the producers.

Despite all this, or maybe *because* of it, the traditional chain persists and continues to grow – in the 1990s, unlike in the 1960s, controlled and directed by the marketing phase. The marketers can exercise control because they have capital and work through a hierarchical governing structure: the chain of 'intermediaries of intermediaries'. Consequently, the coffee producers, although they might try to switch intermediaries, always remain in the same game without incentives to improve the quality of their product or to play honestly. The vicious circle and the low equilibrium continues. Everyone could benefit more from a clearer articulation, but the deficient quality of collective action does not permit this high equilibrium outcome. Those most affected by the low equilibrium are evidently the small-scale coffee producers.

The alternative chain

The challenge for this chain has been to offer an 'alternative' to the traditional chain, or at least to 'develop' the poor sectors so that they can compete within the framework of a renovated traditional chain. It also thrives on other ideas, such as linking producers more directly to consumers. Thus in the 1980s international organizations such as Max Havelaar, Café Direct, Equal Exchange, Mitka and many others built up relationships with local organizations: in the case of Nicaragua, relationships were built up with cooperatives or the marketing enterprises that represent them. Although the amounts vary, they offer additional premiums on the international price of coffee (green bean) as was illustrated in Table 4.1. What is most striking about the alternative chain is that it not only reproduces fundamentally the mode of price distribution within the chain, but also the social practices of the traditional chain. It does not really create a new institutional structure: it does not even recognize the need for one, and therefore does not question the routines and habits of the traditional chain, at least in the case study we performed.

The spirit of compartmentalization between phases persists, although the justifications differ. The marketing enterprise (that is, the directors who nominally represent the coffee producers or cooperatives) hides information, arguing that the cooperative members could criticize the enterprise even when these producers are its legal owners. Another problem is that the enterprise does not have its own processing plant and must therefore contract processing services from another enterprise, which is itself also engaged in marketing. This leads to similar problems and tensions between the enterprise and the processing company as those described for the traditional chain, and the deceit concerning the humidity and quality of coffee may be even worse. By way of illustration, we can indicate that during the 1995/6 cycle, the first-level cooperatives sold part of the coffee to the cooperative marketing enterprise and part directly to the traditional chain. After going through the processing phase, the output sold through the cooperative was valued by the processing company at $5 per bag less than that of the output sold through the market, a difference that could not be justified by real quality differences. It is, however, also clear that producers, on average, sell lower-quality coffee to the alternative chain, since it is an 'alternative', solidarity chain (just as they are reluctant to pay back the credit they receive). The best quality coffee is often diverted to traditional merchants.

In the alternative chain there are also local intermediaries with their costs and their ambiguous roles as local power-holders. With the appearance of the alternative market, cooperative directors surfaced, and almost as a matter of course became new 'intermediaries of intermediaries' linked to an entire hierarchical structure of first- and second-level organizations. The only difference with the traditional intermediaries is that they offer themselves as representatives of the coffee producers. The directors' role is similar, not only because they play the part of 'intermediary' and deduct dollars per quintal of coffee, but also because their mediation has the same social characteristics as in the traditional chain. They have more access to various resources, exercise their role in a despotic, authoritarian manner (for example, they constantly interpret and change the rules of the game; they use credit to get hold of the coffee; they expel members who deal with other enterprises), they hide information, deceive the cooperatives with false promises, and legitimize themselves through their contacts with international organizations (buyers, banks, unions, the government and NGOs). All this allows directors to act without any accountability to the formal owner of the enterprise: the first-level cooperatives and producers. This situation also explains why the operating costs are so high (four times those of the traditional chain).

As a consequence, the previously detected problems of distrust in the traditional chain are not mitigated in the alternative chain – and perhaps even the reverse is true. The fact that the alternative enterprise hides information; that producers are deceived in the processing; that despite receiving a 10 per cent higher fob price, the producer's price is only slightly higher than in the traditional chain – and even less if additional cheating is taken into account; and that the directors of cooperative marketing enterprises operate fundamentally according to similar social practices as the traditional 'intermediaries', means that the few hopes the producers might have had of another institutional model have vanished. And, worse still, neither are they themselves organized properly, nor prepared to move towards another form of organization. All this results in increasing tension between the cooperative enterprise and the producers. The cooperative enterprise naturally expected that, because of its cooperative nature, procurement would not be a problem. Neither was it expected that quality – on the supply side or demand side – would be a problem. However, producers have been shown to supply poor quality, and 'solidarity' consumers have proved to be more exigent than expected. The problems created by this situation evidently put a severe strain on the organizational viability of the entire endeavour.

The experience of the alternative market in its frustrated wish to provide an 'alternative' reveals that institutional changes do not come about automatically with subsidies. Furthermore, it makes us question whether producers should market their products themselves. The case studied reveals that the dream of an autonomous own marketing enterprise does not arise from the rural bases. These are, rather, the dreams of external agents that intervene to encourage development, with interventions that have most often merely deepened the hierarchical relationships so that the new external agents – often those with radical democratic discourse – in fact end up being absorbed by the historical institutional structure. Producers, above all, dream about developing their own farm and therefore in the first place seek better links to the market, in whatever form.

The organic chain

This chain shares the same objectives as the alternative chain in relation to the traditional one, but certainly succeeds in producing better results. It overcomes many difficulties even though it does not cope appropriately with others. The achievements are mainly related to the distribution of information, while the difficulties lie in the social relationships needed to build trust. This chain also offers new elements to evaluate its effectiveness: specialization and flexible organization based on various counterparts.

In the organic chain, more information is provided to the cooperatives, for two reasons. The first is the presence and role of three counterparts: an internal counterpart from one of the cooperatives, a national counterpart from an institution that provides technical–agronomic support for organic production, and an external counterpart that represents the buying organizations. Pressure from these three forces has made the directors of the marketing enterprise improve the distribution of information. The second reason is that, as all the cooperatives produce organic coffee, periodic meetings are held to discuss technical issues and share agronomic information. These provide a forum making them aware of other problems that might persist in the chain as a whole. However, despite the improvement in the distribution of information, various problems persist. Many cooperatives do not manage to assimilate the information, so doubts persist concerning the price and selling costs. Furthermore, despite the pressure of the three counterparts, the directors of the marketing enterprise were unable to provide evidence for audit which could explain what happened to a sum of money supposedly used to bribe government officials. This also reveals that some enterprise managers confuse their role as administrator with that of leader, which often causes serious problems, including corruption.

Organic coffee is processed in a plant which specializes in organic coffee and belongs to one of the cooperatives. What is unique about this is that it allows for a drying-yard test, through which, after measuring the weight (for humidity) and quality of the coffee, a sample quintal of coffee is dried in the yard in the producer's presence. At the end of the day, once the required degree of humidity is obtained and the coffee is cleaned, it is weighed and its quality checked once again, and the parameters applied to the rest of the shipment. This kind of practice avoids possible deceit, shows people that they reap what they sow, and provides an incentive for them to concern themselves more with the quality of their product. However, this test has not yet been applied to all cooperatives and/or producers.

The levels of intermediation have been reduced but have not disappeared. In some of the cooperatives, located in geographically distant regions, directors continue to take advantage of other members' ignorance, which results in similar problems as in the other chains.

Unlike the alternative chain, this one specializes in the marketing and processing of organic coffee through two separate enterprises. The alternative chain does not work in this way, rather there is a multiplicity of activities (for example, marketing, credit, training and organization). The organic chain does not provide credit but supports the cooperatives' efforts to obtain funds directly from other financial institutions; nor does it provide technical assistance/training, which is provided by a national counterpart.

Finally, a good percentage of the producers receive higher prices than in the other chains, the premiums associated with organic coffee reach them in full, there is some distribution of information on the part of the marketing enterprise, and honest operations on the part of the processing plant, a reduction in the levels of intermediation, and a certain institutional security that increases as the counterparts become stronger, all of which has helped to increase the levels of confidence. This translates into lower transaction costs and greater efficiency in the chain. It is important to point out, however, that many structural problems persist. Hopes grow with the growing demand for organic products, but it is also important to remember that conversion from conventional to organic coffee takes years and requires switching from one institutional structure to another, which is not an easy task.

Some more general conclusions can now be drawn from the comparison of the three chains. First, it is clear that the traditional and alternative chains produce a 'low equilibrium trap': the actors behave by promoting self-interest as an optimal strategy, given the lack of cooperation from others. In contrast, the organic chain shows the possibility of a new, 'higher equilibrium' institutional structure: collaboration in the production of a truly organic, high-quality product; accuracy in weighing and measuring the coffee's quality at the processing plant, and the wider dissemination of information indicate that mutual collaboration as an optimization strategy contributes to correctly understood self-interest in a cooperative path throughout the chain. Second, the importance of democratizing information is obvious. The problem here, however, differs among the actors (phases). For producers, the problem is gaining access to information; in contrast, for the other actors it is the way in which the information is handled that has generally been detrimental to the producers and the country. Third, the transition towards a new institutional structure demands an understanding of the weight of hierarchical relationships in the operation of the chains, and the way in which they exert their influence. The more hierarchical, authoritarian and despotic the social relationships, the more difficult it will be to create economically, socially and ecologically efficient chains, or to obtain the results expected of certain policies. The paradox is clear: it is enormously demanding to construct a creative potential capable of overcoming poverty within a culture that presents so many obstacles.

Methodologies to enhance the institutional quality of the coffee commodity chains

In this final section, we turn to the question of how it might be possible to change from the kind of low-equilibrium situation found in the traditional and the alternative chain, to the higher kind of equilibrium found to a certain extent in the organic chain. But before turning to the 'how to' discussion, let us first summarize the main features characterizing the high-equilibrium situation. We identify a need to build mutual confidence, cooperation, transparency, smoothly-flowing information, and appropriate incentives to create a supply that meets international demand. There is also a need to encourage better horizontal organization (local counterpart) and vertical articulation with a sufficient amount of market competition. These would be viable in a renewed institutional structure, which in turn would be more possible if the existing potentialities were taken into account, especially the horizontal spaces for intra-family and neighbourhood cooperation found on the margins of the hierarchical relationships. The issue now is how to do so?

Because of the path dependency we described, we conclude that purely endogenous institutional change is hard to imagine. Rather than providing only a facilitating role, a mode of active intervention ('system shock')[3] is needed. In the case of the coffee commodity chains, the challenge is to replace traditional forms of intermediation based on patron–client relationships with a new form of local organization that invigorates or imposes new forms of intermediation between traditional processors/merchants and the producers. This step would also imply redistributing resources such as technology (know-how) and doing things in a more democratic way. Successful alternative and organic chains then act as a 'system shock' for the traditional chain (disseminating information, for example), so that the poorest producers could develop – individually and in their organizations – a capacity to participate on better terms in the traditional chain. In this sense, a viable proposal cannot be a completely horizontal or hierarchical programme, but rather a kind of pyramid that slowly broadens its base through a brokerage system, including a larger number of rural families. This is a proposal that views development as an issue of social organization, and of conflicts between governing structures; it is this kind of social organization that could achieve institutional change and thus alter the course of poverty.

The framework of action we propose is of the system-shock variety, drawing on features of other successful experiences to combat exclusionary, hierarchical social structures in order to achieve sustainability, such as the Grameen Bank in Bangladesh and Nitlapán's Local Development Fund in Nicaragua (see Chapter 9 of this volume). It starts from the premise that the majority of the actors in the commodity chain cannot be expected to behave altruistically, but are looking after their own (business) interests. Following this hypothesis, the creation of a governance structure with counter–balancing counterparts is critical to sustain transparent access to information for all parties, and the control of opportunistic behaviour in order to permit the continuation of mutually beneficial cooperation on a high-equilibrium path.

Counterparts and enterprise structures

For an enterprise or chain of enterprises to become efficient and effective, to provide for appropriate incentives for enhancing the quality of the product, and to disseminate information and encourage mutual collaboration, a flexible organization with articulated local and external counterparts is necessary.

The organization of the coffee chains or enterprises

An alternative marketing enterprise that wants to articulate with producers should, in our view, respect the following principles. First, it should define the *rules of the game* in such a way that nothing is left to chance or depending on any actor's benevolence; these rules should then be fulfilled and not changed constantly. If they do need to be changed, this should happen only after the new policies to be introduced have been evaluated and tested. Second, it must move *gradually and progressively*; enterprises that begin by trying to do too many things (commercializing, processing, credit and technical assistance, for example) tend to fail, so the enterprise should specialize in one activity and concentrate on one product, at least at the start. Third, it must invest in *building ties* with other enterprises, whether for others to provide the processing, technical assistance or credit services, or to solicit jointly financial resources, or collaborate in technical issues of mutual necessity. The vertical integration of one sector controlling all the phases, or one owner of the whole chain, tends to be inefficient. Fourth, it must create an atmosphere of *permanent improvement* in which each participant in an enterprise has something to contribute, and has the incentive to do so, generating a spirit in which there is real identification with the enterprise. And finally, it must *process and distribute information* through the development of local counterparts and a process of professionalization.

Local counterparts

None of the roles of an enterprise described here are possible without a real local counterpart; what is more, to the extent that more counterparts serve as countervailing powers, there will be a greater distribution of material and non-material resources, and greater effectiveness in neutralizing the effects of the hierarchical legacy. In this sense, the local counterpart represents the interests of the producers, guaranteeing that the rules of the game agreed upon with an enterprise are carried out, maintaining an accounting system of their financial activities so as to pressure for more accurate information, maintaining a fluid and open relationship with the producers (or grassroots organizations), and encouraging the creation of their own counterparts in order to pass on the baton. If this process were to take place, people would once again believe in their own capacity, build confidence among themselves, collaborate and concern themselves with the quality and weight of the coffee, and constitute themselves as real local counterparts with a defined collective stake in the business.

The greatest need for counterparts lies in the interior of the country, where communities are dispersed and hierarchical relationships run deep. This is where most of the coffee production takes place but where, according to figures from Fideg (1995), poverty is greatest. It is not surprising that the organic chain, which has succeeded in creating a local counterpart, is located in the more developed Pacific region of the country. In the interior, there is a double challenge for fomenting local counterparts where there is less of a tradition of horizontal organization.

External counterparts

External counterparts are as important as local counterparts, particularly at the start. The external counterparts are national and international organizations – coffee buyers, certifiers, or institutions that provide credit or technical assistance. Their functions are to support the existence and development of local counterparts and to see that the agreed-upon rules of the game are fulfilled and that information is distributed to the counterparts and rural families. To achieve this, it is important that the coffee buyers have representation in the country to ensure, for example, that the premiums actually reach rural families, or that some auditing mechanisms are established to verify the implementation of policies and principles. If such processes were to take place, they would contribute effectively to making the alternative chain truly alternative and renovating the institutional structure that lies at the heart of poverty and stagnation. All too often, international counterparts are much too distant and passive in this respect.

External counterparts could also be more effective if they were to intervene actively in a 'demand-driven' way, inducing producer actions according to the exigencies and potentialities of the market as they identify them. All too often, they act in a 'supply-driven' way, responding to demands by local producers based on the deficient information of potentialities as they know them. External counterparts could, in this sense, play a crucial role in linking poor producers with profitable international market niches.

Taking the part of a second kind of external counterpart are national organizations, which could enjoy the support of buyers within the framework of fomenting local capacities. For example, organizations such as CENIPAE enjoy great prestige within the country and in

Latin America because of the efficiency with which they certify organic coffee and provide technical assistance. But the majority of organic coffee buyers do not recognize CENIPAE, preferring international organizations such as OCIA, even when they know that this institution does not constantly check the farms and coffee processing plants throughout the year, as CENIPAE does, but only once a year. Considering the hierarchical relationships and the forms in which they manifest themselves described in the preceding two parts, is one visit a year enough to ensure that the coffee is really organic? Associating with organizations such as CENIPAE means becoming part of the country's 'culture of potentiality'.

A third type of external counterpart are the financial institutions, or those that provide technical assistance and advice. As Schumpeter (1961) noted, the development of the financial system can help technological innovation, and thus economic development.

Dissemination of information

The effective dissemination of information does not rely so much on the medium used, such as radio or pamphlets; the important thing is to create counterparts and establish communications between the different phases of the chain. For example, there must be 'round tables' between producers and processors to seek out ways of improving the quality of the product and the determination of weight – for example, reproducing the drying-yard test, and studying control mechanisms to avoid more opportunism. These kinds of meetings would also allow subjects such as intermediation and processing costs to be discussed. On this last point, for example, there is a difference between delivering coffee with the required grade of humidity and cleanliness to the processing plant, and delivering coffee with high humidity and dirt content, since the first implies more work and thus higher costs for the producers, and the second higher costs for the processing enterprise. Also, external counterparts can contribute by creating a coffee-related 'information exchange'. This exchange would concentrate on information related to prices, costs, quality and markets.

Role of the state in promoting private institutions with a public role

The state could also contribute with audits, but the right institutional environment for this currently does not exist. Distrust of the state has increased. However, as a national institution it could promote the

most efficient chains – for example, through credit to reduce intermediation costs, increasing the number of intermediaries, or providing
credit to more efficient and equitable chains, searching for market
niches, disseminating information and offering technical assistance
to enterprises and local counterparts as private institutions with a
'public role'.

The state could also play a more direct and specific role regarding its
own bureaucracy. The bureaucratic steps required for marketing are
numerous and complex, and sharply increase costs. Facilitating these
steps and making the normal paperwork process more open and
accountable would reduce costs and help to avoid corruption through
bribery.

Conclusion

We have established a clear link between the institutional legacy of
hierarchical–authoritarian social relations and the deficiencies of the
concrete governance structure of coffee commodity chains in
Nicaragua. We have seen how this culture of mutual distrust and
opportunism leads to disarticulated 'low-equilibrium' solutions to the
problem of economic cooperation and transaction. However, we also
identified a small commercialization chain of organic coffee that has
managed to avoid many of the negative consequences of the vertical
legacy and thereby was able to achieve a substantially higher level of
efficiency, benefiting all actors in the chain, including the small-scale
organic producers. On the basis of this experience, we also elaborated a
proposal for action in which the need for counter-balancing local,
national and international counterparts was stressed.

Notes

1. In 1996, coffee accounted for 21 per cent of the total agricultural GDP and
   generated 18 per cent of export earnings. It has experienced a spectacular
   boom since that time, but this was largely because of the pronounced
   increase in international coffee prices and of output effects.
2. In the few enterprises that specialize in processing and do not engage in
   trade, these practices seem to be considerably less in order to maintain long-
   term relationships with clients (see Mendoza, 1996).
3. The Sandinista revolution was a 'system shock', and while there were structural contributions such as the agrarian reform process, it sought to replace
   hierarchical relationships based on favouritism with a similar system revolving around the party. In the end, it was not sustainable. Now there are certain signs of a return to pre-Sandinista structures, but under very different

conditions and possibly with greater hierarchy and exclusion, insecurity and poverty.

Bibliography

Boomgard, J., Davies, S. P., Haggblade, S. Y. and Weed, D. C. (1992) 'A Subsector Approach to Small Enterprise Promotion and Research', *World Development*, vol. 20, no. 2, pp. 199–212.

Clairmonte, L. and Cavenagh, B. (1988) *Merchants of Drink. Transnational Control of World Beverages*, Kuala Lumpur: Third World Network.

Gereffi, G. (1994) 'The Organization of Buyer-Driven Global Commodity Chains: How U.S. Retailers Shape Overseas Production Networks', in G. Gereffi and Y. Korzeniewicz (eds), *Commodity Chains and Global Capitalism*, New York: Praeger.

ICO (1995) *Coffee Statistics. January–December 1989 to 1994*, London: ICO.

Martinez, T. (1998) *La pobreza rural en Nicaragua, hacia un desarrollo agropecuario integral*, Managua, Nicaragua: Nitlapán-UCA.

Mendoza, R. (1990) 'Los costos del verticalismo, un FSLN sin rostro campesino', *Envío*, Managua, Nicaragua: IHCA.

Mendoza, R. (1996) *Developing Institutional Change*, Brighton: University of Sussex.

North, D. (1990) *Institutions, Institutional Change and Economic Performance*, Cambridge: Cambridge University Press.

PNUD (1997) *Informe Desarrollo Humano*, New York.

Putnam, R. D. with Leonardi, R. and Nanetti, R. Y. (1993) *Making Democracy Work. Civic Traditions in Modern Italy*, Princeton NJ: Princeton University Press.

Schumpeter, Y. A. (1961) *The Theory of Economic Development*, New York: Oxford University Press.

Wickizer, N. (1943) *The World Coffee Economy*, Stanford: Stanford University Press.

Yeats, A. J. (1981) 'The Influence of Trade and Commercial Barriers on the Industrial Processing of Natural Resources', *World Development*, vol. 9.

Part 2

Land Reform and Land Markets

5
Land Reform and Land Transfers in El Salvador

Hans van Heijningen

Introduction

Between 1992 and 1997 the PTT (Programa de Transferencia de Tierras) land reform programme was implemented in El Salvador within the framework of the Chapultepec peace treaties of 1992. The first part of this chapter deals with the differences between the land-owning elite and the small agrarian producers, which developed historically in the context of the land reform programmes of the 1980s. Apart from their counter-insurgent character and the vertical implementation of the different land reform programmes, their limited effect on unequal land tenure patterns will be emphasized.

The second section describes the execution of the PTT programme and the lack of integrated implementation. This is followed by a preliminary evaluation of the PTT programme, focusing on the limited impact of the reform policies on the structure of land tenure. Its main effect has been a further increase in the number of micro farms. With respect to the present land-use patterns, the participation of land-reform beneficiaries in agriculture and the issue of land and bank debts, the underexploitation of a substantial part of the PTT areas and the lack of profitability in the production of agricultural products – above all, of basic food crops – will be stressed. We conclude with an analysis of the feasibility of land reform through land-market principles, and the possibilities and constraints of the 're-peasantization' strategy applied within the framework of the present internationalized and liberalized economy. The lack of competitiveness of Salvadoran agricultural products on the world market and the absence of policies stimulating production by the Salvadoran government (GOES), will probably provoke a gradual process of 'reproletarization' of the PTT sector.

A brief record of Salvadoran land reform programmes

The land reforms of the 1980s

El Salvador is a small (21 040 km²) and densely populated (262 inhabitants/km²) developing country in Central America, with more than 5.5 million inhabitants.

Traditionally, the economic and social differences between the Salvadoran landlords and the peasant population have been significant. In particular, the rise of the coffee sector, which stimulated the process of privatization of the communal lands of the indigenous population, provoked a strong polarization between the big landowners and the peasant population. This situation has made the rural sector one of the main arenas of political and social struggles throughout the twentieth century.

In 1971, 1.5 per cent of the landlords owned nearly 50 per cent of all agricultural land, a further 50 per cent of landlords possessed only 5 per cent, and more than 110 000 peasant families, representing about 30 per cent of the rural population, did not have any land at all. In an attempt to reduce the growing social and political differences, the Salvadoran Parliament (*Asamblea*) passed a law on land reform in 1976 (Ley de transformación agraria). Nevertheless, because of the strong resistance from the agrarian elite, the law did not have any real impact. By 1980, the number of landless peasant families had grown to 220 000 (Wolpold, 1994). The growing demand for land had also caused a process of fragmentation of small-scale peasant holdings; between 1960 and 1980 the average size of the growing number of micro-enterprises declined from 1.35 hectares to 0.9 hectares.

The absence of 'agrarian frontier' zones (*frontera agrícola*), and the limited capacity of the national economy to absorb the labour reserve, plus the strong population growth in the rural areas, provoked a process of deterioration of the overall living conditions for the majority of the peasant population.

The differences between the rural elite and the peasant sector, together with the continuing process of marginalization of the peasant sector, are generally considered to be the main causes of the armed conflict in El Salvador that lasted from 1980 to 1992. Semi-proletarian peasants played a central role as fighters in the guerrilla organizations united in the Frente Farabundo Marti de Liberación Nacional (FMLN) (Cabarrús 1985, p. 84).

The Salvadoran government, composed of Christian-Democrats and 'young officers', came to power through a military coup at the end of 1979. This government introduced a US-backed counter-insurgent policy based on both land reform and repression of popular resistance movements (Goitia and Galdamez, 1994, p. 139; Arene, 1995, p. 5).

In March 1980, the Junta Revolucionaria de Gobierno issued 'Decreto 153', which formed the starting point for the land reform process. The Salvadoran Institute for Land Reform (Instituto Salvadoreño de Transformación Agraria: ISTA) was charged with the execution of the programme. Agricultural enterprises of more than 500 hectares were confiscated, while their owners were indemnified by the state. The confiscated enterprises were then transformed into production cooperatives and transferred to landless peasants. In return, the beneficiaries were obliged to pay off their lands within a period of thirty years at a fixed interest rate of 6 per cent. They were exempted from these repayments for the first four years.

State intervention (politically conditioned confiscation of lands) and market regulation (indemnification by the state of the owners affected, based on the real value of the confiscated properties and repayment obligations by the new owners to the state) formed the two basic principles of the Salvadoran land reform during the 1980s.

In Phase I of the land reform, more than 31 000 beneficiaries gained access to 315 cooperatives with a total of almost 220 000 hectares of land. Roughly 8 per cent of the peasant families benefited from this policy, while about 15 per cent of the agricultural land was transferred (Fuentes, 1993, p. 14; Ruben, 1993, p. 6).[1]

Phase II of the land reform, which was to include 24 per cent of all agricultural land and about 15 per cent of the rural population, had been planned for farms larger than 100–150 hectares. However, because of a constitutional reform established in 1983, this phase of the land reform programme was never executed. During a period of three years, owners of the respective farms were given the opportunity to sell the surplus parts of their lands or to divide them among family members. By offering them this way out, a structural transformation of the – economically strategic – coffee sector did not materialize (Cabarrús, 1985, p. 88; Garcia, 1995, p. 27).

Nevertheless, the expectation that Phase II would be implemented gave a strong impulse to the development of a land market. More than 70 000 hectares were sold, while almost another 210 000 hectares came into the hands of new proprietors in alternative ways. In total, 17 per cent of landowners were engaged in land transfers during this period (Goitia, 1991, pp. 181–2).

Phase III of the land reform was based on the transfer of small plots of land to individual peasants by the Financiera Nacional de Tierras

Agrícolas (FINATA). This phase involved 70 000 hectares of land, representing about 4.7 per cent of all agricultural land, and some 40 000 beneficiaries (more than 10 per cent of the rural families) qualified for land assignment (Ruben, 1993, p. 2). The procedures regarding the indemnification of owners affected and the financial obligations of the beneficiaries remained the same as during Phase I.

Balance of the 1980s land reform

With the exception of Mexico, the Salvadoran land reform of the 1980s was the most extensive carried out in Latin America. Approximately 290 000 hectares (nearly 20 per cent of all agricultural land) has been distributed to more than 70 000 peasant families (representing nearly 20 per cent of the peasant population).

The peasant sector has by no means been involved in the process of planning and execution of the land reform by the Salvadoran government (Garcia, 1995, p. 24). The top–down approach applied was reflected in serious organizational weaknesses in the new cooperatives, while the necessary process of organizational, economic and productive consolidation has scarcely taken place.

Between 1980 and 1985 more than 40 per cent of the original members of the cooperatives left, while the inflow of new members amounted to 15 per cent a year (Ruben, 1993, p. 6). The economic development of the cooperatives was also critical; only a third of the Phase I cooperatives were able to meet their financial obligations related to the land acquisition process (the so called 'agrarian debts'). According to the bank debts (related to productive credits) the situation was more or less the same (Garcia, 1995, pp. 23–32).

The eventual results of the 1980s land reform programme lagged significantly behind the original goals because Phase II was not executed. One of the consequences was the prolongation – although in a mitigated form – of the differences between the sectors of landowners and the landless peasants. While 13 per cent of the agrarian producers owned 85 per cent of all agrarian lands, 87 per cent – having plots of 3.5 hectares and smaller – possessed only 15 per cent of the total land available.

An important sector of landless peasants did not benefit at all from the land reform of the 1980s. At the beginning of the 1990s, 370 000 families (or two-thirds of the rural population) did not have sufficient land to guarantee their family's subsistence (UNDP, 1995, p. 133). A significant part of this sector has no other economic alternatives;

16 per cent of the agrarian labour force has been reported to be completely jobless, and 56 per cent partially jobless (Ruben, 1993, p. 1).

The PTT programme

The making of the PTT programme

In spite of its political and social importance, the agrarian question was discussed only indirectly in the 'Peace Treaties of Chapultepec' signed by the government of El Salvador (GOES) and the FMLN in January 1992. The reason was obvious: the left-wing resistance movement did not have sufficient political and military power to make a structural transformation of property relations a condition.

Although both parties involved agreed about the necessity to carry out a special land transition programme (Programa de Transferencia de Tierras) for ex-soldiers and ex-guerrillas who were supposed to reintegrate into civil society, there were considerable differences of opinion concerning the scope and depth of the programme. In the New York Agreements of September 1991 (Chapter VII – Articles 1 and 2) both parties had only agreed that rural properties of more than 245 hectares would be considered for expropriation by the state. Representatives of the GOES were opposed to possible constitutional revisions that would facilitate the process of expropriation of other categories of rural properties to the benefit of the PTT programme (FUNDE, 1996, p. 4).

Even after the signing of the peace treaties in January 1992 the GOES and the FMLN were not able to establish an agreement concerning the concrete conditions of the land reform programme. Opposing conceptions regarding the quantity of land involved, the eventual participation of land squatters (*tenedores*) in the programme, and the option of transfer of lands to collectives blocked a potential agreement between the parties involved. While the GOES proposed the Land Bank (Banco de Tierras), the FMLN insisted that ISTA would coordinate the PTT programme (Santamaría, 1995, pp. 506–7).

The UN, in its role as a negotiator, presented a PTT proposal that was later accepted in essence by both parties. The proposal referred to 47 500 beneficiaries (25 000 land squatters, 15 000 ex-soldiers and 7500 ex-guerrillas). Depending on the quality of the land, these beneficiaries would gain access to a total of 122 500 to 166 250 hectares of land. The amount of funds required was calculated at between US$105m and 143m, mainly to be guaranteed by foreign donors. The PTT programme was to be executed completely by October 1993. The Land Bank, established in 1991 to promote a dynamic land market in relation to the 'reformed sector', was appointed to coordinate the programme (Flores, 1994, p. 11). The UN proposal also contained procedures related to supervision and monitoring (UNDP, 1993, p. 14; Santamaría, 1995, pp. 506–7).

The PTT programme, like the 1980s land reform, would be carried out according to market principles. State confiscation would not take place; the owners of both occupied and unoccupied properties would be completely free to decide whether or not to sell (Flores, 1994, pp. 2–5). The beneficiaries of the PTT program would get the opportunity to buy land from the Land Bank under the same financial conditions as during the land reform programme of the 1980s.

The legal recognition of the land-squatter status paved the way for the formal integration of squatters into the PTT programme. Nevertheless, the programme focused primarily on the productive reintegration of ex-soldiers and ex-guerrillas of the FMLN with a rural background who did not have any other rural properties (FUNDE, 1996, p. 4).

Regarding the juridical form to be applied in the transfer of lands, the UN proposed using the formula of *proindiviso*: land would be transferred provisionally to collectives of beneficiaries. This construction would help the beneficiaries to establish definitive property relationships (individually, collectively or a mixed form) within a period of five years (Funde, 1996, p. 6).

The implementation of the PTT programme

The UN time schedule based on the implementation of the programme before October 1993 did not correspond with the real situation in El Salvador. Because of obstacles, including the initial distrust between landowners and the FMLN, the obsolete state of the Cadastre (Catastro) and the Register (Registro de Propiedad), the legal bureaucracy and delays caused by the Land Bank in transferring funds to the sellers of land, the execution of the PTT program was delayed by more than three years. However, in December 1996, almost all of the beneficiaries – whose numbers had gradually declined from 47 500 to 34 700 – had received land.

According to information from UNDP (1995, p. 135) the lack of political interest in the PTT program by the GOES was the principal cause of the delays. Government authorities took no action to tackle the problem of the unnecessary complexity of the land transfer procedures, and in some cases even practiced pure obstruction (Borgh, 1995).

With respect to the financing of the PTT program, the USA – and more particularly USAID – took care of 57 per cent, the Salvadoran government 22 per cent, and the European Union (EU) 21 per cent of the funds involved.

Briefly, the procedure relating to the negotiation of properties and the assignment of lands to beneficiaries was as follows. Any person recognized as a beneficiary on the basis of the inventory of the army and the FMLN, and the subsequent process of verification by CEA-COPAZ (Comisión Especial Agraria of the Comisión Nacional para la Consolidación de la Paz), ONUSAL (UN) and OCTA-MAG (Oficina Coordinadora del Tema Agrario – Ministerio de Agricultura), received a credit document for the purpose of buying land worth approximately US$3500 per person. Army and FMLN executives, formally representing the interests of their respective sectors, contacted owners of occupied and unoccupied properties with the objective of buying them. Where an agreement was reached, the Land Bank fixed the definitive selling price based on the quality of the land for agricultural purposes (according to a system based on seven different categories) and the area of land. In addition, a lawyer or notary checked the documents of ownership, comparing them with the information from the Register and the Cadastre. They also checked that the property was without encumbrance. On account of the deficient functioning of institutions such as the Register and the Cadastre (Flores, 1994, p. 15) the whole procedure, which consisted of ten different formal steps in many cases, involved a minimum of efficiency and a maximum of bureaucracy.

Once all formal conditions had been met, a list of qualified beneficiaries was drawn up, who would eventually be the new owners. Normally, the number of beneficiaries was established by dividing the selling price of the property by the amount of land credit required. In general, little attention was paid to the formation of coherent groups of beneficiaries.

In practice, the execution of the land reform programme had a strong vertical character. Influenced by the war, representatives of the army and the FMLN acted in the way they thought convenient in the name of their rank and file. During the execution of the PTT programme the FMLN beneficiaries (ex-guerrillas and squatters) gradually succeeded in increasing their participation in the process.

Economically, the PTT land programme caused a reactivation of the land market, which had disappeared during the armed conflict, especially in the FMLN-controlled zones. This undermined and destroyed forms of collective management and cultivation that had been developed during the war within the framework of a subsistence economy.

Because of the absence of an established land market, the price of land transferred under the PTT programme varied considerably. While the quality of land in many cases was not a decisive factor, the price per hectare differed from US$485 to US$1930. On average, US$1195 per hectare was paid (Santamaría, 1995, p. 510). During the execution of the PTT programme the price of land tended to rise, while the quality of the land transferred decreased (Flores, 1994, p. 14; Wolpold, 1994; FUNDE, 1996, p. 13). Influenced by the general lack of profitability of agriculture, many landlords proved to be willing to sell land under the PTT programme. Though empirically unproved, a significant part of PTT funds are said to have been invested in the commercial and service sectors.

The lack of an established land market and solid institutional structures paved the way for financial irregularities during the execution of the PTT Programme.[2] Representatives of owners and buyers – often by mutual understanding – frequently charged substantial commissions which were negotiated in the selling price in collaboration with a representative of the Land Bank. Other mechanisms causing the leakage of PTT funds were the falsification of data regarding property extensions,[3] and the overvaluation of lands by Land Bank officials, who collaborated illegally with the vendors. Eventually a significant percentage of the funds managed by the Land Bank is said to have simply disappeared by embezzlement (interview with former EU-project director).

The lack of integrated implementation of the PTT programme

One of the major deficiencies of land reform processes in Latin America is the lack of integrated implementation; generally, land reform programmes have not been complemented by or coordinated systematically with other essential policies regarding productive credit, education and technical assistance, and overall economic and agricultural policies. This important shortcoming causes land reform processes in Latin America generally to be unsuccessful in establishing a productive and prosperous sector of small agrarian producers (Baumeister, 1994a). The PTT programme is by no means an exception to this situation.

With reference to credit, almost 100 per cent of ex-guerrillas and 33 per cent of the – less organized – ex-soldiers received a maximum loan from the GOES of US$1780 (with a fixed interest rate of 14 per cent and a pay-back period of five years starting in the second year). On the other hand, because of governmental opposition, only an estimated 10 per cent of the land squatters succeeded in getting the maximum credit for this category of US$1150 under similar pay-back conditions (FUNDE, 1996, pp. 14–5). Investment plans have never been developed for any of the categories involved, nor has there been any form of assistance or control regarding the use of the funds. In practice, a significant part of these credits was used for consumptive purposes, while its effects in terms of production are considered to be very limited. As a result, an important sector of PTT beneficiaries have in fact run up debts with the financial sector, which disqualifies them for further credit facilities.

According to a report of the Agrarian Commission of FMLN (Comisión de la Tierra) from December 1994, uptill that year, 66 per cent of the ex-guerrillas and 95 per cent of the land squatters had not received any training or other form of technical assistance related to the PTT programme. In contrast to this, the Secretary of National Reconstruction (Secretaria de Reconstrucción Nacional – GOES) indicated that 80 per cent of ex-guerrillas and 40 per cent of ex-soldiers had participated in theoretical and practical courses organized by CENTA (Centro Nacional de Tecnología Agropecuaria) and several NGOs.

Apart from the lack of conditions regarding agricultural training and technical assistance, these elements have never been integrated in the PTT programme. After three years, an important proportion of the 'students' still did not have the title deeds of their lands, and others had not received any credit or technical assistance (UNDP, 1993, p. 68). In addition, the educational and training facilities were reported to have a strong top-down character (FUNDE, 1996, pp. 16–7).

The PTT programme: preliminary balance

Land tenure

Under the PTT program, 98 000 hectares of land were transferred to about 37 400 beneficiaries. Compared with the land reform carried out in El Salvador in the 1980s, the extent of the PTT program was modest.

In spite of the land reform programmes of the 1990s and past decades, which have resulted in the transfer of an estimated 27 per cent of the total agricultural area to a similar percentage of the rural population, the polarized differences between the land-owning

Table 5.1 Results of the agrarian reform programmes in El Salvador

Programme	Area	Area (%)	Beneficiaries	Beneficiaries (%)
Phase 1	220 000 ha	15	31 500	8
Phase 3	70 000 ha	5	40 500	10
PTT	98 000 ha	7	37 400	9

Source: Based on Fuentes, 1993, p. 14; Ruben, 1993, pp. 2–6; UN, 1997, p. 1.

elite and the sector of landless peasants still continue to exist. So far, the main effect of the land-reform policies has been a strong increase in the number of small-scale rural producers; 87 per cent of them own 3.5 hectares of land or less, which in the present circumstances is not sufficient to guarantee the maintenance of a rural family.

The concentration of land in the hands of a small minority of agrarian producers and the strong population growth in the rural areas are the reasons why in the late 1990s there are still 300 000 families without land, or insufficient land to support themselves. Less than a third of the tillers own the land they cultivate, while about half of the producers belong to the category of tenant farmers (Flores, 1994, p. 4). About 75 per cent of landless peasants are forced to undertake part-time additional work outside the rural sector in order to support their families. Apart from the profound economic transformations and the severe loss of influence of the agricultural sector on the economy as a whole, the present pattern of land tenure and labour division within the rural sector 'does not differ dramatically from the agrarian situation at the beginning of the war' (UNDP, 1995, p. 133).

As mentioned before, the land market in El Salvador does not function adequately. This is caused by the concentration of land in the hands of a small minority, the lack of buying power of the vast majority of rural producers, and the complexity and high costs involved in the process of selling and buying lands (Goitia, 1991, pp. 175–85). A further liberalization of the land market without tackling directly underlying socio-political contradictions is unlikely to have any positive effect on the sector of small-scale rural producers.

Land use

With respect to the use of lands transferred under the PTT programme, about 50 per cent seems to offer excellent conditions for agriculture. Nonetheless, in 1996, only 25 per cent of the total PTT area was cultivated effectively![4] Almost 90 per cent of the cultivated PTT area was used for the production of basic food crops (especially maize) which represents one of the less profitable activities in agriculture (FUNDE, 1996, p. 26). Apart from this the productive results of the different categories of PTT beneficiaries were significantly below the national average.

Many areas where the PTT programme has been implemented face problems of deforestation. Several factors play a role: a lack of interest among the beneficiaries in maintaining the fertility of their plots, the critical economic situation of the new owners, and the attractiveness of earning some 'fast and easy money' by selling wood. Nevertheless, the effects of deforestation are significant: erosion, loss of soil fertility and damage to water systems are closely connected to this phenomenon (FUNDE, 1996, p. 23).

Participation in agricultural production

The limited use of the productive potential of the PTT area by its beneficiaries can be explained in part by a number of specific factors. Many of the properties transferred under the programme demonstrate serious shortcomings in terms of production facilities: inaccessible roads, non-functioning water systems, broken machinery, absence of means of transport, storage and processing facilities, and limited access to markets are the rule rather than the exception.

The absence of adequate property relationships is another factor that has a negative impact on the integration of the beneficiaries in agricultural production. The *proindiviso* model has contributed to a situation in which many of them did not and do not consider themselves to be the real owners of the land. Apart from the question of whether beneficiaries are interested mainly in working individually, or collectively, the vast majority of them wish to be owners of their own piece of land. At the time of writing, PTT properties are split up formally on the initiative of the GOES.

Another factor restraining the integration of an important sector of PTT beneficiaries in agriculture concerns their specific situation as ex-soldiers and ex-guerrillas. For economic and social motives, a number of this group has no interest in becoming integrated into agricultural production. Nor do they possess the psychological or professional capacities to incorporate themselves into this sector (UNDP, 1993, p. 32; Keune, 1996). The female PTT beneficiaries, who make up about 30 per cent of the group, received no special attention during the execution of the PTT programme.

Land and bank debts

At the end of 1996, the average agrarian debt (land debt) per capita for beneficiaries of the PTT program was nearly US$3000 (Hemisphere Initiatives, 1997, p. 45); the total agrarian debt of the PTT beneficiaries was US$82m (FUNDE, 1996, p. 14). Given the originally established financial conditions from the fifth year onwards the PTT beneficiaries would have to pay an annual amount of about US$100 to remove this debt.

The average income of a PTT beneficiary during the production cycle of 1993–4 was just above US$400, an amount not even sufficient to cover the basic food requirements of a rural family (FUNDE, 1996, pp. 38–9).

At the beginning of 1997 initiatives by the FMLN, the GOES and USAID led to a redemption of the agrarian debts in favour of the PTT-beneficiaries. However, until the end of 1997 vehement political contradictions prevented any concrete resolution of the agrarian debts, which by then amounted to the equivalent of US$250m; while a parliamentary majority and FMLN-orientated peasant organizations struggle for a radical debt redemption, the government and ARENA party are not willing to agree, arguing that this measure would undermine the critical economic situation of the country and would give the wrong signal to the entire Salvadoran private sector.

Structural changes in agriculture and society

At first sight, comparing the PTT programme with the Salvadoran land reform programme of the 1980s and with other Latin-American land reform experiences, might appear to be adequate, but from an analytical perspective this is unsatisfactory; both function and impact of agriculture within the Salvadoran economy as a whole have changed thoroughly. Before estimating the future potential of the PTT sector, this context that has recently emerged will be analyzed.

The function and impact of agriculture within the Salvadoran economy

Both capitalist and socialist development theories traditionally considered agriculture to be fundamental to the entire economy in Central America; in one way or another, agriculture would have to generate the required economic surplus for economic diversification and industrialization.

Within the dominant neo-liberal context, the process of economic globalization has provoked a kind of 'unannounced reform' (Fuentes, 1993, p. 14); not only the characteristics of the Salvadoran economy as such, but also the function and impact of the agrarian sector on the national economy has changed profoundly.

Because of the form of integration of El Salvador into the world economy, the country has lost a great part of its traditional role as a provider of agricultural products. El Salvador and other Central American countries have gradually been transformed into importers of food and agricultural products from the industrialized countries.[5] In spite of all rhetoric, the so-called green revolution and the application of transnational technological models have deepened the gap between capitalist agriculture and the peasant economies of these countries (García, 1985, p. 64).

The downfall of the agricultural sector in Central America is not only the result of free economic competition on a world market level; Central American agriculture is also confronted with forms of unfair competition from abroad. While El Salvador and other countries of the region have been forced by the World Bank and the IMF to liberalize their markets, agrarian producers from the USA and Canada – supported by state subsidies and protected by their respective governments – have strengthened their position on the Central American food market (Arias and Rodríguez, 1994, p. 115).

While the value of El Salvador's imports and exports increased by factors of 8.7 and 3.2, respectively, in the period 1970–93, the volume and value of traditional agrarian export products (coffee, cotton, sugar and meat) in 1992 were significantly below the levels of 1975. The cotton and beef sectors in the 1990s are undergoing a serious crisis, while the importance of coffee for the Salvadoran economy has been heavily reduced. With respect to the basic food crops (maize, beans and rice) the situation is also critical because of the competition from foreign producers, the low level of technology applied and – in relation to this – the limited size of the national food market. On the other hand, the potential growth of non-traditional agrarian crops[6] such as sisal and tobacco in no way provides sufficient compensation for these negative tendencies (Baumeister, 1994b, p. 73; Arias and Rodríguez, 1994, p. 118).

Without taking into account the impact of agro-industry, the impact of the agricultural sector on the economy as a whole has decreased dramatically: between 1980 and 1994 the proportion of agriculture in the Gross National Product (GNP) diminished from 28 to 9 per cent (Hernández and Goitia, 1995, p. 46). Economically, the agro-export sector has lost its predominance; the total amount of family remittances from the USA to El Salvador (more than 1000 million US dollars) at present not only exceeds the value of all traditional agroexport products (coffee, cotton, meat and sugar) but also of the whole of the Salvadoran export sector. The conclusion seems to be justified that agriculture in El Salvador not only suffers a severe but also a structural crisis.

Governmental economic and agricultural policies

The policies of the GOES with respect to the agrarian sector derive in general from the structural adjustment programme which began, in 1988–9 (Plan de Desarrollo Económico y Social).[7]

The adjustment policy for the agrarian sector reveals itself mainly through the privatization of state enterprises and institutes engaged in storage, processing, commerce and banking (Goitia and Galdamez, 1994, pp. 153–4). The establishment of the Land Bank in 1991 fits within the same framework of privatization and liberalization.

Meanwhile, the macro-economic policy of the GOES has led to a significant fall in relative prices for agricultural products. Various factors have played a role: the overvaluation of the currency, tax rates which favour the industrial sector, the policy of deregulating the credit market and rates, and the introduction of a value added tax (Impuesto de Valor Agregado; Arene, 1995, p. 10).

The withdrawal by the Salvadoran state from the agricultural sector has strengthened the dependence of small-scale agrarian producers on traditional commerce, agro-industry and the financial sector. However, not all services that in the recent past were guaranteed by the state, have been taken over by private enterprise. Credit facilities and technical assistance in particular have become inaccessible for a vast majority of small producers[8] (Baumeister, 1994b, pp. 77–8).

Within the framework of the late-1990s world economic system, the GOES has very limited options to develop its own economic policies. This limited 'autonomous' space is not, at the time of writing used to promote a reactivation of the agricultural sector, but to support the financial and commercial sectors, which tend to be increasingly involved in speculative rather than productive activities (Arene, 1995, p. 14).

The decline of rural society

Until recently the 'agrarian question' in Central America was considered to be crucial, from both a political and a social perspective; power elites or important factions were based in the rural sector, while political stability – at least for a significant part – depended on the ability of governments to handle the social and economic contradictions effectively within the rural sector.

Before 1980, El Salvador was an agrarian country; about 60 per cent of the population lived in the countryside and more than 50 per cent of the economically active population (EAP) was engaged in agriculture. In the late 1990s, the proportion of the population living wholly in the countryside is calculated at about 25–35 per cent, while the labour force engaged in agriculture has declined to 28 per cent of the EAP (Umaña, 1996, p. 15).

The present world economic transformations have put an end to a period of a hundred years of coffee domination in El Salvador: 'traditional agrarian society has been blown to pieces'. Only fragments of it are still there, but within a new social structure (Umaña, 1996, pp. 14–18). The armed conflict, although not the main factor, has certainly accelerated this process of transformation; apart from speeding up the process of migration from the countryside to the cities and the USA, the war has seriously affected the agrarian production capacity.

Not surprisingly, the critical situation in the agrarian sector has had severe repercussions on the social and economic situation of the producers and the labour force involved. Real minimum wages in the rural sector in 1992 represented only 33 per cent of the 1978 level (Arene, 1995, p. 6). According to a study of the United Nations Development Programme, undertaken in 1986, more than 50 per cent of the rural population lives in poverty, and about 60 per cent is reported to suffer from some degree of malnutrition (Goitia 1991, p. 172). The critical situation in large areas of the countryside manifests itself in many ways, including high rates of crime and violence.

The reduction of the economic impact of agriculture and the decline of rural society also have repercussions at the political level. Recent debates about the debt issue illustrate that agriculture is no longer considered to be a fundamental sector for the economy as a whole, but is seen as a problematic economic and social issue.

The impact and future potential of the PTT programme

With respect to the situation mentioned above, the PTT programme at best offers a temporary survival perspective for the beneficiaries and their families (Wolpold, 1994, p. 5). In the 1990s, a significant proportion of the beneficiaries produce basic food products for family consumption. The average income of the beneficiaries is far below the legally established minimum wage (FUNDE, 1996, pp. 42–67). Production methods linked to subsistence agriculture generally have a negative impact on land productivity and the environment.

In spite of the structural crisis in agriculture, a significant part of the population still depends, directly or indirectly, on this sector (UNDP, 1993, p. 28; UNDP, 1995, pp. 125–8). On the other hand, sectors such as the assembly industry, services and tourism – identified by World Bank studies as potential growth sectors – by no means offer the non-agrarian employment opportunities required by the rural poor who have been expelled from the countryside.

The critical socio-economic situation of the small agrarian producers, and the current and potential social and political repercussions of this situation, demand the elaboration of 'inclusive' development strategies; government policies should be aimed primarily at creating survival – not to mention development – perspectives for the benefit of the marginalized masses (see also Arias and Rodríguez, 1993, p. 135 and FUNDE, 1996, p. 3). Changing governmental policies that focus exclusively on the promotion of dynamic markets (Baumeister, 1994b, pp. 60–1) requires taking distance from the unilateral dictates of the World Bank and the IMF. This requires, at the same time, a strengthening of the political and social organizations with a grassroots perspective.

Those who suffer most from the lack of policies aimed at stimulating agrarian production are the PTT beneficiaries. For this reason, the future of the majority within this sector is most insecure. In a report of the Peace Accords of April 1996, the secretary general of the FMLN, Sánchez Ceren, concluded that the ex-guerrillas belonging to the PTT sector had not succeeded in dragging themselves out of poverty. In the near future it would be 'very likely that they [would] give up their productive activities to work as part-time unemployed day laborers' (FMLN, 1996).

As mentioned earlier, the social phenomena which in the 1970s led to a situation of crisis, political violence and war have presented themselves again in the Salvadoran countryside (Arias and Rodríguez, 1994, p. 119; Hernández and Goitia, 1995, p. 46). Nevertheless, both the international context and the structure of the Salvadoran economy and society have been entirely transformed during the same period. Old problems require new solutions, which under the present circumstances not only seem to be difficult to realize but even hard to perceive.

Notes

1. The last national agricultural inventory took place in 1971 (UNDP, 1995, p. 133). Because of this, a considerable part of the data presented here is based on extrapolations and estimations.
2. The way the PTT programme was executed is not atypical by Central American standards. The low level of economic development, the absence of established markets, the lack of political stability, and weak institutional structures generally cause the human factor to have a strong impact on all types of economic transactions.
3. The assignment of agricultural credits in El Salvador is based, among other factors, on the extent of farm lands. This is why owners have an interest in inflating artificially data regarding land extensions. Since the

measuring capacity of the Salvadoran *cadastre* was almost non-existent until recently, the institution used a heavily manipulated database.

4. The phenomenon of fallow lands is not exclusive to the PTT sector. The non-cultivated area of land belonging to Phase I production cooperatives is estimated at around 25–30 per cent (Arene, 1995, pp. 8–30). In 1993, about 21 per cent of the land belonging to private farms larger than 50 hectares was also not cultivated (FUNDE, 1996, p. 20). Apart from the uncultivated agricultural areas, another symptom indicates the limited use of the agrarian production potential: within agriculture there is a clear tendency towards more extensive forms of land exploitation (Ruben, 1993, p. 6).

5. Peasant production in the whole of Central America is in crisis: about 40 per cent of the food consumed in the region comes from abroad (Arias and Rodríguez, 1994, p. 116).

6. Although so-called 'non-traditional' agrarian exports have shown significant growth since the late 1980s they cannot form the basis of a reactivation of the agricultural sector as such. The international demand for these types of product is structurally too limited, while the markets involved – monopolized for the greater part by transnational enterprises – are considered to be too unstable. Apart from that, the expansion of this sector has a negative effect on the internal capacity of the countries concerned to meet their national food demand (Arias and Rodríguez, 1994, p. 127; Baumeister, 1994b, p. 69; UNDP, 1995, p. 132).

7. Until the end of the 1980s, USAID had for political reasons postponed the execution of structural adjustment policies through an impressive volume of loans and donations (Ruben, 1993, p. 11). Before implementing these policies the left-wing resistance movement had to be neutralized to prevent another 'Communist take-over' in Central America.

8. According to the UNDP (1995), only 20 per cent of small agrarian producers have access to bank credit, and a further reduction of this percentage was considered very probable. The exclusion of small producers from credit systems has led to a strong increase in informal credit systems, with about 80 per cent of small producers being involved.

Bibliography

Arene, A. (1995) 'La nueva estructura de la tenencia de tierra y la necesidad de una nueva oportunidad al desarrollo agropecuario en El Salvador', in R. Maeda and S. Roggenbuck (eds), *Situación Agraria y cooperativismo en El Salvador*.

Arias, S. and Rodríguez, R. (1994) 'Peasant Agriculture and development alternatives in Central America', in K. Biekart and M. Jelsma (eds), *Beyond Protest*.

Banco Mundial (1997) *El Salvador, estudio de desarrollo rural: resumen ejecutivo*, Fusades, San Salvador.

Barry, D. and Cuéllar, N. (1997) 'Las transformaciones del agro salvadoreño y la efectividad de las políticas sectoriales', *Prisma 21*, San Salvador.

Baumeister, E. (1994a) *La reforma agraria en Nicaragua (1979–1989)*, Third World Centre, Catholic University of Nijmegen, The Netherlands.

Baumeister E. (1994b) 'Agrarian Structures and Small Producers: Review and Prospects', in Biekart and Jelsma (eds), *Beyond Protest*.

Biekart, K. and M. Jelsma (eds) (1994b) *Beyond Protest: Peasantry in Central America*, Transnational Institute, Amsterdam, The Netherlands.

Borgh, C. van den (1995) 'El Salvador: op weg naar een duurzame vrede?', *Derde Wereld*, Third World Centre, Catholic University of Nijmegen, The Netherlands, November.

Cabarrús, C. R. (1985) 'El Salvador: de movimiento campesino a revolución popular', in P. González Casanova, *Historia política de los campesinos latinoamericanos*, Siglo XXI, México.

Flores, M. (1994) *Tierra: conflicto y paz en El Salvador*, paper presented at, International Congress of Americanists, Stockholm, Sweden, July.

FMLN (Coordinación nacional del sector campesino) (1995a) *Propuesta nacional abierta al sector agropecuario de un marco de política agraria*, San Salvador, El Salvador, October.

FMLN (1995b) *Elementos básicos sobre los programas de inserción*, San Salvador, El Salvador.

FMLN (1996) *Balance del cumplimiento de los Acuerdos de Paz*, Salvador Cerén, FMLN, San Salvador, El Salvador.

FMLN (1997) *Ponencia sobre políticas, iniciativas y acciones para el sector agropecuario 1997–2000*, Antonio Alvarez, Comisión de Seguimiento de los Acuerdos de Paz–FMLN, San Salvador, El Salvador.

Fuentes, M. (1993) 'Ajuste y reforma institucional del sector agropecuario', *Prisma*, nos 3–4.

Fundación Para el Desarrollo (FUNDE) (1996) *El programa de Transferencia de Tierras*, San Salvador, El Salvador.

García, A. (1995) *Modelos operacionales de reforma agraria y desarrollo rural en América Latina*, Edit. IICA, San José, Costa Rica.

Garcia, J. J. (1995) 'La reforma agraria y sus resultados', in R. Maeda and S. Roggenbuck (eds), *situación agraria y cooperativismo.*

Goitia, A. (1991) 'Reforma agraria con orientación de mercado', in R. Ruben and G. van Oord (eds) *Más alla del ajuste.*

Goitia, A. and Galdamez, E. (1994) 'El Salvador: movimiento campesino', in K. D. Tangerman and I. Ríos Valdés (eds), *Alternivas campesinas.*

González Casanova P. (1985) *Historia política de los campesinos latinoamericanos*, Siglo XXI, México.

Hernández, P. J. and Goitia, A. (1995) 'La realidad actual del cooperativismo agropecuario en El Salvador', in R. Maeda and S. Roggenbuck (eds), *Situación agraria y cooperativismo.*

Keune, L. (1996) *Sobrevivimos la guerra*, Adelina Editores, San Salvador.

Lazo, F. and Ruíz Moiza, C. (1996) *El Salvador en cifras y trazos*, Equipo Maíz, San Salvador.

Maeda, R. and Roggenbuck, S. (eds) (1995) *Situación agraria y cooperativismo en El Salvador*, Imprenta Criterio, San Salvador.

Montesino Castro, M. S. (1996) 'Las recomendaciones de política económica para el subsector de granos básicos', *Realidad, revista de Ciencias Sociales e Humanidades*, UCA, San Salvador, July–August.

Murray, K. (1994) 'Rescuing Reconstruction: The Debate on Post-war Economic Recovery in El Salvador', *Hemisphere Initiatives*, May.

Navas, M. C. (1995) 'Mujer cooperativista en El Salvador', in R. Maeda and S. Roggenbuck (eds), *Situación agraria y cooperativismo.*

Pelupessy, W. (1993) *El mercado mundial de café*, DEI, Costa Rica.

Petsch, M. (1993) 'El programa de la transferencia de tierras: una profundización del minifundio', in *Tendencias actuales de la resolución del conflicto salvadoreño*, ASACS, San Salvador.

PNUD (1996) *Evaluación de la situación actual, estrategias y programas para el desarrollo de las áreas del Programa de Transferencia de Tierras*, San Salvador.

PRISMA, (1996) *El Banco Mundial y el Banco Interamericano de desarrollo*, San Salvador.

PROCESO, (1997) *La crisis del agro y el plan de reactivación agrícola del gobierno*, UCA, San Salvador, no. 743, January.

Ruben, R. and van Oord, G. (eds) (1991) *Más alla del ajuste*, MAK–Den Haag/ DEI-Costa Rica.

Ruben, R. (1993) *Land Reform and the Transformation of the Peasantry in El Salvador: Perspectives for the Consolidation of Land Reform Cooperatives*, Paper for the IX ASERCCA Annual Conference, Maastricht.

San Sebastián, C. and Barry, D. (1996) 'La deuda del sector agropecuario: implicaciones de la condonación parcial', *Prisma*.

Santamaría, R. (1995) 'El problema agrario y los acuerdos de paz: un estado permanente de incumplimiento y conflictos', *ECO*, May.

Tangerman, K. D. and Ríos Valdés, I. (1994) *Alternativas campesinas*, Latino Edit./CRIES, Managua.

Umaña, C. (1996) *Un nuevo mapa para El Salvador*. Edic Tendencias. San Salvador.

UN (1997) 'Unidad de apoyo al enviado del secretario general El Salvador', *Programa de Transferencia de Tierras; escrituraciones al 21/03/97*, San Salvador.

UNCTAD (1995) *1994 Handbook of international trade and development statistics*, New York–Geneva.

UNDP (1993) *Launching New Protagonists in Salvadoran Agriculture: The Agricultural Training Programme for Ex-combatants of the FMLN*, San Salvador.

UNDP (1995) *Adjustment Toward Peace: Economic Policy and Post-war Reconstruction in El Salvador*, San Salvador, May.

Wolpold, M. (1994) *Land In Sicht? Die landbesitzfrage nach dem Friedensabkommen in El Salvador*, Seminar Landfrage, Fluchtlingehilfe Mittelamerika, Berlin.

6
Property Rights, Missing Markets and Agricultural Diversification: Consolidation of Agrarian Reform in Masaya, Nicaragua

Ben D'Exelle and Johan Bastiaensen

Introduction

Property rights and the fate of agrarian reform are much debated issues in late 1990s Nicaragua, and the focus of these debates centres almost exclusively on the legal dimensions of the problems. After various phases of confiscation, land redistribution and reprivatization, the legal situation of land property has become an inextricable Gordian knot. Counter-agrarian reform scenarios are often believed to involve the expulsion of the poorest agrarian reform beneficiaries, who, lacking adequate legal titles, have been ousted by previous owners, who claim to be the legal owners. Such expulsions, whether or not backed by legal rulings, have occurred occasionally, but are not the dominant scenario. A larger share of counter-agrarian reform takes place through less visible and practically uncontested market processes, and these can be expected to continue in the future unless appropriate measures are taken to support the economic activities of the poor landowners rather than those focusing on the legal status of the land. In this chapter we shall present an analysis of some of the issues involved in the agrarian reform zone of Northern Masaya. Our general reflection will be illustrated with case studies of different types of producers in the region.[1]

Agrarian reform and counter-agrarian reform

Description of the study area

Our study region – the northern part of the department of Masaya – is situated in the western, and most populated region of Nicaragua. It is located between the river Tipitapa, two large lakes and the Carazo plateau. It has an area of about 160 Km^2 and is densely populated with between 160 and 300 inhabitants per km². Because of the proximity of the capital and other important cities in the Pacific region, and the relatively good road infrastructure, the inhabitants enjoy privileged access to urban markets. This is of great importance to the character of local economic activities (Antillón, 1996, p. 75). Generally, the region of Masaya is characterized by a warm, dry climate, irregular rainy seasons and fertile soils. Environmental problems consist of wind and water erosion and desiccating rivers. Furthermore, soil fertility has decreased severely because of intensive monocultivation in private *haciendas* and cooperatives, as well as the recent depletion of the land by insecure land reform beneficiaries. The main crops are fruit, vegetables, staple foods (maize, beans, sorghum and dry rice, for example) peanuts, sesame and wood. Cattle production is also important in the region. A diversity of producers inhabit the study region: poor agrarian reform beneficiaries, of whom 90 per cent lives in a regimen of formal collective property but are *de facto* engaged in individual production; peasants with highly diversified production systems who are well-integrated into local markets and whose ancestors have always disposed of land; and larger agricultural entrepreneurs (Nitlapán, 1995, p. 17; Nitlapán, 1994a, pp. 19–20).

The process of land reform in northern Masaya

The poor semi-proletarians of Masaya played a crucial role in the Sandinista agrarian reform process. In the region, and particularly in the densely populated southern *minifundio* zone where small-scale farmers dominate, a substantial demand for land existed because of the fragmentation of the inherited land. However, under the initial agrarian reform law, practically no land was available for redistribution in the region.

In 1985, out of frustration with the lack of response to their demand for land, the poor of southern Masaya invaded the mainly private cotton plains of northern Masaya and forced the Sandinista government to legitimize their illegal endeavour. This event forced a national breakthrough in agrarian reform policy in favour of more drastic land redistribution in areas of great need. The numerous restrictions on expropriable land in the initial law were officially lifted in 1986. In northern Masaya, the overall process is estimated to have benefited some 1200 families, with the redistribution of a total of about 6000 *manzanas* of land (1 mz = 0.7 ha). This implies an average of 5 mz of land per family (Nitlapán, 1996a, p. 10).

Most of the agrarian reform granted access to land on condition that producer cooperatives were formed with a collective usufruct right to the land. This was not only inspired by socialist ideological preferences, but was also held to be a necessary guarantee to safeguard 'modern' production on these large farms. The choice of productive activity was determined by the ministry of agriculture according to the regional production plans. In practice, this implied continued emphasis on mechanized and input-intensive monocultivation, at first of cotton and later of high-yielding maize and sorghum. Sometimes, but not always from the beginning, members of the cooperatives were allowed to till a small individual plot for staple food production. Production on these farms was amply financed with cheap credit in exchange for (staple) produce at low official prices. Exploitation was often at a deficit, so that recurrent debt characterized most cooperatives. This problem was 'solved' through the almost automatic condonation of pending debts at each anniversary of the revolution. The articulation of the agrarian reform cooperatives with their labour force often did not differ much from that of the previous private *haciendas* with their semi-proletarian workforce. Most of the members continued to live in their hamlets of origin and travelled occasionally to the farm when work had to be done. Often it was discouraged and even prohibited to live on the farm itself. As a result of the lack of identification of members with 'their' cooperative, the rotation of membership was also very high. Current membership is almost never the same as the original members whose names appear on the agrarian reform titles.

The reality of the agrarian reform cooperatives began to change profoundly with the initiation of the economic stabilization process in 1988. The abandonment of the wartime planned economy, under which the cooperatives of Masaya had been maintained without regard to underlying profitability considerations, radically transformed their economic environment, and the distorted price structure was gradually adjusted to match that of international markets. Subsidies – and cheap and abundant credit in particular – were cut back. The consequences for the cooperatives were dramatic. Input-intensive, mechanized monocultivation turned out not to be viable under the new economic conditions. Debts accumulated even more rapidly than in the previous period, whereas the government was much more reluctant to condone them and started to cut access to additional finance for the cooperatives. This plunged most of them into a life-threatening liquidity crisis that reflected the underlying structural problems of the inherited production system.

The spontaneous response of most of the reform beneficiaries was to parcel the cooperatives' land. In this way, the members tried to guarantee food self-sufficiency, and some additional income in view of the reduction or disappearance of regular wage payments from the cooperative. On their individualized plots, a short-term survival strategy determined production choices. This was partially because of the absence of clear individual property rights within the cooperative, and the growing insecurity over the collective property of the cooperative after the election victory of the anti-Sandinista opposition. This insecurity concerning the tenure regime spurred a 'tragedy of the commons' dynamic, in which unsustainable short-term optimization prevailed over medium-term rationality. Furthermore, outright lack of minimal resources and liquidity confined production to annual (mostly staple) crops and caused a dramatic decline in the application of external inputs and nutrients. The sharp reductions in fertilizer applications led to deterioration of the inherited land resources and contributed to a substantial reduction in crop yields. This, of course, contributed to a further deepening of the crisis. In reaction, some members opted for a return to a semi-proletarian life outside the cooperative. For this reason, some of the weakest cooperatives disintegrated to such an extent that it was relatively easy for the previous owners to recover their farms.

Today's challenges for the agrarian reform beneficiaries

Many more beneficiaries, however, are trying to find a way out of the present crisis. But a way out practically always requires the previous establishment of clear and secure individual rights to the land. In the late 1990s, many cooperatives are therefore involved in a process of simultaneous land titling and decollectivization. Only in a limited number of cases has this process already been successfully concluded, with members disposing of registered individual land titles. Many more cooperative members are still in the midst of the legal process, but can be considered to have reached a satisfactory level of security concerning individual property rights. Once a cooperative is parcelled out and beneficiaries start to consolidate small individual farms, it becomes particularly difficult for anyone, even the state, to return the land to another producer. This 'agrarian reform from below' (Nitlapán, 1994a) indeed evokes a local legitimation of full individual property rights that is absent under the cooperative arrangement. As indicated by Ruben (1997), the cooperative organization resembles the structure of a sharecropping arrangement. Under this dominant sharecropping arrangement, the sharecropper's usufruct rights over the land are limited to one production cycle. Investment in the establishment of permanent crops or land improvement therefore does not make much sense. From the traditional model of the arrangement it follows that no claim can be made on any such improvement in land productivity. Quite the opposite is true for the perception of individual farm property: any personal effort towards farm improvement (*mejoras*) entails stronger rights over the land. Its proceeds can always be claimed, even when the land has to be returned to its legitimate owner. One can therefore observe a self-reinforcing circle of farm investments (fences and housing in particular) and the security of the individual title. In the light of this legitimation process 'from below', the threat of legal expropriation of agrarian reform land for cooperatives that have entered the decollectivization path does not seem to be particularly great.

The challenges for the new individual proprietors are, however, immense. Many of them own a 4–6 mz plot of 'bare land', often depleted through years of overexploitation. At best, the low-yielding staple food production on such plots can provide a supplement to family consumption needs. The temptation to lease the land or to sell out altogether becomes great for those families living at the edge of survival. Pressured by one emergency or another, they all too often sell at ludicrously low prices. Estimates indicate that 10 per cent of the redistributed land under the Sandinista land reform has already been sold this way (Nitlapán, 1996a, pp. 10–11). Unless a transition can be made towards a more intensive and diversified peasant farm, perspectives for the consolidation of the land reform process do not look bright. The scenario of a reversal of the land redistribution process through the land market is much more probable and real than that through legal expropriation.

The establishment of a viable family farm on 4–6 mz of land is a difficult, but not impossible, task. The first precondition is, of course, sufficient security of ownership. The transition requires a substantial investment on the farm, which will not be undertaken without minimal security concerning property rights, even when investments may serve the purpose of strengthening this security once acquired. A second condition is the transfer of the producer to his/her farm. A producer who continues to live more than 10 km away from his/her plot can only avoid destruction and theft of crops with great difficulty, especially when they are higher-value crops. Fencing constitutes another crucial requirement, which together with basic housing infrastructure constitutes the bulk of the required initial farm investment. Without barbed wire, it is impossible to plant trees or to cultivate any permanent crop. In the dry season, cattle are allowed to graze freely and can legitimately destroy any crop that is not protected by barbed wire or other fences. Only when the farm is properly fenced and the producer lives on his/her parcel, do investments in higher-value activities such as root crops, fruit, vegetables, poultry, pigs and trees become possible. It is precisely these higher-value crops that are necessary to establish a minimally viable family farm on 4–6 mz. In fact, it represents the typical production system of the viable historical peasants of southern Masaya who until now have avoided excessive fragmentation of their plots.

The investment required to initiate the biological accumulation process towards a viable diversified farm is not very great. Preliminary calculations by Nitlapán estimate that less than US$1500 suffices to put a small farm on its way towards a viable production system (Nitlapán, 1996a, p. 13). However, for many of the poor and decapitalized agrarian reform beneficiaries, even this low threshold is insurmountable. They lack own resources, face few off-farm labour opportunities and have deficient access to credit markets, especially for long-term credit. As a consequence they are often blocked by a liquidity constraint. Consolidation of land reform might therefore depend on the provision of adequate support for these producers to initiate this investment process. The viability of this strategy will also be enhanced to the extent that increasing numbers of profitable productive activities become available. Although viable production systems are possible with high-value crops for which commercial networks do already exist, perspectives might substantially improve should new product markets become more widely available. In practice, throughout Masaya traditional peasants are already making substantial adjustments to their production systems and taking steps towards the innovation of both products and commercialization networks. Besides specialized fruit and vegetable crops for the capital and even for export, the production of tree products seems to offer interesting possibilities. Given the increasing scarcity of firewood in the Pacific region, the proximity of artisan production in Masaya and the need to take measures against erosion and excessive drought, production of fast-growing trees/fences represents a promising activity for the poorer peasants.[2] One of the problems with the transition towards such diversified and innovative agroforestry systems, however, is once again the need to bridge the gap between current consumption needs and future revenues from the trees.

Strategies of agricultural households

Before we undertake a small illustrative analysis of the issues involved in the transition process towards a viable family farm by means of three case-studies, we first elaborate on the production and survival strategies of agricultural households in Masaya. Given the context of deficient credit and product markets, these strategies will depend on expected financial returns as well as subjective household opportunity costs, particularly those affected by risk aversion.

The high climatological and market uncertainty that characterizes the region forces households to resort to a wide range of risk-mitigating mechanisms to protect the welfare of their members. *Ex ante* risk-reducing strategies, such as income diversification and reverting to less risky technologies and products, are widespread in the region. In particular, the diversification of income sources and activities with low covariate risk reduces both predictable seasonal fluctuations and unpredictable price and climate fluctuations (Sadoulet and de Janvry, 1995, pp. 166–7). Poor agrarian reform beneficiaries typically look for non-agricultural income sources during the dry season, and try to combine agricultural and non-agricultural productive activities with petty commerce and wage work to survive. Moreover, faced with the choice between low-value staple crops and higher-value annual cash crops, they often prefer the staple crop. Even when climatological risk is also quite high for the staple crops, poor peasants tend to cope better with the technology for traditional staple crops. A further important advantage is that price risk is partially eliminated, even when large parts of the food crops are sold at low prices. This poorer household's anti-risk strategy can be seen to represent a kind of 'low equilibrium', where risk mitigation leads to non-optimal product choices in terms of expected returns. This contrasts with the 'high equilibrium' anti-risk strategy of the established peasant farms that diversify by cultivating a variety of high value perennial and annual cash crops. In the 'high equilibrium', the trade-off between expected returns and *ex ante* anti-risk mitigation disappears almost completely.

Agricultural households in the region also resort to several *ex post* risk management strategies (Valdivia *et al.*, 1996, pp. 1329–31). In crises, the richer households can usually rely on the liquidation of assets and often have easier access to emergency borrowing. Poorer households rely relatively more on intensified petty commercial activity and increased labour sales, including temporary migration to Costa Rica. Gifts among friends and neighbours and other, more formalized, non-market arrangements of mutual insurance are also relied upon. It must, however, be stressed that, with the disintegration of the cooperatives, the poor agrarian reform beneficiaries lost the fixed and secure cooperative wage component in their income. This clearly entails a more severe risk exposure for former cooperative members. Given restricted access to credit and limited opportunities for remunerative wage labour, poorer households in the region are strongly constrained in their capabilities for *ex post* risk management. These households therefore have a greater need for *ex ante* risk mitigation, which further strengthens the 'low equilibrium' income diversification strategy.

For the consolidation of the agrarian reform, it is necessary to transform this low-equilibrium 'diversification for bad reasons' into a high-equilibrium 'diversification for good reasons'. Some authors state that this 'diversification for good reasons' must even lead to a capturing of gains from specialization at the household level (Von Braun and Pandya-Lorch, 1991, p. 20). Nevertheless, as long as markets are mainly imperfect and uncertain, complete specialization is unacceptably risky, and a capitalized and highly diversified production system is likely to offer the best opportunities for agricultural development (Ellis, 1996, p. 244).

The transition to this 'high-equilibrium' diversification requires biological accumulation and initial farm investments such as fencing and basic housing to protect perennial and high-value crops. These investments require liquid resources and entail opportunity costs in terms of current consumption that must be sacrificed for higher revenues in the future, such as in the case of long-term investments in tree production. Since most agrarian reform beneficiaries struggle on the edge of survival, both the lack of resources and their high subjective discount rates make this transformation hardly feasible for them. It could be argued that many investments only require a small increase in labour intensity, and that off-farm labour too could generate the needed liquidity. However, the establishment of perennial crops often implies a reduction in current production, and the availability of sufficiently remunerative wage employment in the region is doubtful. The stalemate could, however, also be broken by the provision of longer-term credit as it is envisaged, for example, in the 'Los Arboles Valen' (LAV) initiative (see the Annex on pp. 112–13). Annual consumption credit, guaranteed by the future revenues of high-value perennial crops, could help to bridge the gap between current survival and optimal diversification and investment. The major problem with making this kind of financial service available is primarily institutional: that is, how to develop a socio-economic network that allows control of adverse selection and moral hazard problems at reasonably low transaction costs (see also Chapter 9, this volume). Generalized distrust and social exclusion characterizes the region and makes the articulation of a credit institution with local clients problematical, especially in relation to the kind of credit that is needed here.

Case studies of the different producers in the rural zone of northern Masaya

The general tendencies described above can be illustrated by a number of case studies of different types of producers in the study-region. We present data on three case studies based on the 1995 agricultural cycle: two contrasting examples of agrarian reform beneficiaries on recently parcelled and depleted land; and one example of a diversified and sustainable production system of an historical peasant, who serves as a kind of 'role model' for the agrarian reform beneficiary. Table 6.1 summarizes the data of these case studies.

The non-viable, decapitalized agrarian reform beneficiary (Type 1)

Our first case study refers to a former female member of the cooperative 'La Victor Gonzalez No. 2', whom we shall call Carmen. In 1994, the cooperative's property was parcelled out among its members. Carmen received a 4 mz plot of 'bare' land still without title but going through the process of legalization. She estimates its value at C$6000 per mz. She is 40 years old and a single parent of three young sons. Because of the struggle for survival, she has very little time left to engage in community organizations or activities. She fights her struggle pretty much on her own. Her house is located on borrowed land near to the parcel, which is not fenced. Cattle can therefore enter during the dry season so that it is impossible to plant trees or to grow any perennial crop. The production unit has very little capital. In this particular case too, family labour is scarce and gender-constrained.

Lack of resources and liquidity characterize the farm. Production is limited to annual crops. In 1995, she cultivated maize as a food crop during only one agricultural cycle and smaller areas of *pipián* (a local horticulture crop) and sorghum for broom-making as cash crops. Because of climatological and farm conditions, crop yields were quite low. Carmen combines her agricultural activity with income from other sources, mainly as an agricultural wage labourer. On her parcel she obtained an average net revenue per day of about C$11 only slightly higher than the average sub-subsistence wage of C$10 that she

Table 6.1 Typology of peasant producers: resources, income composition and investments

	Type 1: Decapitalized agrarian reform beneficiary	Type 2: Agrarian reform beneficiary in transition	Type 3: Small diversified peasant farmer
Assets			
1. Land	4 mz	5 + 6 mz	6 + 1 mz
	(6000 C$/mz)	(8000 C$/mz)	(14 000 C$/mz)
2. Family labour	1	2	3
3. Capital	3125 C$	39 800 C$	132 800 C$
	(781 C$/mz)	(3618 C$/mz)	(18 971 C$/mz)
Infrastructure	3000 C$	5300 C$	90 000 C$
Farm implements	125 C$	3720 C$	6840 C$
Perennial crops	Very little	30 000 C$	32 380 C$
Livestock	–	780 C$	3580 C$
Income			
1. Total current value	3620 C$	6340 C$	14 558 C$
of production	(905 C$/mz)	(1268 C$/mz)	(2080 C$/mz)
Annual staple crops	2200 C$	6340 C$	3000 C$
Annual cash crops	1420 C$	–	1340 C$
Perennial crops	–	–	10 218 C$
Livestock	–	n.a.	n.a.
2. Total production	1695 C$	1205 C$	4200 C$
costs			
3. Gross current	1925 C$	5135 C$	10 358 C$
agricultural income	(481 C$/mz)	(1027 C$/mz)	(1480 C$/mz)
4. Off-farm income	1600 C$	–	5350 C$
5. Total gross family	3525 C$	5135 C$	15 708 C$
income			
Investments			
	–	0.25 mz sweet pepper	0.25 mz flowers
	–	0.25 mz trees/fences	0.25 mz trees
	–	0.5 mz plantain	

Notes: In 1995: 1 US$ = ± 8C$; n.a. = not available; MZ = Manzana; 1 Manzana = 0.7 ha.

earned with wage labour. The combination of wage labour and additional income and food security from her land, as well as the relative preference for the better-known low-value staple crops over riskier, but potentially higher-value cash crops is consistent with our previous analysis of a low-equilibrium anti-risk strategy. In this particular case, it could be observed that the lack of agricultural skills in particular affected the production of the vegetable *pipián*. Total gross family income for this household amounted to only C$3525, which is barely sufficient to survive.

At present, Carmen does not have sufficient capacity to maintain or invest in her production unit. Lack of resources, of family labour and of access to financial sources (long-term credit or own resources), plus legal uncentainty about her plot make the necessary investments in soil maintenance unfeasible. She continues to deplete her already exhausted land, so production yields have decreased spectacularly. Productivity of maize fell from 25 cwt/mz to only 11 cwt/mz. She has no opportunities to make investments in basic farm infrastructure or to establish high-value perennial crops. She is trapped in the 'low equilibrium' of annual production with a preference for low-value staple crops. Low farm production forces her to look for off-farm labour income. She will be able to continue this semi-proletarian strategy until accumulated debt or some kind of emergency forces her to sell her property. Because of very imperfect and non-transparent land markets, she can be expected to sell out at a low price should she be forced to do so.

The agrarian reform beneficiary in transition (Type 2)

Poor agrarian reform beneficiaries are condemned to non-viable production systems unless they are provided with the opportunity to make the jump to a more intensive production system. For this purpose, sufficient basic capitalization is needed. Credit and trees/fences – of which the basic capital is built up – play a crucial part in the transition process towards a viable (that is, diversified and renewable) production system. The second case study refers to an agrarian reform beneficiary who is engaged in such a transition process.

Compared to Carmen, this second farmer, who we shall call Franco, is socially much better connected. Franco is chairman of the 'Union of Agricultural and Cattle-breeding Cooperatives' in San Ramón as well as a member of the 'Campesino a Campesino'[3] and the 'Los Arboles Valen' projects. His family consists of two adults, and three daughters and one son, all too young to work. Franco's wife possesses a plot of 5 mz obtained under the agrarian reform process and parcelled since August 1994 with legal title in process. The lot is located 15 minutes' walking distance form their house. Franco possesses another 6 mz of agrarian reform land within walking distance that he has cultivated individually since 1992. He has to put up just C$350 to obtain an individual title. Family labour is scarce in the production unit since Franco lost an arm during the war and his wife is often unable to work because of health problems. His land is valued at C$8000/mz and his total capital is estimated at C$39 800.

During the 1995 agricultural cycle, he grew 2 mz of maize, 0.25 mz of rice and 1 mz of manioc on the parcel of 5 mz. The gross current agricultural income amounted to C$5135, implying an estimated revenue of about C$16 a day. In following years, his income was expected to rise, since plantain and sweet pepper would be harvested in 1996, and fruit production (avocado, lemon, mango and oranges) should bring additional revenue from 1997 onwards. The other parcel of 6 mz does not produce any immediate income. On this plot, trees are planted along the contour lines in order to counteract erosion and to offer shadow and forage for a small amount of livestock planned for the long term. Many new trees are growing on both plots.

Although he still does not have an official individual property title, Franco has already fenced most of his land. This was partially financed by a C$5000 credit from the 'Los Arboles Valen' project. These fences are an important step, since they reduce problems concerning demarcation lines and casual intrusions by cattle. At the same time, they raise the value of the parcel, offer protection against erosion, and produce forage and wood. In the near future, Franco plans to cultivate more perennial crops that will improve and maintain soil fertility and diversify production. Capital will be accumulated and his production system will become biologically more solid and sustainable. He receives the required technical assistance from the 'Los Arboles Valen' promoters and in the near future he will pay off the credit by selling part of his tree stock that is presently growing. The particularity of scarce family labour in this case has encouraged him to switch totally from traditional agriculture to perennial crops. The presence of the necessary basic infrastructure, such as water – he is building a well on his plot – and electricity removes the last obstacle to moving to his individual parcel. There is a good chance that this somewhat better-endowed agrarian reform beneficiary is on his way to a viable diversified and renewed production system. It is clear that Franco's social connections, resulting in access to credit and technical knowledge, are also contributing decisively to his successful transition.

The small diversified peasant farmer as 'role model' (Type 3)

The last case study here refers to a 57-year-old farmer, whom we shall call Rafael, and whose family consists of two adults, two studying sons, an adopted daughter and a grandson. His sons help him whenever possible, and sometimes some day-labourers are hired to sow or harvest.

Two, and sometimes even three, agricultural cycles are obtained. He has always possessed a private individual plot of land. In this way he can rely on his broad experience and knowledge. His grandparents' farm covered 40 mz but because of fragmentation by inheritance, Rafael inherited only 6 mz: 2 mz around his house and 4 mz at walking distance. He possesses another 1 mz of agrarian reform land with title, and in 1995 rented an additional plot of 1 mz. His house is built of concrete, has a tiled floor and a zinc roof. The value of his land is estimated at C\$14 280/mz and his farm is fairly capitalized with an estimated value of C\$132 800.

In 1995, he cultivated maize as an annual food crop, and sorghum and tomatoes as cash crops. The production of 1 mz of highly-priced tomatoes failed totally because of excessive rainfall. Fruit production (*nancites*, *jocotes*, *mamónes*, mangos, tamarinds, *pitahayas* and bananas) counted for more than 40 per cent of total income. The sale of *nancites* and *jocotes* formed a permanent income flow, enabling the purchase of food from July until October, and from March into April, and sometimes he sells a little firewood. Around All Saints, he sells flowers at a considerable profit. Even when negatively affected by the loss of 1 mz of tomatoes, gross current agricultural income still amounted to C\$10 358, or an estimated revenue of C\$21 per day per worker. Off-farm income of the family was C\$2300, and Rafael received compensation of C\$3050 as a promoter of LAV. In this way, total gross family income amounted to C\$15 708, sufficient to cover all family and social costs, and finance further investments.

Rafael's system is experiencing dyamic change under the new conditions of structural adjustment. More profitable high-value crops, such as fruit, flowers or trees, are gradually being grown in place of staple and tuber crops. After 1995, Rafael made a radical change from low-yielding maize to larger areas of flowers and firewood production. Any remainder of the 'low equilibrium' strategy under which 'secure' staple crops are preferred for anti-risk reasons has been completely overruled by considerations of expected return. New crops are introduced to capture higher-income-earning opportunities, and risky cash crops, such as tomatoes, are complemented by less risky high-value activities, such as fruit and trees. In this way, the farm has the capacity to resist negative shocks such as those caused by the loss of the tomato crop. The tree stock in particular constitutes an interesting *ex post* risk management mechanism. Furthermore, this diversification component also smooths income flows and thereby counteracts possible temporary liquidity shortages.

Fragmentation of plots through inheritance further obliges peasants of this type to intensify permanently their production system. In this context, Rafael has plans to buy two cows and at the same time he is experimenting with new, high-value crops such as mint. He is also interested in hiring some additional land and in augmenting his agricultural activities with other economic projects. It is clear that he has transformed his production system from a very traditional to a highly diversified and viable production unit based on root crops, fruit, vegetables, poultry, pigs and trees.

Conclusion

The agrarian reform fundamentally changed the unequal distribution of land that existed in Nicaragua, and opened perspectives for a more equitable rural development. However, the collectivization of production and property by the Sandinista agrarian reform did not permit the full exploitation of the economic potential of small and medium-sized production units. At the end of the 1980s, cooperatives turned out to be non-viable under the new economic conditions, and peasants themselves started to subdivide the common cooperative land in order to survive. Through lack of liquidity, many agrarian reform beneficiaries became caught up in a vicious circle of low production and decapitalization leading to unsustainable production systems. Unprofitable staple food production on 'bare' plots forces them to look for additional income sources. Many of them will be able to continue this semi-proletarian strategy of 'low equilibrium' income diversification until accumulated debt or some kind of emergency forces them to sell their property.

Reality shows that counter-agrarian reform tendencies work mainly through these kinds of market processes rather than through legal expropriation. To counteract this regressive process, agrarian reform beneficiaries should be able to make a transition to a more intensive and diversified peasant farm. Individual titles are the first step in initiating this transition process. Second, investments are needed to initiate a capitalization process so that the basic capital needed to cultivate the land in a sustainable way can be accumulated. If basic services of water and electricity are available, producers can migrate to their individual plots. Finally, higher-value activities such as root crops, fruit, vegetables, poultry, pigs and trees should be introduced to diversify and intensify production. However, for many agrarian reform beneficiaries living on the edge of survival, this transition remains unfeasible. Complementary to the struggle for property rights, attention must be drawn to the necessary support for the proprietors in order to make the transition possible.

That such a transition makes sense is indicated by the dynamic viability of the established small-scale peasant production systems that provide the role model for the agrarian reform beneficiaries. Even where commercial networks for high-value crops do already exist, perspectives for this type of producer might further improve in the future if innovative and secure product markets are developed. Throughout the Masaya area, traditional peasants are already making substantial adjustments in their production systems and taking steps towards the innovation of both production and commercialization networks.

Annex: the *Los Arboles Valen* project

This project is concentrated in the rural zone of Masaya and contributes to the diversification and consolidation of local, small-scale production systems. It focuses mainly on the basic investment process of agrarian reform beneficiaries that is essential to make the transition towards viable, diversified and renewed production systems. Tree production is promoted as a commercial crop, including firewood, hardwood and fruit production. Another objective of the project is to develop a viable institutional framework, embedded in the social organization around agroforestry dynamics, and to provide the members with (consumption) credit guaranteed by the investment in the tree stock. At the same time, peasants are provided with technical advice about agroforestry activities, and participatory research and interaction is organized among them. In practice, two major practical components can be identified: the promotion of different kinds of tree production, and support for the initial establishment of fences and hedges.

The project finances activities of the members, with loans of six and three years, respectively, guaranteed by the number of trees (Nitlapán, 1994b, pp. 16–20). For the promotion of tree production, the fund accords annual consumption advances against the future harvest. This guarantees a regular minimum income flow for the producer during the years prior to the harvest. In this way the producer's cash flow is balanced over the years, and the problem of the high subjective discount rate is counteracted. The annual advance per tree during the first five years varies according to the kinds of tree and the system of planting. The annual interest amounts to 8 per cent with a repayment term of six years (ibid., pp. 22–5). In June 1996, 329 000 new trees were financed in this way, with a total area of 660 mz planted by 305 families.

The credit earmarked for the construction of fences aims at reforestation and investment in basic infrastructure on the plots of agrarian reform beneficiaries. In this way, the project corresponds to an important demand from the producers and stimulates tree production. Credit guarantees do not use trees as a collateral, but require other guarantees frequently used in credit systems, such as the legal contract, the agrarian pledge, and solidarity groups. The major potential sanction is probably 'social' exclusion from the overall dynamic surrounding the agroforestry network in the hamlets. To maximize effectiveness, the users of the credit have to fulfil conditions that indicate their degree of solvency and their progress in the transition to viable sustainable production systems. They need to have started the process of legalization of their plot and to be living on their parcel of land, or very near to it. They must not have any outstanding debts or be in arrears with any financing institution. The average amount of loan per producer amounts to US$440, and the annual interest here again amounts to 8 per cent with a repayment term of three years. In June 1996, 141 500 yards of fencing had already been financed, encircling 664 bordered *manzanas*. The repayment of the interest on the credit and the principal amounted to 96 per cent and 86 per cent, respectively (Nitlapán, 1996a, pp. 10–12).

Transformation of the structure of the total project was planned for 1997, to ensure greater participation by an 'Association of Agroforestry Producers' and other actors as guarantors of the fund. This stage will be developed gradually as producers consolidate their organizational and representative capacities as a local association. The fund will be transformed to a limited liability partnership, in which the producers, Nitlapán and other actors interested in the production and commercialization of tree products will have a share (ibid., pp. 28–9).

Notes

1. These case studies refer to the 1995 agricultural cycle and were made possible through a research grant from the University Foundation of Development Cooperation (USOS) of the UFSIA, University of Antwerp. The 'Los Arboles Valen' ('Trees have a value') project of Nitlapán afforded access to interesting data and facilitated contact with local farmers. This project offers long-term credit to support primitive capital accumulation and reforestation to make peasant farms more diversified and viable. Nitlapán is a research and

development institution connected to the UCA – the Central American University of Managua.
2. For example, in 1995, with 1100 eucalyptus trees an annual income of US $200 could be obtained by selling firewood and an additional US$65 by selling piles (Nitlapán, 1996b, p. 16). Nevertheless, this income is still relatively low because transporters pay low prices and get the greater part of the final consumption price, but it should be increased if local farmers get more negotiation power.
3. 'Campesino a campesino' is a project of the UNAG (National Union of Farmers and Cattle-breeders) which promotes the interchange of farm implements and other capital among peasants.

Bibliography

Antillon, T. (1996) *Crisis, arborización y conservacionismo: la configuración socio-económica de la reproducción de los recursos forestales en el Pacífico nicaragüense*, Managua, Universidad Centroamericana.
Ellis, F. (1996) *Peasant Economics: Farm Households and Agrarian Development*, Wye Studies in Agricultural and Rural Development, 2nd edn, Cambridge University Press.
Nitlapán (1985) 'Los campesinos Nicaraguenses dan un giro a la reforma agraria', *Envío*, Nicaragua: IHCA, yr 4, no. 51, pp. 1–19.
Nitlapán (1994a) 'Descolectivización: reforma agraria "desdo abajo"', *Envío*, Nicaragua: IHCA, yr 13, no. 154, pp. 17–23.
Nitlapán (1994b) *Los Arboles Valen: proyecto de promoción de la producción forestal para la diversificación comercial de las fincas periurbanas de Masaya y Managua*, Managua: Nitlapán–UCA.
Nitlapán (1995) 'La propiedad agraria y la establidad', *Envio*, Nicaragua: IHCA, yr 14, no. 165, pp. 15–23.
Nitlapán (1996a) 'De parceleros palmados a campesinos finqueros', *Envío*, Nicaragua: IHCA, yr 15, no. 173, pp. 10–14.
Nitlapán (1996b) *Memoria del seminario 'El Crédito y la Reforestación'*, Masaya: Nitlapán–UCA.
Nitlapán (1996c) *El Campesino-Finquero y el potencial económico del campesinado nicaragüense*, Managua: IHCA.
North, D. C. (1990) *Institutions, Institutional Change and Economic Performance*, Cambridge: Cambridge University Press.
Ruben, R. (1997) *Making Cooperatives Work. Contract Choice and Resource Management within Land Reform Cooperatives in Honduras*, PhD thesis: Free University of Amsterdam.
Sadoulet, E. and de Janvry, A. (1995) *Quantitive Development Policy Analysis*, Baltimore, MD: Johns Hopkins University Press.
Validivia, C., Dunn, E. G. and Jette, C. (1996) 'Diversification as a Risk Management Strategy in an Andean Agropastoral Community', *American Journal of Agricultural Economics*, no. 78, pp. 1329–34.
Von Braun, J. and Pandya-Lorch, R. (1991) *Income Sources of Malnourished People in Rural Areas: Microlevel Information and Policy Implications*, Working Paper on Commercialization of Agriculture and Nutrition, no. 5, IFPRI.

7
Transformation of Cooperative Organizations: Pathways of Change for Agricultural Production Cooperatives in León-Chinandega, Nicaragua

Jos Vaessen, Orlando Cortéz and Ruerd Ruben

Introduction

Decollectivization processes within the agricultural cooperative sector can be observed all over the world and in the 1990s have received attention in the academic literature within the context of the transformation of former socialist regimes (Deininger, 1993; Csaki and Kislev, 1993). Adjustment processes within cooperative organizations in Latin-American countries with a tradition of land reform have also been widely documented (Carter, 1987; Carter *et al.*, 1993). Regarding the causes and directions of these adjustments, much uncertainty still exists, since comparative data bases are scarce. Most studies are reluctant to mark single drastic political or macroeconomic changes as the causes or determinants of the processes of cooperative change (Melmed-Sanjak and Carter, 1991).

The heterogeneous patterns of cooperative change evidently allow for closer analysis of intrinsic characteristics in relation to the different directions of cooperative change. Csaki and Kislev (1993), in their analysis of the cooperative transformation in the former socialist countries in Europe, illustrate processes of cooperative change where members partly substitute individual for collective production. Instead of completely abandoning the cooperative structure, many former members maintain ties with the collective framework, for several reasons. Input availability and marketing opportunities are often noted as motives for members to maintain these ties and protect themselves against missing markets (Bardhan, 1989; Carter, 1987). Access to information and risk diversification opportunities are additional factors for farmers to maintain ties with a cooperative organization at the secondary level (services) or sometimes at the primary level (production). In many cases, collective production is continued on a lesser scale in smaller groups and under different contractual agreements, thereby avoiding intrinsic problems of cooperative production related to moral hazard and free-riding behaviour (Putterman, 1985).

The agricultural production cooperatives in Nicaragua are called *Cooperativas Agrícolas Sandinistas* (CAS). In this chapter, the patterns of change within the sector of the CAS in the north-western region of León-Chinandega in Nicaragua (also referred to as Region II) are described using a comparative data set from two different years (1989 and 1997).[1]

The first section of the chapter outlines the empirical background of the decollectivization process in Nicaragua. The second section sketches some of the theoretical notions about the production cooperatives and the factors that influence the shifts in contract choice within these organizations. The third section presents the results of the analysis of the comparative data set. The goal is to describe the directions of change and to gain more insight in the rationality behind the changes. The lack of comparative empirical data on patterns of cooperative change has resulted in few testable hypotheses in the academic literature (Bonin *et al.*, 1993). Therefore, the effort of relating differences in group characteristics and member characteristics of agricultural production cooperatives to the heterogeneous directions of change is sometimes a precarious process, and one should be cautious with directions of causality.

Empirical context

Both external and internal factors may influence drastically the performance of production cooperatives. In Nicaragua, and in Region II in particular, a number of external factors have left clear marks on the development of the cooperative sector. The promotion of CAS by the Sandinista government in the 1980s was accompanied by large subsidies and strong control by the state over the CAS, since these were considered to be 'superior forms of economic organization' in the agricultural sector (Cortez, 1995). By 1986, the Sandinista government had loosened its grip on the cooperative sector, mainly because of the economic crisis and the intensified war with the Contras. Forced by the severe economic crisis, the Contra war and the international trade embargo, in 1988 the Sandinista government initiated structural adjustment policies, resulting in a tendency towards reduced state control and price liberalization (Catalan, 1994; Spoor, 1995). Despite restrictive monetary policies executed by the Chamorro government

(1990–6) and a continuation of the liberalization process, economic development continued to stagnate while the marginalization of various groups and sectors in society worsened (Catalan, 1994).

The CAS in Region II were not only affected by the general economic crisis and the effects of the adjustment policies, but also by the cotton crisis. In the first half of the 1980s, cotton was the most important commercial crop in Region II and also very important for the CAS in this region. The massive application of chemicals, declining soil fertility and an increasing incidence of diseases and pests began to undermine the success of the cotton monocultivation model in Region II. The sudden fall of international cotton prices in the late 1980s, further aggravated by hyperinflation and an overvalued córdoba, devastated the commercial production of cotton as well as other commercial crops, thereby leaving the agricultural sector of Region II in a crisis (Siles, 1992; Spoor, 1994). Relative prices of inputs changed in the period 1989–94, as machinery and chemical inputs became much more expensive compared to labour. These changes in relative prices between the late 1980s and the early 1990s as a result of adjustment policies induced changes in the production systems as agricultural producers moved away from cotton production towards the production of cereals and livestock (Clemens, 1995; Spoor, 1994). In particular, owners of small and medium sized farms, like the members of the CAS, substituted labour for capital and often moved away from commercial crop production towards more labour-intensive cereal production. After 1990, the credit which in the 1980s had been abundantly distributed among the CAS, became severely restricted. With the political change in 1990, conflicts over land rights increased, as political parties started discussing the validity of the land reform titles issued by the Sandinista government and former land-owners began to reclaim their lands (Amador and Ribbink, 1992). Even under the new government of president Alemán (1996–), the land titling problem remains a big issue which continues to hamper incentives for local agricultural development.[2] In general terms, it can be stated that the cotton crisis, the overall economic crisis which started in the late 1980s, the insecure land tenure, and reduced government support (including restrictive credit policies) are the most important external factors that have had an impact on the tendencies of disintegration and parcellation among the CAS in Region II.

Analytical framework

Putterman (1985) defines agricultural production cooperatives as: 'farm enterprises in which the labour of a group of farm households is pooled under an output or net revenue sharing arrangement'. A more appropriate definition for agricultural production cooperatives in developing countries is provided by Ruben (1997): 'agrarian production cooperatives can be seen as groups of farm households working together in a complex framework of interlinked transactions'. Farmers can choose to allocate time and resources between their own private production, collective production and off-farm activities.

Prospects for survival of production cooperatives depend to a large extent on the economic performance of the cooperative organization (see, for example, Bonin *et al.*, 1993; Porter and Scully, 1987). The performance of the cooperative again depends on the internal arrangements and rules that provide incentives for collective production. The theoretical framework focusing on these internal organization aspects is called contract choice theory. This is a fairly recent theoretical framework which is being used increasingly for the analysis of resource management in common property regimes (Hayami and Otsuka, 1993; Ruben, 1997; Ruben and Van de Berg, 1997). Contract choice refers to the different combinations of individual and collective activities within an institution such as the production cooperative. These different combinations shaped by internal arrangements and rules can be altered in order to increase incentives and improve cooperative efficiency (Ruben, 1997). Changing expectations of members with regard to the performance of the cooperative can lead to changes in contract choice.

Contract choice from the point of view of the individual producer implies two basic aspects. The first aspect refers to the rational allocation of time and resources to activities in order to satisfy the specific mix of household objectives (Ellis, 1988). The second aspect refers to the selection and negotiation of the most favourable institutional arrangement or contract with respect to the delivery and remuneration of inputs and the distribution of outputs for a certain activity. The two aspects influence each other simultaneously, since the objective function of a producer implies a certain activity mix with subsequent institutional arrangements. On the other hand, the existing 'supply' or 'context' of institutional arrangements can make certain activities more or less favourable in terms of output, input (service, subsidy) or insurance aspects. In that case, the 'supply' of contractual alternatives influences the time and resource allocation within the limits of the personal objective function.

Membership of a production cooperative can offer several benefits to a potential member. Stable income from collective activities, social services, access to inputs and information for individual production are some of the benefits that might be superior to alternative contractual agreements and might motivate potential members to join the production cooperative or prevent members from leaving the organization. Once they are a part of the cooperative, members bargain with each other in order to make the multiple contractual arrangements as beneficial as possible to themselves.[3] Moreover, the institution and the internal arrangements underlying the institution (in this case, the production cooperative) will be shaped in such a way as to obtain maximum benefit from the institution in terms of each member's specific objective function. In the case of disappointing performance of collective production, members might decide not only to shift their contract choice towards other contracts (and activities) but also to start using the institution in a different way in order to satisfy their specific objective functions. Holding on to risk diversification possibilities, access to information, inputs and land will restrict the contract choice in the sense that the shift towards individual production does not necessarily imply a complete retreat by members from the cooperative framework. Consequently, shifts in contract choice, in this case defined as the choices to continue collective production or to maintain ties with the collective framework, are essentially endogenous variables. These processes of shifts in contract choice towards a different use of the cooperative institution or contract, as well as shifts towards other contracts outside the cooperative (or within the cooperative at the individual, informal level) are processes that are at the core of this chapter.

Melmed-Sanjak and Carter (1991) describe the shift in contract choice in relation to the external environment. The presence of external political or economic factors that threaten the future profitability of the agricultural production cooperative might reduce members' expectations on the future profitability of collective production. For individual members, factor productivity of their individual production is used as a measure of their opportunity costs of labour. Against these opportunity costs they weigh the attractiveness of off-farm employment and involvement in collective production (Ruben, 1997). A reduction in members' expectations of collective production shifts their attention towards their private parcels, or in some cases to off-farm work. Consequently, competition for time and resources draws labour away from collective activities. In addition, this might lead to free-riding behaviour (that is, reduced labour efforts by members who continue to receive a share of the collective profits as do other members) with subsequent lower productivity in collective production. This further affects members' expectations and might eventually lead to the rational response of parcellation (Carter, 1987; Melmed-Sanjak and Carter, 1991). Thus, while internal labour discipline problems affect cooperative performance directly, external political or economic factors have a direct influence on both cooperative performance and internal labour discipline.

Besides the contract choice theoretical framework, the theory of induced technical change (sometimes called induced innovation) developed by Hayami and Ruttan (1971) can offer some insight into the changes that have been taking place in the sector CAS in Nicaragua. Hayami and Ruttan argued that there are multiple paths of technological development, and that the appropriate path for a country or region is a function of resource endowments. In societies where labour is relatively scarce and consequently more expensive, farmers optimize productivity per unit of labour. Land is used more extensively and agricultural research is directed at labour-productivity-enhancing technologies (for example, mechanization). In contrast, in societies where labour is relatively abundant and cheaper while land is relatively scarce and expensive, farmers will optimize productivity per unit of land. Consequently, agricultural research will be focused on land-productivity-enhancing technologies (for example, improved seeds or fertilizers). This presents the basic idea of induced technical change. It should be noted that the theory is more refined and has received much criticism as well as new impulses for improvement (Koppel, 1995). One of the fundamental shortcomings of the theory is the fact that each agroclimatic zone in principle represents a different production function, and, because of differences in transaction costs, each farm faces its own specific vector of input and output prices. It is beyond the scope of this chapter to go into the discussion around induced technical change, so we shall focus here on a brief interpretation of the framework for the changes that have been taking place in the CAS sector.

It can be argued that the CAS sector in the 1980s was embedded in an institutional environment that confronted the CAS with an artificially high availability of machinery and capital intensive inputs. Factor prices were artificially low for this group of inputs in relation to labour, which led to an irrationally high use of the former. After the reduction in government support, the CAS were left with severe budgetary problems. In the late 1980s and the beginning of the 1990s, chemical inputs started to reflect real scarcity values, and suddenly became much more expensive for the CAS. In addition, the restriction of credit in the agricultural sector confronted many CAS with problems of collective performance. The fact that the CAS often lacked commercial attitudes and skills and were accustomed to capital-intensive production methods made it very difficult for many of them to make the shift towards more labour-intensive collective production with a more rational use of capital-intensive inputs. Individual production was much more suited to following the trend of induced technical change, because the scale, the types of crops and the types of technology were better suited to labour-intensive production. The inability of the CAS to readjust collective production according to the changes in relative factor prices, partially explains the performance problems and the massive shift in contract choice towards individual production.

Comparing cooperative structures

Brief methodology

Contract choice theory analyses as an endogenous variable the decision whether or not to continue to produce collectively. The decision depends on the outcome of a bargaining process among members, each having evaluated collective performance in relation to their specific objective functions. While not knowing the specific objective function of each member, we can relate the question of whether or not to continue to produce collectively with a number of variables with regard to member characteristics and organizational characteristics. Although several econometric techniques are available to treat such decisions, the precariousness of the data set obliged us to choose an elaborate approach to describe contract choice, taking into account different sets and types of variable.[4] Therefore, as a first step to gaining insight about the heterogeneity of the CAS, they are classified into a number of distinct groups, based on their current characteristics.[5]

The 62 CAS of the 1997 sample are classified into three groups, based on the existence of collective activities in the cooperative. The three groups are identified as COL (collective), SER (services) and DIS (disintegrated).[6] First, we shall take a look at the general changes which have taken place within the CAS in Nicaragua since the late 1980s. Then, cooperative characteristics and member characteristics will be examined in relation to the shifts in contract choice. The classification of the CAS into distinct groups and the directions of change towards these groups are referred to as 'pathways of change'.

General changes: 1989–97

To provide an overview on general changes within the CAS sector in Region II, Table 7.1 compares 1989 and 1997. The table confirms the trends of decollectivization and parcellization as described earlier.

Table 7.1   Production cooperatives in Region II: resources and membership

Cooperative characteristics (mean; standard deviation)	1989 (n = 72)	1997 (n = 62)	t-test for significant differences (n = 62)
Total area (mz)[a]	481.7 (537.4)	354.4 (407.8)	2.62**
Number of members	18.3 (10.4)	12.4 (6.2)	5.45**
Area per member (mz)	23.6 (18.0)	28.0 (28.7)	−1.70*
Percentage of members related to each other[b]	58 (28)	59 (33)	−0.61
Percentage of male members	92 (15)	90 (15)	0.97
Percentage of founder members	42 (25)	56 (30)	−4.31**
Number of collective livestock	71.9 (113.6)	10.5 (36.7)	4.29**
Units of collective machinery	8.8 (6.6)	3.6 (5.5)	6.48**
Collective production (per cent of CAS engaged in coll. production)	100%	20%	Not valid[c]

Notes: *significant at the 0.10 level.   **significant at the 0.05 level.
[a]mz = manzana; 1 manzana is 0.7 ha.
[b]Also referred to as family grade. The question underlying the variable is: how many members are family of each other?
[c]The variable is a dummy with 1 if the CAS is engaged in collective agricultural production, and 0 if the CAS has no collective production.
Source: Database 88/89 (DEA, 1989) and NIRP field work in Region II, April–May 1997.

The total area and the number of members have declined significantly. Former members leaving the CAS often took with them a piece of land. Although land titles were often not formalized or recognized, some members were able to sell their parcels informally.[7] Surprisingly, the share of members with family ties did not increase. While members marry other members, and children have the right to succeed their father or mother, the CAS did not evolve into fully extended family enterprises. Probably because of the crisis, children of members started to pursue their fortunes elsewhere. The share of founder members increased, which can be explained by the fact that non-founders were often excluded from the initial collective title. Therefore, while having no claim to collective land and low claims to other collective resources, non-founder members were the first to leave the cooperative. The drastic decline in collective livestock and collective machinery is in line with the overall tendency of decollectivization and parcellation. The latter tendency is also clearly illustrated by the fact that in 1997 only 20 per cent of the still-existing CAS were involved in any form of collective production. Evidently, the trend of massive decollectivization took place between 1989 and 1997, since in 1989 100 per cent of the CAS were still involved in collective production. The fact that in 1989 all the cooperatives in the sample were engaged in collective production does not mean, however, that production was totally collective. In many of the CAS decollectivization and parcellization tendencies had already been going on for years, while other CAS remained completely collective organizations.

Production systems changed considerably, as the share of collective production declined drastically and the production of cotton disappeared totally. However, livestock, basic grains (maize, sorghum and rice) and some other crops (soya, sesame and sugarcane) were, and still are, the main crops in the CAS in Region II. The economic crisis and the changes in relative prices have led to a decrease in the production of commercial crops. Individual production, hampered by similar problems as collective production and relying on relatively abundant labour, is concentrated on food production. Individual production systems are primarily based on basic grains (mainly maize and, to a lesser extent, sorghum), and to a much lesser extent livestock and other crops.

Cooperative characteristics and contract choice: 1989–97

Table 7.2 shows that the number of members per CAS was not significantly different between the groups in 1997. Moreover, the overall decline in members per CAS has been similar for all the CAS. Family grade (percentage of members related) and gender (percentage of male members) are similar between groups and did not change between 1989 and 1997. The next variable shows a very interesting tendency. Although the membership decline was similar for CAS in the COL and DIS group, in the DIS group (and the SER group) a concentration of founder members manifested itself. Perhaps founder members from the DIS and SER group had higher claims to collective resources. With the disappearance of the collective system, non-founder members of, especially, the DIS group were more-or-less driven out of the CAS. The loss of income from collective activities and the inferior claims on collective resources moved these members to leave the CAS in greater numbers than did the founder members. Although no significant differences were found, apparently members who left CAS in the SER and DIS groups took land away with them. In the COL group, leaving members could not issue claims on collective resources. This is shown by the larger area per CAS in the COL group in 1997. A functioning system of collective activities protected non-founder members and

Table 7.2   Evolution of cooperative characteristics, 1989–97

Variable (mean values)	Year	Group 1: COL	Group 2: SER	Group 3: DIS	ANOVA F-stat.	Significant difference between groups (Tamhane and Games-Howell)
Number of	1989	21.2	19.4	17.7	0.624	Not significant
members	1997	12.5	12.8	12.2	0.938	Not significant
Percentage						
of members	1989	57.1	54.8	59.9	0.198	Not significant
related	1997	57.1	57.8	60.6	0.937	Not significant
Percentage						
of male	1989	93.7	87.0	94.1	1.246	Not significant
members	1997	87.7	88.9	92.2	0.533	Not significant
Percentage						
of founder	1989	30.5	36.6	46.1	2.470*	1 and 3*
members	1997	35.9	56.2	64.6	4.840**	1 and 3**
Total area	1989	469.1	422.6	532.2	0.244	Not significant
(mz)	1997	419.2	281.8	364.2	0.419	Not significant
Area per						
member	1989	21.9	23.9	24.5	0.102	Not significant
(mz)	1997	41.1	23.3	25.1	1.789	Not significant
Number of						
coll.	1989	59.5	40.3	90.2	1.187	Not significant
Livestock	1997	46.1	2.90	0.12	10.071**	1 and 2**, 1 and 3**
Number of	1989	13.2	8.10	8.00	3.318**	1 and 2**, 1 and 3**
coll.						
Machinery	1997	12.3	2.80	0.82	55.966**	1 and 2**, 1 and 3**

Notes: *Significant at the 0.10 level. **Significant at the 0.05 level.
Source: Database 88/89 (DEA, 1989) and NIRP field work in Region II, April–May 1997.

discouraged founder members from triggering their claims. The system of collective activities provided the members with sufficient security and income to discourage claims on resources by those who left.

The decline in collective livestock and collective machinery is similar to that of land. In the COL group, collective livestock production has been maintained but in the SER group, and especially in the DIS group, livestock has either been divided among members or sold. The average number of livestock per CAS in 1989 was higher in CAS from the DIS group than in CAS from the COL and SER groups. The fact that livestock fits into a strategy of personal accumulation and security probably makes collective livestock systems more vulnerable to decollectivization tendencies than collective cropping activities. This is shown by the large decline in collective livestock in the DIS group between 1989 and 1997. Collective machinery is maintained in the COL group. CAS from this group in 1989 were already significantly better endowed with machinery than CAS from the other two groups. In the SER group, some CAS maintain the provision of machinery services to their members. The low average number of machines per CAS in 1997 in this group is because of the incidence of other services. CAS which provide other inputs or loans to their members are also classified in this group, although most of them had already divided their machinery (or left it to deteriorate).

Looking at the internal organization and some additional characteristics of collective production in 1989, some interesting factors related to the shifts in contract choice can be identified (see Table 7.3). The first variable, advance payments to members, is not significantly different between groups. However, the existence of a sanctioning system seems to be important. Although the majority of the CAS employed a sanctioning system in the case of non-compliance with labour activities, in the COL group *all* the CAS had a functioning system of sanctions.

The next two variables support a very important conclusion. In the COL group, almost no CAS provided inputs to their members for individual production and *none* of the CAS from this group made their machinery available to members. In both the SER and DIS groups, approximately half of the CAS provided one or both of these services to their members. The provision of services by the CAS to their members has promoted the development of individual production and clearly influenced the parcellation and decollectivization processes within these CAS. Making available collective pastures for individual use has been the same among the groups and has apparently had no influence on the direction of change.

Besides the relative vulnerability of livestock-orientated CAS, another connection can be made with respect to the production system. Successful cotton-producing CAS, many of them belonging to the COL group in 1989, require a more strict and diversified organization of labour compared to many other CAS. Moreover, they tend to own more machinery. This might have contributed to a better labour discipline, a higher probability of successful cooperative performance and subsequently better prospects for the continuance of collective production.

Table 7.3　Internal organization and the cooperative production system, 1989 (frequencies and association tests)

	Group 1 COL (%)		Group 2 SER (%)		Group 3 DIS (%)		Significant association[a]	Goodman and Kruskal Tau
Advance	No:	7.7	No:	20.0	No:	20.0	Not valid	No
payments	Yes:	92.3	Yes:	80.0	Yes:	80.0		
to members								
Sanctions	No:	0	No:	37.5	No:	30.0	Not valid	Yes
	Yes:	100	Yes:	62.5	Yes:	70.0		
Input	No:	92.3	No:	43.8	No:	55.0	Yes**	Yes**
provision	Yes:	7.7	Yes:	56.3	Yes:	45.0		
to members								
Machinery	No:	100	No:	43.8	No:	52.5	Yes**	Yes**
for use by	Yes:	0	Yes:	56.3	Yes:	47.5		
members								
Individual	No:	23.1	No:	31.3	No:	35.0	No	No
live stock	Yes:	76.9	Yes:	68.8	Yes:	65.0		
in collective								
pastures								
Production system								
Basic grains		30.8		50.0		25.0	Not valid	Yes*
and other								
Cotton		38.5		12.5		7.5		
and other								
Livestock		7.7		18.8		27.5		
and basic								
grains								
Livestock		23.1		18.8		40.0		
and other								

Notes:　*Significant at the 0.10 level. **Significant at the 0.05 level.
[a]Based on the association tests of Pearson, likelihood ratio, Phi, Cramer's v, Contingency Coefficient.
Source:　Database 88/89 (DEA, 1989).

Table 7.4 shows some additional cooperative characteristics for 1997. First of all, in the COL group almost no land sales took place, which confirms the findings in Table 7.2. In the SER and DIS group, in 50 per cent and 64 per cent of the CAS respectively, land sales occurred. The loss of income from collective activities, insufficient income from individual production and restricted entry in the labour market were motives for many members to sell their parcels. Land was sold to previous landowners or other members from the CAS (Jonakin, 1994). Clear

Table 7.4 Cooperative behaviour and management regimes, 1997 (frequencies and association tests)

	Group 1 COL (%)		Group 2 SER (%)		Group 3 DIS (%)		Significant association[a]	Goodman and Kruskal Tau
Land sales (individual or collective)	No:	92.3	No:	50.0	No:	36.4	Yes**	Yes**
	Yes:	7.7	Yes:	50.0	Yes:	63.6		
Partial division of collective land[b]	No:	53.8	No:	0	No:	6.1	Not valid	Yes**
	Yes:	46.2	Yes:	100	Yes:	93.9		
Total division of col. land	No:	91.7	No:	12.5	No:	18.2	Not valid	Yes**
	Yes:	8.3	Yes:	87.5	Yes:	81.8		
Collective debt	No:	38.5	No:	81.3	No:	72.5	Yes**	Yes**
	Yes:	61.5	Yes:	18.8	Yes:	27.5		
Off-farm work in dry season	No:	84.6	No:	56.3	No:	39.4	Yes**	Yes**
	Yes:	15.4	Yes:	43.6	Yes:	60.6		

Notes: *Significant at the 0.10 level. **Significant at the 0.05 level.
[a]Based on the association tests of Pearson, likelihood ratio, Phi, Cramer's v, Contingency Coefficient.
[b]Minimum condition for a clear division of land between members, as defined here, is a more-or-less fixed geographical distribution of land among the members, which is recognized by (more-or-less) all the members. Sometimes the division of land is based on an oral agreement between members; in other cases official individual land titles have been assigned to the parcels.
Source: NIRP field work in Region II, April–May 1997.

divisions of land have occurred significantly more in the SER and DIS group than in the COL group. The SER group and the DIS group show no differences in that respect, giving evidence that production in the former group is also based on the individual parcel, although in a still-existing cooperative framework. The division of land, one of the initial steps in the decollectivization process, has been the engine for many other processes such as the division and sales of livestock and machinery, and the increased mobility of members.

The debt variable shows a clear association between collective debt and continuance of collective production. It would be going too far to conclude that collective debt is pressing farmers to continue collective production, which otherwise is considered not to be viable. However, repaying the collective debt is a clear motive. Unfortunately, the relationship is disturbed by the fact that the debt variable includes short-term outstanding debt (1996/7) and long-term outstanding debt.

However, CAS that used to be involved in commercial cotton production and were affected by the cotton crisis are often faced with
debts stemming from this period. Other studies also mention that
cotton-orientated CAS, which after the crisis faced, and still are
facing, substantial collective debts, are continuing to produce collectively to pay back their debt (Siles, 1992; Jonakin, 1994).[8] In several
CAS, the members expressed a wish for formal parcellation of the cooperative land. However, in many cases the collective debt was the basic
obstacle to being able to do so. In their study on the decollectivization
of production cooperatives in a Peruvian valley, Melmed-Sanjak and
Carter (1991) also note this phenomenon. The off-farm labour variable
(limited to the dry period) suggests that members from the COL group
are internally ensured of employment, while in the SER and DIS groups
members seek employment elsewhere. Of course, one could also reason
the other way around: that is, members with substantial off-farm
employment activities are not willing to sacrifice their off-farm source
of income for a labour discipline in a collective production framework
with lower expected returns.

Member characteristics and contract choice: 1997

Table 7.5 shows members' household and farm characteristics, specified
for the three groups of CAS. Family sizes differ significantly between the
COL and the DIS groups but there are no significant differences in age
and education of the head of the household. The bigger family size in
the DIS group is related to larger private parcels, which are able to sustain a larger family. The fact that more members from the SER and DIS
groups work outside the CAS than from the COL group could suggest
comparative investment advantages in the private parcels (even more
so in the case where members receive or have received support from the
CAS for individual production). However, total area per member (see
collective area per member in Table 7.2) in contrast to total individual
area per member (see Table 7.5), is higher in the COL group than in the
SER and DIS groups. This illustrates the importance of collective income
for members in the COL group. Members from the other two groups
compensate their loss of income from collective activities by working
more on their individual parcels and outside their own farms.

Significant differences in the amount of individual land between
the COL group and the SER and DIS groups show the differences
in parcellation, but no differences in individual livestock can be
observed. This seems odd, in view of the fact that in 1989 the numbers
of collective livestock in the DIS group was much higher than in the

Table 7.5 Individual member characteristics, 1997

Variable (mean values)	Group 1 COL	Group 2 SER	Group 3 DIS	ANOVA F-stat.	Significant difference between groups (Tamhane and Games-Howell)
Family size	5.2	5.5	6.1	2.865	1 and 3*
Education (yrs)	3.1	2.8	2.8	0.376	Not significant
Age	44.8	43.5	46.3	1.051	Not significant
Size private parcel (mz)[a]	8.1	15.7	19.1	6.772**	1 and 2*; 1 and 3**
Percentage of the parcel for agriculture	47.6	60.1	60.5	1.737	Not significant
Total area per member (mz)[b]	8.9	17.3	22.9	7.152**	1 and 2**; 1 and 3**
Number of individual livestock	5.7	5.6	6.8	0.334	Not significant

Notes: *Significant at the 0.10 level. **Significant at 0.05 level.
[a]This number refers to the actual amount of land the member is using or 'owns' in the CAS and excludes collective land.
[b]This number refers to the total amount of land the member 'owns' inside and outside the CAS.
Source: NIRP field work in Region II, April–May 1997.

COL group. The decline in collective livestock is not reflected in members of the DIS group having more individual livestock in 1997. There are two reasons for this. The first is that livestock, like land, were sold to repay collective debts. The second explanation is that livestock was divided unfairly between members in favour of a small group of influential members (the management of the CAS). This tendency by the management of the CAS towards exploitation has been described in several other studies (see, for example, Siles, 1992).

Table 7.6 shows additional member characteristics. Remittances are not a basic source of income for members of the CAS. There are no significant differences between the groups. Nor does the organization grade differ between groups. In general, about 25 per cent of CAS members are affiliated to a rural organization. The proportion of members possessing farm machinery is clearly higher in the SER and DIS groups, fitting perfectly into the decollectivization trend. The credit variable shows that the independent producers in the SER and the DIS groups are more likely to receive individual credit than the members from the COL group, but the difference is not significant. The advantage of collateral (private parcel) has increased the proportion of CAS members from the SER and DIS groups having access to the credit market.

As suggested by previous studies, the performance of a CAS is related to the background of the members because this influences their experience in working together and subsequently the probability of being able to deal with free-riding problems (DEA, 1989; Ruben, 1997). Table 7.6 shows no differences in background between the groups. Either this finding contradicts the statement of the influence of the background of members on cooperative performance, or one can doubt the direct relationship between economic performance of a CAS and the shift in contract choice, in this case the willingness to continue collective production.[9]

The significant association of the production system with the group classification can be explained by the fact that in the COL group 30 per cent of the members have no individual production, and that in the SER and DIS groups more members cultivate labour-intensive commercial crops. The ability to diversify agricultural production for members in the SER or COL groups has increased because of the distribution of collective resources. Moreover, the need to diversify agricultural production has been stimulated by disappointing results in collective production. This has subsequently reduced members' willingness to cooperate and thereby promoted the shift in contract choice towards parcellation and disintegration. Loss of income from collective activities has encouraged farmers to work more intensively on their own private plots. The risk hazard obliged CAS members from the SER and DIS groups to diversify their income by working more off-farm and making a wider variety of products.

Pathways of change

Summarizing the findings of the previous section we can identify three distinct pathways of cooperative change. Lack of resources might delay the formalization of the parcellation process. Similarly, a collective debt might be a motive to continue some collective activities at a lower level of intensity. The unresolved question of formal land titles does influence members' decisions to stay,[10] but it is not sufficient to explain the shift in contract choice towards parcellation (for example, shift to individual production). This section tries to structure the findings of the previous sections. Figure 7.1 summarizes the three pathways of change,

Table 7.6 Contract choice and member characteristics, 1997 (frequencies and association tests)

	Group 1 COL (%)		Group 2 SER (%)		Group 3 DIS (%)		Significant association[a]	Goodman and Kruskal Tau
Remittances	No:	95.3	No:	89.5	No:	89.3	No	No
	Yes:	4.7	Yes:	10.5	Yes:	10.7		
Membership of	No:	75.0	No:	72.4	No:	79.8	No	No
organization[b]	Yes:	25.0	Yes:	27.6	Yes:	20.2		
Own farm	No:	97.7	No:	79.3	No:	68.4	Yes**	Yes**
machinery	Yes:	2.3	Yes:	20.7	Yes:	31.6		
Credit in the	No:	75.0	No:	56.9	No:	59.6	No	No
past three years	Yes:	25.0	Yes:	43.1	Yes:	40.4		

Main activity before joining the CAS

Non-agricultural labourer	13.6		5.2		5.3		Not valid	No
Agricultural labourer	63.6		58.6		63.2			
Independent producer	20.5		19.0		23.7			
Other	2.3		17.2		7.9			

Production system

No individual production	29.5		3.4		6.1		Not valid	Yes**
Basic grains	47.7		67.2		62.3			
Livestock and basic grains	15.9		10.3		14.0			
Horticultural crops and basic grains	6.8		19.0		17.6			

Notes: *Significant at the 0.10 level. **Significant at the 0.05 level.
[a]Based on the association tests of Pearson, likelihood ratio, Phi, Cramer's v, Contingency Coefficient.
[b]Membership of UNAG excluded.
Source: NIRP field work in Region II, April–May 1997.

which will be treated in this section by distinguishing between two levels: organizational change and individual shifts in contract choice.

Organizational change

Looking at the overall shift in contract choice within the sector CAS, we found that in the 1990s the CAS faced restricted institutional

132

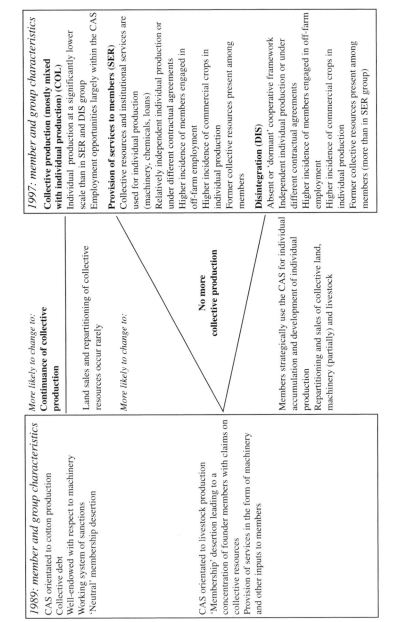

Figure 7.1 Three pathways of cooperative change

support and were confronted with high-risk circumstances. The better-endowed (in terms of machinery) and well-organized CAS (in terms of sanctioning and supervision systems) have proved to be the most likely to consolidate their collective production activities. They offered the best protection against adverse external conditions and the best con-tractual alternative in terms of guaranteed income from collective pro-duction compared to other contractual agreements available for CAS members. CAS oriented towards commercial crop production (in the 1980s, especially cotton) seem to have a comparative advantage in terms of labour organization, and subsequently a better protection against the risk environment compared to livestock-orientated CAS.

Moreover, livestock fits in better with personal strategies of accumu-lation and security. The provision of productive services during the 1980s has stimulated individual agricultural production and made the shift in contract choice towards parcellation and disintegration much easier. CAS from the disintegration group have already stopped the provision of services to members, since collective resources have been exhausted and fully distributed among members. CAS from the services group have continued to provide services to members. One could con-clude that the services group is just an intermediate group of CAS that have abandoned their collective production and are soon about to give up their patronage network in a further step towards 'total' disintegra-tion. However, this would be a premature conclusion. As stated earlier, some CAS, when moving from collective production towards only services, improved and enlarged their service network. In this case one cannot talk about an intermediate phase towards disintegration but rather a conscious change towards a specialization in services. However, new institutional linkages should be made and old ones should be renewed if the small CAS from the SER group want to avoid total exhaustion of cooperative resources. If not, they would eventually end up in 'total' disintegration.

Individual shifts in contract choice

Apart from the direct influence of adverse external circumstances on organizational change, the CAS are largely being changed from within by their members, who respond rationally to the cooperative and the external environment from the point of view of their own specific objective functions. Individual contract choice is influenced directly by members' judgements concerning expected benefits from the CAS, such as risk diversification options, access to services, or income from collective production. The CAS from the collective group have been able to maintain a collective organization with continued prospects and incentives for collective production. Membership turnover has been higher than in the other groups, and free entry of members has prevented a concentration of founder members with superior claims to collective resources. Because of disappointing prospects for collective production, CAS from the other two groups have fallen prey to claims on collective resources by members. Provision of services to members, whether or not negotiated by the founder member, further stimulated existing tendencies towards parcellation and shifts of contract choice towards individual production. Having secured their position within a CAS, the founder members were pioneers in a strategy of individual accumulation of collective resources in order to diversify and improve their agricultural production, or to secure means for security or self-financing potential. Less fortunate members within the services or dis-integration group were confronted with loss of employment and low opportunity costs of individual production, which obliged them to perform wage-labour work or engage in other (non-) agricultural activities in order to ensure a secure income. In some cases, restricted access to labour markets made it difficult for members to find other income-earning possibilities to compensate for the loss of income from collective activities. To ensure their survival these members often sold parts of their individual land.

Discussion

This chapter has tried to describe the processes of change that have taken place in the production cooperatives in Nicaragua. By comparing data from 1989 and 1997 pathways could be constructed to gain insight into some of the causes of these processes of change. Contract choice theory has proved to be a useful tool for shedding light on the rationality of these processes. Because of the heterogeneity among members *within* the CAS it has been difficult to relate member characteristics to the three pathways of change, which are initially based on cooperative characteristics. The need for a more member-focused methodology to study the shifts in contract choice within processes of decollectivization is essential. The model of pathways is useful in describing and elucidating complex relationships of association between characteristics of the CAS and directions of change. However, the enormous variety of member and cooperative characteristics disturbs many general relationships and puts a constraint on the practical use of this methodology. In addition, variables such as ideology and social interaction are issues that have certainly influenced the changes in the CAS and have not been sufficiently taken into account here.

One of the most important findings of this chapter is the elucidation of rational responses of members who move away from a collective model, which under the specific circumstances has proved not to be viable. Although in specific circumstances some CAS continue to operate successfully, the majority of the cases have shown that, especially in the field of services and access to the labour market, the CAS have lost their comparative advantages in relation to other alternatives. Service cooperatives in Nicaragua offer the same potential for benefits in terms of services and patronage as the CAS, while not suffering from internal labour discipline problems related to collective production. With the loss of income from collective activities and a declining importance of the cooperative framework of the CAS, access to wage-labour markets and adequate access to inputs are two important fields that merit attention for policy intervention targeted at small farmers such as the (ex-)members of the CAS.

Notes

1. This chapter is based on data collected by the authors in April–June 1997 within the framework of a research project, 'Resource Management and Contract Choice in Agricultural Cooperatives', financed by the Netherlands–Israel Research Programme (NIRP). The data from 1989 are based on the same sample stemming from previous research in the Region II on production cooperatives which was financed by the Ford Foundation (DEA, 1989; Carter and Luz, 1990). Data from 1989 refer to the agricultural cycle of 1988/9 and data from 1997 to the cycle of 1996/7. The authors would like to thank Zvi Lerman, Michael Carter, Gustavo Siles and Estela Alemán.
2. For a concise summary on government policies towards the CAS, see Cortez (1995).
3. Coase (1937) was one of the first to write on bargaining processes under common property regimes. Contract choice theory and new institutional economics have benefited from his work and many refinements have since been developed (see, for example, Hoff *et al.*, 1993).
4. For a review of the statistical foundation of the methodology used in this chapter, see Vaessen (1997). A logistic regression function was estimated in order to determine which variables influence the decision whether or not to continue collective production. The results were not satisfactory, as the causality was reversed in the case of the most significant variables.
. The choice to classify CAS on the basis of their current characteristics is based on two underlying features. First, it is supposed that the nature of the cooperative organization is the result of a process of negotiation and choices made by *current* members, most of them having been around for some time. Second, it is suggested that the current classification is based on a 'static picture' of the actual status of the CAS which is influenced by processes that

have already begun. Therefore, another 'static picture' representing the situation in 1989 may indicate some of the factors associated with the direction of change experienced by the CAS to reach their current status.

6. 'COL' group: collective production (livestock and/or agriculture); 'SER' group: no collective production, but services to members; and 'DIS' group: no collective production or services. The classification is based on the existence of collective production and the provision of services to members, which means that these variables are not included in the 1997 variables.

7. Jonakin (1997) describes the land sales of peasant farmers in Nicaragua, who, faced with restricted entry into labour and capital markets, are forced to sell parts of their land in order to survive.

8. Members state that having a collective debt makes it necessary to continue to produce collectively. Apparently, paying back collective debts with private production is not considered to be an option. Possible reasons for this are legal obstacles or distrust among members.

9. It is difficult to determine empirically the influence of agricultural performance on the shifts in contract choice. Here, it is reasoned that the CAS that are better-protected against adverse external conditions (production system, internal organization) are more likely to be successful in collective agriculture. For a detailed analysis of agricultural performance in relation to contract choice in Region II, see Vaessen (1997).

10. Because of inexperience or lack of knowledge, members might not be able to face the risky 'outside' world of independent farming. Even in the case of low prospects for successful collective production, members may decide to continue engagement in collective agricultural activities. No direct relationships with respect to education or social background related to shifts in contract choice could be established (Cortez *et al.*, 1997).

Bibliography

Amador, F. and Ribbink, G. (1992) *Nicaragua: Reforma Agraria, Propiedad y Mercado de Tierra*, ESECA-UNAN: Managua.

Bardhan, P. (ed.) (1989) *The Economic Theory of Agrarian Institutions*, Oxford: Clarendon Press.

Bonin, J. P., Jones, D. C. and Putterman, L. (1993) 'Theoretical and Empirical Studies of Producer Cooperatives: Will Ever the Twain Meet?', *Journal of Economic Literature*, vol. 31.

Carter, M. R. (1987) 'Risk Sharing and Incentives in the Decollectivisation of Agriculture', *Oxford Economic Papers*, vol. 39.

Carter, M. R. and Luz, K. (1990) *What is to be done about Land Reform Cooperatives in Nicaragua?*, Department of Agricultural Economics, University of Wisconsin-Madison, Staff Paper No. 118.

Carter, M. R., Melmed-Sanjak, J. and Luz, K. (1993) 'Can Production Cooperatives Resolve the Conundrum of Exclusionary Growth? An Econometric Evaluation of Land Reform Cooperatives in Honduras and Nicaragua', in C. Csaki and Y. Kislev (eds), *Agricultural Cooperatives in Transition*, Boulder, Col.: Westview Press.

Catalan, O. (1994) 'Control de Hiperinflación y Ajuste Estructural en Nicaragua', in J. P. de Groot and M. Spoor (eds), *Ajuste Estructural y Economía Campesina: Nicaragua, El Salvador, Centroamérica*, ESECA-UNAN: Managua.

Clemens, H. (1995) *Economic Adjustment Policies, Agricultural Technology and Environment: The Case of Small Farmer Production in Nicaragua in the Early Nineties*, CDR-ULA: Costa Rica.

Coase, R. H. (1937) 'The Nature of the Firm', *Economica*, vol. 16.

Cortéz, O. (1995) 'La Parcelización y la Gestión del Estado', *Economía Agrícola*, ESECA-UNAN: Managua.

Cortéz, O., Ruber, R. and Vaessen, J. L. (1997) *Quien se queda y quien se va?*, Working paper, ESECA-UNAN: Managua.

Csaki, C. and Y. Kislev (eds) (1993) *Agricultural Cooperatives in Transition*, Boulder, Col.: Westview Press.

DEA (1989) *Cooperativas de Producción en la Región II: Del Acceso a la Tierra hacia la Efficiencia Económica, Resultados y Desafíos*, Unpublished manuscript, UNAN: Managua.

Deininger, K. W. (1993) *Cooperatives and the Breakup of Large Mechanized Farms: Theoretical Perspectives and Empirical Evidence*, World Bank Discussion Paper No. 218, Washington.

Ellis, F. (1988) *Peasant Economics: Farm Households and Agrarian Development*, Wye Studies in Agricultural and Rural Development, Cambridge University Press.

Hayami, Y. and Otsuka, K. (1993) *The Economics of Contract Choice – An Agrarian Perspective*, Oxford: Clarendon Press.

Hayami, Y. and Ruttan, V. W. (1971) *Agricultural Development: An International Perspective*, Baltimore, MD: Johns Hopkins University Press.

Hoff, K., Braverman, A. and Stiglitz, J. E. (1993) *The Economics of Rural Organization – Theory, Practice and Policy*, Oxford University Press for the World Bank.

Jonakin, J. (1994) *Las Cooperatives de Producción Nicaragüense: Una Investigación del Uso de la Tierra, Deuda y Mercados de Tierra*, Staff paper, Tennessee Technological University.

Jonakin, J. (1997) 'The Interaction of Market Failure and Structural Adjustment in Producer Credit and Land Markets: The Case of Nicaragua', *Journal of Economic Issues*, vol. 31.

Koppel, B. M. (ed.) (1995) *Induced Innovation Theory and International Agricultural Development: A Reassessment*, Baltimore, MD: Johns Hopkins University Press.

Melmed-Sanjak, J. and Carter, M. R. (1991) 'The Economic Viability and Stability of Capitalized Family Farming: An Analysis of Agricultural Decollectivization in Peru', *Journal of Development Studies*, vol. 27.

Porter, P. K. and Scully, G. W. (1987) 'Economic Efficiency in Cooperatives', *Journal of Law and Economics*, vol. 30.

Putterman, L. (1985) 'Extrinsic versus Intrinsic Problems of Agricultural Cooperation: Anti-incentivism in Tanzania and China', *Journal of Development Studies*, vol. 21.

Ruben, R. (1997) *Making Cooperatives Work: Contract Choice and Resource Management within Land Reform Cooperatives in Honduras*, Amsterdam: PhD thesis, Free University of Amsterdam.

Ruben, R. and van den Berg, M. (1997) 'Land Reform and Resource Management within Agricultural Production Cooperatives', in J. P. de Groot and R. Ruben (eds), *Sustainable Agriculture in Central America*, New York: Macmillan Press.

Siles, G. (1992) *Sistemas de Producción en CAS de la Región II de Nicaragua*, PhD thesis, Universidad Central de Villas, Cuba.

Spoor, M. (1994) 'Transformación Agraria en Nicaragua: Mercados y Racionalidad Campesina', in J. P. de Groot and M. Spoor (eds), *Ajuste Estructural y Economía Campesina: Nicaragua, El Salvador, Centroamérica*, ESECA-UNAN: Managua.

Spoor, M. (1995) *Agrarian Markets in Nicaragua: The Transition from Interventionism to Laissez-faire Revisited*, Proceedings Congress 'Agrarian Questions', Wageningen, May.

Vaessen, J. L. (1997) *The Transformation of Cooperative Organisation in Nicaragua: Contract Choice, Pathways of Change and Agricultural Performance among Agricultural Production Cooperatives*, M.Sc. thesis, Development Economics, Wageningen Agricultural University.

Part 3
Rural Financial Markets

8
Rural Finance and Poverty Alleviation in Central America: Evolution and Challenges

Osvaldo Feinstein

Introduction

This chapter presents a comparison between the view dominating rural finances in Central America during the 1970s and the 'new paradigm' of the 1990s, highlighting several challenges. It focuses on a trade-off that has emerged in the evaluation of several rural finance projects in Central America: the trade-off between outreach and targeting (TOBOT). We analyze some key factors behind the TOBOT, discussing possible ways to overcome it. The chapter starts with a brief presentation on the evolution of the approach to rural finances in the context of rural poverty alleviation. The second section discusses a set of challenges associated with this evolution; and the third and final section discusses the trade-off between outreach and targeting, and the corresponding challenges.

Evolution of the approach to rural finances in the context of rural poverty alleviation

Since the 1970s there has been an evolution in the approach (or paradigm) to rural finances in the context of poverty alleviation in Central America. To compare the key features of the 'old view' (1970s) and the 'new view' (1990s) Table 8.1 will be useful. The 1980s were a transition period (not at all a 'lost decade', as it is frequently referred to, despite the significant institutional changes that took place during those years). Strong criticism was made of the prevailing 'mode of intervention' in rural finances. It became clear that the traditional, supply-driven approach was neither effective nor efficient. The second column of Table 8.1 shows the characteristic features of the emerging alternative

Table 8.1   Comparison of views on rural finances and poverty alleviation in Central America

Aspect emphasized	Old view (1970s)	New view (1990s)
Institutions	Public development banks	Private banks, NGOs
Financial flows	Disbursements	Recoveries
Type of financial service	Credit	Rural financial services
Driven by	Supply	Demand
Expected impact on	Production and welfare	Borrowers' income and financial institutions' sustainability
Supervision	External supervision	Internal supervision (peer group pressure)
Importance of credit	Credit as sufficient condition	Necessary but not sufficient
Activity by sector	Agriculture	Rural (agriculture and non-agriculture)
Unit	Farm	Microentreprise
Economic activity	Production	Production and consumption
Type of targeting	Targeting by activity	Targeting by social groups
Gender	Gender 'blindness'	Gender awareness

paradigm. The 'new view' emphasizes the role of private banks and NGOs, the importance of broader financial services (including savings as well as credit), focusing on demand rather than on supply (additional comparisons of the two paradigms can be found in Table 8.1). It should be mentioned that whereas the 'old view' was frequently associated with a paternalistic approach, a populist bias is sometimes linked to the 'new view'. The time seems ripe for a new approach that goes beyond those driven alternatively by supply or by demand, integrating supply and demand in a comprehensive framework.

Another way in which the evolution in rural finances can be described is by establishing a contrast between the relative emphasis placed upon three fundamental issues in experiences in rural finances: outreach, targeting and sustainability. Table 8.2 shows that contrast. Whereas in the 1970s the emphasis was on outreach, and particularly on disbursements, in the 1990s there is also concern with sustainability, raising in turn the possibility of important trade-offs between these different aspects (see below).

The emphasis on disbursements has not only been a result of pressure generated by the donors, but also by Central-American governments, who showed the number of loans disbursed to 'medium and

Table 8.2 Evolution of outreach, targeting and sustainability priorities in rural finance and poverty alleviation programmes 1970–90

	Outreach		Targeting	Sustainability
	Disbursements	**Access**		
1970s	Yes	No	Yes	No
1980s	Yes	No	No	Yes
1990s	Yes	Yes	Yes	Yes

small farmers' as an indication of their concern with social and economic development, and used these credit programmes (including the corresponding write-offs of the debts) as instruments to obtain political support. At that time, targeting was pursued as part of this 'political economy operation', to 'signal' (indicate) the social group to which these loans were directed.

The criticism of the 'naïve approach' to agricultural credit that started in the later years of the 1970s and continued well into the 1980s (in which the Ohio State School played an important role), together with the budgetary restrictions that started to become increasingly binding on Central-American countries during the 1980s, and the new wave of privatization, led to a development of a new type of rural finance intervention, not restricted to credit and no longer based on public development banks.

A growing concern with sustainability of the financial institutions started to emerge, thus emphasizing repayments and positive interest rates. Although the critique was effective in showing what did not make sense, the alternatives were not that clear. Several initiatives were developed, in some cases replicating experiences that were thought to be successful in their own context (such as the Grameen Bank), but very few evaluations of rural financial interventions have been carried out in Latin America. It is therefore unclear what has worked and what has failed. Furthermore, these evaluations and related studies have had only restricted circulation, so they are not widely known.

Emerging challenges

One of the challenges is to find ways to evaluate, synthesize and then disseminate the rich stock of experiences in Central America concerning rural finances for poverty alleviation. Some constructive answers to this knowledge challenge are in the process of emerging: the Central-American-based Multi-Agency Regional Unit for Technical Assistance (RUTA), joining efforts with the Dutch bilateral development cooperation, has started an initiative that could play an important role in establishing what are the best practices in this field and disseminating them. The Regional Program for the Development of Evaluation Capabilities in Latin America (PREVAL), which is being implemented by the Inter-American Institute for Cooperation on Agriculture (IICA), is also likely to be able to contribute to this area during 1998. Furthermore, there are several studies that provide valuable information on experiences in Central America – such as Wattel *et al.* (1994), Glaessner *et al.* (1995) – and elsewhere – for example, Schneider (1997), and Hulme and Mosley (1996). Finally, it is appropriate also to mention in this context the recent Focus Note Series issued by the Consultative Group to Assist the Poorest (CGAP), on best practices in microenterprise finance.

The second challenge is to overcome the trade-off between innovations that reduce borrowers' costs, but increase lenders' costs, and vice versa. Opening bank branches is a typical innovation carried out in the past which reduced borrowers' costs but increased those of lenders. We can call this the transaction costs challenge, and one of the keys to its success is the introduction of appropriate information systems that allow financial institutions to speed-up loan-processing tasks, thus increasing the number of clients that can be serviced in a given period, and consequently providing opportunities for cost reductions. This would also reduce the time it takes for clients to get their loans (see Feinstein, 1997). Some advances have already been made along these lines, but there is also a significant knowledge gap on this matter. So the first and second challenges are linked.

The development of appropriate forms of government intervention in rural financial markets is another challenge. In the past, the presumption of market failure was immediately taken as an argument in favour of government intervention. However, experience has shown that government failure is also a very concrete possibility. On the other hand, financial liberalization without any intervention is not advisable. Even orthodox 'neo-liberal' economists, such as M. J. Fry, acknowledge that there is a role for governments to play in the area of prudential regulation and supervision (Fry, 1997, p. 760). Therefore, we are also facing a challenge to develop appropriate forms of government intervention, taking into account the failure of traditional policies in rural finances.

A fourth challenge has to do with collateral substitutes. One of the main factors blocking the access of the rural poor to rural financial services has been a lack of traditional collateral. There have been several experiences with collateral substitutes such as 'solidarity groups' and loan guarantee funds. Some 'experts' consider that these are *the* solutions to the collateral challenge. But, again, the results of these and other collateral substitutes have been mixed, working in some contexts and not working in other realities (Hulme and Mosley, 1996; Wattel *et al.*, 1994). As in the case of the previous challenges, we face here a knowledge gap and there is an important need to tap the existing stock of information, and sift, evaluate and synthesize it, to transform it into valuable knowledge.

The remaining part of this chapter will be devoted to clarifying an important issue in rural finances in Central America that has emerged in recent years and that, upto now, has hardly been discussed. This is the trade-off between outreach and targeting. An understanding of this trade-off will show that there is also a targeting challenge and a realistic credit demand estimation challenge.

Trade-off between outreach and targeting (TOBOT)

A typical pattern to be found in several rural credit projects and programmes may be described by the following sequence: during the first two years of implementation, disbursements are at a very low level, whereas targeting proceeds as expected (leakages to the non-target group are kept to a minimum); so during years 3 or 4, as the project reaches its mid-term, the pressure to disburse increases. Targeting criteria are then frequently relaxed: for example, by expanding the project area or increasing the income ceilings defining project beneficiaries. At this stage, most project staff allocate their efforts to activities leading to increased disbursements; so, finally, disbursements increase substantially; but marketing problems arise, leading to increased delinquency, and thus to unsustainability.

The first three stages of this pattern, which correspond to the TOBOT, can be illustrated by Table 8.3, constructed on the basis of several cases corresponding to credit projects in Central America. Note that in Table 8.3 the first two years of implementation targeting proceeds as expected, but disbursements are at a very low level. Then the pressure to disburse increases, the targeting criteria are relaxed, and practically all project staff are requested to allocate their time and efforts to facilitate the disbursement of funds. So by year 5 the funds are disbursed, but targeting has deteriorated and sustainability is also jeopardized because of the consequences of 'loan-pushing' in terms of marketing

Table 8.3   Numerical illustration of trade-offs between outreach and targeting (TOBOT) in a typical credit project in Central America

Year of implementation	Disbursements (as % of total amount of project funds)	Targeting (% of funds disbursed allocated to target group)
1	3	99
2	5	98
3	45	60
4	75	57
5	100	55

problems and increased delinquency. To these negative effects on sustainability one could add those arising from the 'politics of rural credit' (Drèze *et al.*, 1997, p. 77). However, the argument here is that the pressure to disburse leads (i) to a decrease in the quality (or disappearance) of the supporting services (such as extension), for all manpower is used to disburse the loans; and (ii) to 'bad loans' (either to people who will not be able to repay unless they are also provided with complementary services, at least for a certain period of time, or to people that are not willing to repay in a context of weak enforceability).

Examination of the time profiles of disbursements and 'targeting' also indicates the 'trade-off'. In Figure 8.1 the argument is presented visually by using a 45° line along which there would be zero leakages (as all the amount disbursed would be directed towards the target group). As disbursements proceed, the distance between the 45° line and the targeting – disbursements curve increases, showing the increased leakages. Note that this section is not addressing the 'normative' question whether to target or not to target, but rather the 'positive' question concerning the dynamics of outreach (in terms of disbursements) and targeting (or, to be more precise, of a specific type of targeting which involves a set of criteria such as income-level ceilings or land ceilings of the prospective clients).[1] Though 'outreach' is generally measured by number of loans made and/or number of borrowers (see, for example, Von Pischke 1996, p. 227), if there is a loan-size ceiling (as is frequently the case in rural poverty alleviation interventions), 'disbursements' can be considered as a proxy for 'outreach'.[2]

However, the clarification of the positive issue (the TOBOT) may help to approach the normative question with more insight, because it is often not realized that targeting by a set of criteria that try to direct

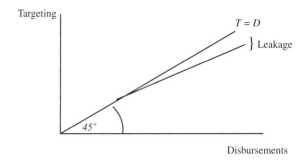

Figure 8.1   Increasing leakage as disbursements increase

the loans to a specific clientele might become so burdensome in practice that it would jeopardize the disbursement of funds and, given the internal logic of the institutions involved (international and national), it then tends to become ineffective. The problem might not be with targeting as such but rather with the specific modality of targeting. Given the difficulty of ranking targeting mechanisms a priori (Grosh, 1994, p. 159 *et passim*), there is a need for a concrete analysis of the situations, bearing in mind the feasibility of the proposed targeting mechanism. This leads to the targeting challenge, going beyond the Scylla of voluntarism (thinking that any targeting criteria will work) and the Charybdis of nihilism (thinking that no targeting criteria or mechanism will work). The works quoted in this chapter provide some orientation on potentially useful targeting approaches, such as self-targeting and geographical targeting.

It should be noted that one of the reasons allowing the TOBOT to emerge has been the frequent and considerable overestimation of credit demand. This has been caused by several factors: a confusion of credit requirements with cash requirements associated with technical packages, which implies that other sources of funds are negligible. This is particularly inaccurate in the case of Central America, where remittances are important. Another factor is that, for an estimation of credit demand, assumptions have to be made concerning the future, and under conditions of high uncertainty (concerning markets and rates of interest) the margin of error might be quite high.

Furthermore, there is also an incentive compatibility issue that frequently is not apparent: the lack of incentives for the staff of financial institutions to lend to the rural poor. Thus what might appear as a lack of credit demand might in fact be a problem on the supply side. This 'identification problem' is seldom perceived, and sometimes even 'the donor's' staff argue that high interest rates or some other factor is likely to be the explanation for the lack of disbursements.

Finally, the widespread view that credit is an extremely powerful tool for poverty alleviation has been also a factor leading to an overestimation of credit demand. Rather ironically, some evaluations in Central America have shown that in projects with several components, when credit was available, the projects were not working with and for the poor (given the restrictions imposed by the national financial institutions), whereas when funds for loans became unavailable, extension and other services began to be directed towards the poor.

Therefore, there is a challenge to estimate credit demand realistically. Awareness of several factors that frequently lead to overestimation should be developed.

Last, but not least, the traditional emphasis on disbursements, recovery rates and even on income might be at least partly due to the lack of alternative indicators. In this context, I would like to mention a last challenge: that of developing alternative key indicators. One of these has to do with the process of 'social intermediation', in which NGOs play a crucial role and for which they have comparative advantage. The consolidation of groups resulting from this process not only facilitates the access of the rural poor to financial services with lower transaction costs for the lender, but should also be seen in the perspective of social capital accumulation. For example, an evaluation of credit projects in Honduras has shown that a significant percentage of groups of poor small farmers, which were formed mainly to facilitate credit delivery, were still operating several years after the project's implementation, and were involved in multiple activities. An indicator such as 'number of consolidated groups' should be adapted to the specific context. This can and should be used. This indicator is also useful in order to perceive clearly the trade-offs between group formation and group consolidation (Feinstein, 1995), and it may facilitate the design of projects that attempt to contribute to build up social capital.[3]

This wider perspective puts the efforts made and the results achieved by rural finance interventions into a broader context, going far beyond disbursements and targeting and well into sustainable rural poverty alleviation.

Summing up, in order for rural finances to become an effective and efficient tool for poverty alleviation in Central America, it is essential to develop and disseminate the knowledge gained from decades of experience in the region and elsewhere. This will facilitate the process of proposing appropriate forms of government intervention and the introduction of innovations that could reduce lenders' and borrowers' transaction costs as well as collateral alternatives. Further crucial challenges are the design of feasible targeting mechanisms and the development of realistic credit demand estimates. Finally, the elaboration of key indicators corresponding to the expected effects and impact are of fundamental importance to provide adequate signals during the implementation of rural finance interventions, for impact assessment and to draw lessons from experience.

Notes

1. A recent paper by Gelbach and Pritchett (1997) arrives at negative conclusions on the normative question (but with a rather fragile argument), whereas the most detailed analysis of targeted social programmes in Latin America, by Grosh (1994, p. 159) argues in favour of targeting; several of the papers in van de Walle and Kimberly (1995) are also relevant for the normative issue.
2. One could reframe the argument in terms of a trade-off between disbursements and targeting (TODBAT), but given that the trade-off between outreach and sustainability has been very much discussed in the literature (and it is still an important issue), it seems worthwhile focusing on the TOBOT, taking 'disbursements' as a proxy for 'outreach'. The results of the paper are not affected by reformulating the argument with outreach measured by number of loans made and/or number of borrowers.
3. Johan Bastiaensen (1997, p. 4) has pointed out in the case of Nicaragua the tremendous lack of social capital that could facilitate the synergy between local rural producers, the adjusting markets and the state. By contributing to the development of local capabilities for collective action, for example through the consolidation (rather than the mere formation) of groups of the rural poor, rural financial interventions can contribute towards modifying the local institutional environment (which therefore becomes partly endogenous). Thus the apparently technocratic point made in the text concerning indicators might help in operationalizing a political economy approach.

Bibliography

Bastiaensen, J. (1997) *Governance for Finance in Rural Nicaragua. Analysis of the Network of Local Banks Promoted by Nitlapán*, Paper presented at the XI Annual Asserca Conference, Portsmouth.

Cuevas, C. E. (1996) 'Enabling Environment and Microfinance Institutions: Lessons from Latin America', *Journal of International Development*, vol. 8, no. 2, pp. 195–209.

Drèze, J., Lanjouw, P. and Sharma, N. (1997) *Credit in Rural India: A Case Study*, LSE-STICERD, The Development Economics Research Programme, no. 6.

Feinstein, O. N. (1995) 'Comments on "Measuring the Performance of Agricultural and Rural Development Programs"', in R. Piccioto and R. Rist (eds), *Evaluation and Development*, Washington DC.

Feinstein, O. N. (1997) *A Transactions Cost Approach for Microfinance Project Assessment*, Background paper prepared for the CGAP Working Group on Impact Assessment Virtual Conference.

Fry, M. J. (1997) 'In Favour of Financial Liberalization', *Economic Journal*, vol. 107, no. 442, pp. 754–70.

Gelbach, J. B. and Pritchett, L. H. (1997) *More for the Poor is Less for the Poor, The Politics of Targeting*, Policy Research Working Paper, no. 1799, Washington DC: World Bank.

Glaessner, P. J., Lee, K. W., Sant'Anna, A. M. and St. Antoine, J. J. (1995) *Alivio de la Pobreza y Fondos de Inversión Social. La Experiencia Latinoamericana*, Washington DC: Documento para Discusión del Banco Mundial, 261 S.

Grosh, M. G. (1994) *Administering Targeted Social Programs in Latin America*, Washington, DC: World Bank.

Hulme, D. and Mosley, P. (1996) *Finance Against Poverty*, London: Routledge.

Johnson, S. and Rogaly, B. (1997) *Microfinance and Poverty Reduction*, Oxford: Oxfam.

Schneider, H. (1997) *Microfinance for the Poor?*, Paris: IFAD/OECD.

Van De Walle, D. and Kimberley, N. (eds) (1995) *Public Spending and the Poor*, Baltimore, Md: Johns Hopkins University Press.

Von Pischke, J. D. (1996) 'Measuring the Trade-off between Outreach and Sustainability of Microenterprise Lenders', *Journal of International Development*, vol. 8, no. 2, pp. 225–39.

Wattel, C. J., Ruben, R., Caballero, E. L. and Krikke, E. (1994) *Financiamiento Rural Alternativo*, Tegucigalpa, Guaymuras.

Zeller, M., Schreider, G., Von Braun, J. and F. Heidhues. (1997) *Rural Finance for Food Security for the Poor*, Washington DC: IFPRI.

9
Institutional Entrepreneurship for Rural Development: the Nitlapán Banking Network in Nicaragua
Johan Bastiaensen

Introduction

The recent history of Nicaragua is characterized by pronounced economic regress. The termination of the war and the initiation of adjustment policies in the 1990s were not sufficient to redress the dramatic conditions. Only recently has the economy shown a few modest signs of recovery. Stagnation and poverty continue to reign, particularly in the rural areas. Inspired by North (1990), we believe the fundamental causes for the rural disarray can be attributed at least partially to the malfunctioning of economic institutions. The troubled history of recent decades has produced a series of shocks that have disrupted the 'total package of formal and informal constraints and enforcement aspects' (North, 1990, p. 87) thereby creating the present-day disequilibrium. The challenge of rural economic recovery is therefore one of institutional rearticulation in the midst of a disrupted authoritarian patron–client inheritance.

As Hoff *et al.* (1993, p. 22) indicate, alternative financial organization-building could be thought of as an instrument of social innovation. It is in the light of this hypothesis that we undertake an analysis of the experiences of Nitlapán[1] in building a more 'democratic' and entrepreneurially viable financial organization that serves small and medium-sized producers. The first section develops a brief tentative interpretation of the rural institutional crisis and the need for institutional change. Subsequently, Nitlapán's financial network and its governance structure are described. The concluding sections relate this governance structure and its historical genesis to the inherited institutional environment and make some comments on the possibilities for institutional change by means of financial organization-building.

A tentative interpretation of the crisis of rural institutions and the need for institutional change

The vertical inheritance

There is little doubt that before the Sandinista revolution the dominant pattern of socio-economic organization in the Nicaraguan rural villages can be characterized as being 'local despotism' of the patron–client type (Marchetti, 1994). From an economic governance point of view, such vertical governance structures are not the most supportive for dynamic rural development. As is stressed by Putnam (1993, pp. 174–5), vertical patron–client structures present only a 'second-best' solution to the problem of social order and cooperation. While it must be preferred over total Hobbesian chaos, it does not constitute the most effective governance structure to foment economic growth.

An important flaw of the vertical governance structure is the patron's monopolization of contacts with the external world. This distorts information flows between the local and the external environment, and hampers the development of integrated networks of mutual cooperation for technological learning, supply of inputs and commercialization. The dyadic relationship of the patron with his clients also undermines the development of horizontal social ties. Solidarity ties are often confined to family and kinship networks. These typically co-exist in the same territory, but develop only a few relationships with each other. Worse still, between kinship groups belonging to different patron–client networks, a fierce political or religious competition often strains relations and makes them conflictive. 'Weak ties' stretching over the entire local society, considered to be crucial for a vibrant local economy, are poorly developed.

Another deficiency is a consequence of the unchecked power of the patron. This distorts incentives and is inimical to the prevalence of a stable 'rule of law'. 'Upward' imposition of rules and sanctions is impossible, and the patron can impose arbitrary decisions on the clients. For the powerless clients, this creates an unpredictable environment in which success and survival depend on the arbitrary benevolence of the patron and not on their own efforts. This undermines personal incentives.

The vertical constellation is supported by inherited meaning systems. These contain a conception of a natural and divine order that leaves little room for advancement through individual productive effort (Houtart and Lemercinier, 1992, p. 101). In this world view, welfare and happiness depend on a kind of individual symbolic exchange with an authoritarian God as well as the unquestioned patron. The object of this involves loyalty and intrinsic ethical qualities of personal behaviour, and not individual or collective productive efficacy. Such legitimizing world views are necessary to sustain the patron–client relationship, since intrinsically the model creates strong incentives on the part of the client to shirk in his/her relationship with the patron. Viewed from a 'principal–agent' perspective, the patron–client relationship is indeed problematical, since the patron is both obstacle and avenue for a better life. Logically, the attitude of the dependent client is ambiguous and balances between loyalty and passive resistance, sliding into opportunistic abuse whenever possible.

The post-revolutionary crisis

The inherited vertical structure of rural society was only partially changed by the Sandinista revolution. The latter curtailed the power of many traditional landlords and thereby dissolved existing patron–client relationships. These were substituted for by state–paternalistic governance structures which, however, continued to match the traditional pattern of clientelistic social organization. Top-down information and benefits were passed on to clients by politically loyal local leaders acting as intermediaries (Marchetti, 1994, p. 6). In general, few alternative horizontal forms of political and social organization among equal citizens were created. However, the Sandinista revolution and the transition period that followed its defeat entailed changes that did undermine the effectiveness of the vertical governance structures.

The land reform process is the first important event that drastically reduced the relative efficiency of vertical governance. After different phases of land redistribution, the remaining landlords now control less than 15 per cent of the total land area. Vertical patterns evidently become less appropriate if 'patrons' control a smaller part of the income-generating resources. As Lipton (1993, p. 642) indicates, land reform contributes to an increasing incompatibility between inherited governance structures and the requirements of rural development. This need for complementary institution-building is the reason why he speaks of land reform as commenced, but not finished business.

The shock of the revolution also contributed decisively to the redefinition of popular identity and provided for an acceleration in the modernization of world views. An increasing number of people considered themselves to be actors of their own destiny and equal citizens of the nation. This made vertical governance structures increasingly ineffective, since many started to reject the naturalness of their dependence. This was translated into a reduction of discipline and obedience, and with the erosion of revolutionary morality, also into a legitimation for abuse wherever it remained unsanctioned. This was even more so after the electoral defeat of the Sandinistas, when knowledge and rumours about the abuses of both old and new 'patrons' were popularized. As a result, the inherited authority of patrons was increasingly delegitimized and the enforcement of compliance by any authority became problematical.

This leaves Nicaragua in the kind of 'worst of all situations with respect to contract enforcement' referred to by Hoff *et al.* (1993, p. 21). 'Second-best' vertical governance no longer functions properly, but its wreckages that constitute today's governance structures are far away from 'first-best' horizontal structures. As a consequence, the late 1990s social order is characterized by a high degree of insecurity, distrust and chaos. This increases transaction costs and leaves many opportunities for collective action and investment unseized. Up to now the cry for liberation of the *güegüense*[2] seems to have resulted solely in a disruption of the oppressive structures and not in a positive and viable alternative project. In the short run, this leaves the average rural Nicaraguan worse off than under the previous vertical structures.[3]

The need for institutional innovation

Since the inherited vertical arrangements no longer function properly, an important challenge for rural development is to innovate local institutions. This should result in horizontally structured, civic and rule-governed local polities, since a return to the previous vertical structures hardly seems possible and, if indeed it were possible, would only re-establish a second-best solution. Horizontal forms of social capital can be expected to contribute more to development than vertical structures (Narayan and Pritchett, 1997, pp. 3–7). They improve the capacity for local collective action and therefore create better opportunities for the diffusion of information and knowledge, the creation of risk-sharing mechanisms, and the realization and maintenance of local public goods. A crucial type of such public goods are stable and mutually reliable governance structures for economic transactions with outsiders. These reduce transaction costs and allow for a mutually responsive articulation between actors in the micro- and macro-structures of the economy. The question on how to contribute to the envisaged institutional transition from the disrupted vertical to viable horizontal governance structures therefore becomes a crucial policy issue. Nitlapán agrees with P. Evans that 'norms of cooperation and networks of civic engagement among ordinary citizens can be promoted by public agencies and used for developmental ends' (Evans, 1996, p. 1124). Accordingly, it views its financial programme as a semi-public institution that aims 'to transform local social organization' (Nitlapán, 1994, p. 30). In the following sections, we shall evaluate Nitlapán's initiative as an attempt at such institutional entrepreneurship.

The Nitlapán banking network

A brief overview of the financial landscape[4]

The context of the financial configurations in Nicaragua is evidently marked by frequent rural institutional changes. Before the Sandinista revolution, small-scale rural producers were excluded from formal credit and relied mainly on self-financing. Only a few better-off peasants managed to gain access to the national development bank, provided a guarantor (that is the local patron) was prepared to provide surety. The poorer section depended on informal and often interlocked financial transactions with local patrons such as sharecropping arrangements and forward sales. The patron was also the source of occasional emergency loans. The structure of the financial configuration thus coincided with the overall vertical institutions of rural society. When smaller-scale rural producers had access to credit, it was mediated by local patrons and enforcement was guaranteed by the repressive patron–client pattern.

This situation changed partially during the revolution. The Sandinistas used massive and heavily-subsidized credit as a planning and procurement instrument. This made cheap credit available for the majority of rural producers. From a governance point of view, one could say that a 'distant paternalistic national patron' had replaced the local patrons. Enforcement of repayment was only a minor preoccupation of the Sandinistas. It even became a political habit to condone uncancelled debts at each anniversary of the revolution. Credit became a synonym for subsidy, since its real cost was negative and repayment was only for those without the political leverage to evade their obligations. In this way, the traditional financial governance structures were replaced by unsustainable structures that completely eroded credit culture.

This period of abundant and cheap credit came to an abrupt end with the initiation of stabilization policies at the end of the 1980s. Monetary programming made official credit scarce and expensive (with real interest rates of over 20 per cent per annum). Also, branches and loan volumes of the national development bank were cut back drastically. In 1992, some 85 per cent of (smaller) rural clients were excluded after a recapitalization of the virtually bankrupt public bank. However, because of the institutional erosion, rent-seeking behaviour continued to prevail among the remaining clients. By not repaying the credit of the development bank, an enormous subsidy was monopolized by the rural rich. Ultimately, this unsustainable and unwanted situation led to the closure of the development bank in 1997.

Despite a high rural demand for financial services and the liberalization of the financial sector under the structural adjustment policies, the private sector was not able to fill the gap left by the retreat of the development bank. The previous period of subsidized credit and general turmoil created an institutional vacuum in which high transaction costs made rural credit operations extremely difficult. Some of the gap for the small clients was filled by private NGOs. Many of them, however, repeated a similar pattern of clientelistic grant–credit confusion that was omnipresent in the previous Sandinista financial climate (Mendoza, 1993, p. 4). Only recently, a number of more professionally run financial NGOs took on the task of reconstructing viable rural financial governance structures. One of them is the Nitlapán system.

Nitlapán's banking network

Nitlapán's banking network consists of eighteen semi-independent and mainly rural local banks and one central refinancing unit: the Local Banks Fund (LBF). The LBF is the main source of loanable funds for the local banks (US$1.4 million in 1996) and charges an interest rate of 8 per cent per year. For these loans, the LBF depends on its equity capital, made up of non-governmental aid and a soft development loan with an interest of 2 per cent per annum. Locally, LBF loans are supplemented with share capital provided by client-members (US$250000 after one year), accumulated local profits (US$15000) and the remainder of initial capital gifts (US$100000). The local banks on average apply an interest rate of 27 per cent to the clients.

In 1996, the network provided a total of US$2.6 million in loans to 4688 clients. The greater percentage of these clients (60 per cent) were poor producers: subsistence farmers with little or no land or cattle, and with non-farm households depending on wage labour and artisan or petty-commercial activities. The rest of the clients were medium-sized peasants, peasant entrepreneurs and rural traders; 60 per cent of the clients were male. Three-quarters of the loans were short-term credit of less than 18 months, while the rest was extended for periods up to three years. Clients are free to use credit for what they want, but the local banks try to link their portfolio to locally concerted 'development policies'. These try to avoid excessive concentration on highly prof-itable petty commercial activities and give attention to agricultural and processing activities as well as strategic investments for rural commerce (transport and storage for example). In 1996, 44 per cent of the loans were directed to agricultural and livestock activities; 46 per cent to rural and petty commerce; and 10 per cent to small-scale industrial, artisan and service activities.

Since the mid-1990s a substantial effort of enterprise and organiza-tion-building has been made. The first component of this effort was intense local promotion to make sure that the rules of the system were known and accepted by the clients. This involved the continuous spreading of information about the 'rules of the game' and the con-scious cultivation of an image of solidity, transparency and trustwor-thiness by the 'bank'. The second component involved the creation of the organizational structure and training of the different actors in the banking system. At the same time, a modest but solid physical infra-structure (well-protected offices with a largely symbolical strongbox, a computer and required furniture) was constructed. Equally important was the creation of a standardized and computerized information sys-tem that allows permanent monitoring of the local banks and the clients by the LBF.

The banking system strives for entrepreneurial sustainability. At the time of writing, strong sustainability has not yet been reached, although in financial terms a profit of US$50000 has been achieved. According to Nitlapán's calculations, in 1996 the subsidy dependence index (see Yaron, 1992, p. 51) was 1.2, implying that the average inter-est rate of 26 per cent should rise to 57 per cent in order to reach the break-even point at full market opportunity costs. Even though the cri-terion of strong financial sustainability should not be accepted,[5] Nitlapán's planning aims at a further reduction of this index. The objective is to reach a total portfolio of US$16 million and 12000 clients by the year 2001. According to the projections, this would enable the system to function without subsidy, provided that the current repay-ment rate of 94.7 per cent can be maintained without a proportional increase in monitoring and enforcement costs.

The organization of the bank

As we have indicated, the financial network of Nitlapán is a two-tier system with a refinancing unit (LBF) at the central level and eighteen semi-independent village banks at the local level (see Figure 9.1). The operational link between the two levels is the bank official: the local

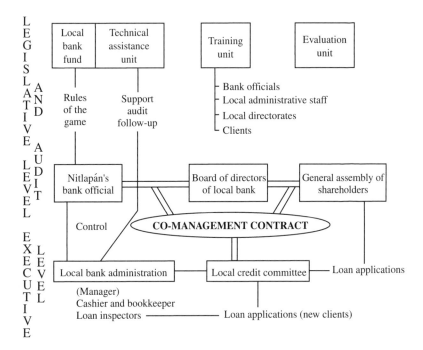

Figure 9.1   Actors and procedures of the Nitlapán banking network

representative of the LBF. A secondary link is established by the technical assistance unit. This unit gives practical support to the local administrations and audits their bookkeeping. At the central level, an independent evaluation team (not working exclusively for the LBF) and a training unit also operate.

The bank official, assisted by the administration, negotiates a yearly co-management contract with local directors who are elected by the general assembly of client-shareholders. This co-management contract stipulates the conditions on which the loans from the LBF are extended to the local bank. Within the boundaries of increasingly standardized rules, each bank negotiates a specific co-management contract. In 1996, the general rules defined a minimum amount of US$100 and a maximum of US$5000; imposed a reserve requirement of 5 per cent as a delinquency provision; stipulated a target interest of 18 per cent per annum for productive and 30 per cent for commercial activities; compelled the purchase of local shares by means of an automatic 7 per cent deduction of each loan; and established the procedures for loan guarantee policy. The specific negotiation of each contract serves two complementary purposes. The first is to adapt and detail the specific policies within each particular context. The second is to go through an obligatory annual process of participation and consultation of the 'rules of the game', with both local directors and the general assembly. This annual ritual is complemented by the spread of decentralized information in local assemblies and house visits by local inspectors and the bank official.

Within the framework defined by the co-management contract operations are executed by a small and usually part-time administration. This consists of a cashier, a bookkeeper and a number of inspectors. The cashier and the bookkeeper register the operations with respect to loans and share deposits. The semi-voluntary inspectors, who work for a daily allowance of twice the rural wage, spread information about the bank, identify new clients and loan applications and perform *ex post* monitoring of a limited number of clients under their supervision. Up to 1996, this local staff was assisted by a voluntary board of directors and a credit committee. Much the same as in other initiatives (Uphoff, 1993, p. 618), however, it proved difficult to sustain the initial levels of voluntary commitment that had played a critical role at the start. The work of volunteers had therefore to be taken over by paid staff. It was also felt necessary to free the bank official from too close an involvement in day-to-day operations. This would allow him/her to dedicate more attention to complementary development animation and to expand client networks in this perspective. For both reasons, the local administration was supplemented by a local manager chosen from among the most committed directors or the better-schooled local youngsters.

In 1996, client selection and loan approval was still mainly performed by a voluntary credit committee. Members of this committee are chosen to safeguard representation by the relevant social sectors and the territory of the local bank. In this way, local knowledge is pooled for the screening of the projects as well as the solvency and trustworthiness of the clients. Since the credit committee has to comply with the co-management contract, the bank official is present to monitor and approve the decisions. The inspectors perform a pre-screening task, since they prepare the loan applications for the (new) clients. In this manner, the role of the credit committee, which was crucial at the start, is later gradually played down and the local management takes over an increasing quantity of routine decisions. It is expected that the formal credit committees will disappear in the future.

Directors and members of the credit committee will become referecs at the service of the local management in order to screen new clients.

Enforcement and incentives

In order to safeguard the contractual compliance of the clients, a number of incentive and enforcement mechanisms are put in place. First, all clients have to sign a formal promissory note. The system also creates economic incentives to repay on time. Interest is due on balances, and delinquent debtors are charged additional interest of 2–3 per cent on any arrears. More important is the progressive principle. This principle implies that both at the client and the bank level compliance with the contractual terms is rewarded by a right of access to higher and longer-term loans. Inversely, non-compliance is punished by suspension of access to new loans. At the bank level, this implies that compliance with the co-management contract is rewarded with higher annual loans as well as access to longer-term credit lines. In this way, banks are collectively motivated to comply in order to pursue a dynamic growth path in terms of outreach and increasing possibilities to extend loans for investment. The progressive principle is also applied at the client level through a rating system. Only the best-rated clients obtain the right to participate fully in the growth path of the bank and are allowed to demand increasing volumes for longer terms.

Another incentive is created by the obligatory purchase of shares. Since 1996, any client who takes a new loan, has 7 per cent of the amount deducted in order to buy local shares. These shares can only been withdrawn after three years, and their value is indexed to the US dollar. In the first place, these shares constitute a personalized reserve provision against delinquency that contributes to the capitalization of the local banks. They also give a right to dividends when profits are generated by the local bank. Given the spread in interest rates and the positive repayment rates, many local banks managed to pay dividends of over 10 per cent after the first year. Initially, most clients saw the new obligation simply as an additional cost of the loans. With the first dividend payment, this perception rapidly changed and the share mechanism enhanced client identification with the 'their' bank. This contributes decisively to the legitimacy of contract enforcement measures.

In line with this strategy, the system of Nitlapán aspires to engage in the collection of voluntary savings. The spontaneous reactions to dividend payments pointed out a substantial demand for money-saving opportunities. As well as being a proof of local trust, savings would further enhance local identification with the 'cause of the bank' and thereby foster the virtuous trust cycle. The collection of savings does, however, pose serious legal problems, since it requires legal recognition as a financial enterprise. In the absence of specific supervisory rules, it is at the time of writing impossible to reconcile the objectives of the financial system with the standardized reserve requirements for private banks.[6]

Further components of enforcement policy are material and social guarantees. New poorer clients usually have to form joint liability groups. The combination of small initial loans with the progressive principle at the group level then induces careful mutual *ex ante* selection and *ex post* monitoring. With time, in some of the banks, smaller clients can gain access to loans without the condition of group liability. In these cases, one or another durable consumer item (for example, a television set or a bicycle) has to be pledged as collateral or the client has to look for a solvent guarantor. The few larger clients need to take a registered mortgage, usually on a building.

Tenacity in the application of the 'rules of the game' is also considered to be important for success in enforcement. Therefore, local banks systematically take a hard stand towards delinquent debtors, and in case of delinquency an escalating battery of measures to pressurize people are put into action. This follows the slogan of the system that 'there are no bad debtors, just bad debt collectors'. Because of this systematically unforgiving attitude of Nitlapán, some condemned it as a merciless institution without consideration for the poor.[7] It is, however, clear that rigidity in the application of the rules contributed decisively to the system's image of impartiality and seriousness, and this is necessary to guarantee access to credit for the poor in the future.

The historical genesis of the financial network's governance structure

The governance structure described above resulted in a promising state of affairs: a substantial and increasing outreach with a clear majority of smaller clients, a reasonable recuperation rate of 94.7 per cent, and a break-even operation in present-day financial terms. This opens up a realistic perspective for future growth and sustainability. Most analyses of 'finance for the poor' would stop here; since the dominating perspective concentrates almost exclusively on the financial enterprise-building dimension. Even when this is evidently important, however, the evaluation of impact must go beyond finance. Given the crisis of rural institutions in Nicaragua, it is particularly interesting to investigate the relationship between the financial governance structures and the broader institutional environment. To evaluate this 'institutional entrepreneurship' dimension of Nitlapán's structure, we shall now first analyze its historical genesis. The 1996 governance structure is the intermediate result of a permanent learning process that gradually managed to cope with the difficulties created by the inherited vertical structures in crisis. This analysis will not only explain the particular nature of the financial governance structure, but also produce insights on the strained relations with the local institutional environment. These insights will then be further developed in a final part that discusses the avenues for broader institutional innovation through financial organization-building.

Coping with the institutional crisis

When Nitlapán started to work in Masaya in 1987, it refused to get involved in development projects. The institute was very aware of the distortions generated by externally mediated aid enhancing clientelistic dependency, and associated local divisions and jealousy. The initial endeavour was therefore to engage in popular education and local organizational capacity building. However, the economic crisis after 1988 forced the institute to engage more actively in local problem-solving processes. Since the liquidity crisis made access to credit one of the pressing constraints, the institute started to create a financial system, at first in the form of rotating funds. The initial governance structure of these funds was poorly developed and relied primarily on trust in what were considered to be promising 'natural leaders'. The initial intervention model tried to foster autonomous local organizations managed by these leaders. For this purpose, the latter were provided with technical and leadership training. At the same time, independent local village funds were capitalized with 'seed capital'. It was hoped that this could transform Nitlapán's 'cold' external aid money into collectively managed 'hot' village money.

Despite Nitlapán's options to the contrary, the identified leaders were almost exclusively Sandinista. Given the political constellation at the end of the 1980s, it was only the Sandinista leaders who had had contact with the visiting extension workers. It proved to be very difficult for anyone in the rural areas to imagine an initiative that was not politically linked to the revolution, and even harder to imagine that it would be directed towards all locals without political or religious distinctions.[8] In spite of their training and the principles of the initiatives, the

Sandinista leadership saw no problem in restricting access to their political clients, friends and relatives. Worse still, with the purpose of reinforcing their leadership position, they presented the fund as a benefit mediated through their connections.

In this first phase, repayment rates were dramatically low (between 50 per cent and 70 per cent). Local Sandinista patrons were not inclined to enforce repayment obligations strictly. Often the main incentive mechanisms, in particular the progressive principle and joint group liability, were not clearly explained nor properly implemented, and the local directors were often the least convinced of the advantages of repayment. They thought their local prestige depended more on their capacity to raise immediate benefits than on an insecure perspective of a sustainable financial system. Their multiple experiences with official Sandinista credit and NGOs partially explained their scepticism. Nitlapán had not yet reached a minimum scale nor established its reputation and therefore did not foster much more trust than other 'aid offers.' Another important problem was that, for opportunistic reasons, the leaders themselves were the least willing to repay. As predicted by the analysis of the patron–client structure, local leaders and their favourites figured prominently among delinquent debtors. Their control over information and their power to avoid sanctions convinced them that they could abuse the system. In a few cases, the abuse also took the form of more spectacular corruption. One leader made use of the money from loans for his personal commercial activities and did not repay the sum when his activities were eventually detected. In an urban bank, the local directors engaged in charging clients a substantial commission fee for each loan.

These circumstances made it impossible to construct a sustainable credit system, and corrective action was required. At first, Nitlapán tried to articulate better 'rules of the game' and to enhance compliance with these rules within the original framework of self-management. However, recuperation rates did not improve sufficiently, outreach continued to be politically restricted, including the predominantly non-Sandinista banks that had been opened in the interior, and cases of abuse by local board members continued to emerge. Attempts to promote control by the local assembly of client-members were not successful, since the tradition of patron–client relations did not support the idea of leadership accountability. Therefore the organization of local checks and balances in the management of the banks did not succeed. Locals easily accepted the discourse of their leaders and were not very interested in participation.

The necessity of external intervention

All this led to the conclusion that the trust vested in the local leadership under the option for self-management was not warranted. The impact of the sectarian, vertical governance structures invalidated any attempt to impose transparent and objective rules of the game. Nor did it allow access for all the clients, independent of their network affiliation. Stronger external intervention by Nitlapán was therefore necessary to create an active countervailing power to the local leadership and its associated social dynamics. This was not easily accepted by the initial leaders, who rightly recognized an attack on their power position. They demystified Nitlapán's new discourse of co-management and protested against the shift from 'assisted self-management' to the top-down imposition of the 'rules of the game'. However, many of the local leaders were delegitimized when Nitlapán began to unravel and publicize the leaders' delinquency. The erosion of the predominant position of the original Sandinista leadership and the growing disapproval with politics in general also contributed to weakening the politicized leadership. The profound change in the rules of the game was accompanied by a concomitant replacement of local directors that marked a definite change in the functioning of the local banks.

This change was, however, not primarily characterized by a change in the initial leadership. In fact, some of the original leaders remained. But governance problems should not be attributed to a lack of ethical or managerial qualities among the leaders. On the contrary, given the socio-cultural conditions, it must be acknowledged that no leader could be expected to behave differently in the absence of external constraints. The problem is therefore identified as one of designing appropriate governance structures that do not allow space for behavioural deficiencies. As explained above, decisive external intervention incorporated in the co-management system of Nitlapán's banking network now supplements and enhances local checks and balances on the actors of the network.

Institutional innovation through finance

A realm of civic, transparent and rule-bound rural governance

Nitlapán's banking network proves that even in the adverse context of rural Nicaragua it is possible to create an innovative, non-clientelistic corporate culture embracing a national enterprise and local villagers. The co-management system succeeded in restoring local credit culture at an acceptable cost to the financial enterprise. The accumulated social capital around the local financial organization sufficiently reduces transaction costs to make rural financial transactions with poorer clients a viable prospect. At the same time, the governance structure of Nitlapán's local banks was to a large extent able to delink access to financial services from politically or religiously conditioned clientelistic mediation. Also, most of its enforcement mechanisms do not rely on patron–client dependency, but rather on a mutually sustained legality. In this way, it is gradually constituting a socially and culturally innovative organizational layer of local society.

Without invalidating this general conclusion, it must be stressed that in the Nitlapán network the tendency to return to the vertical dependency remains omnipresent. Some aspects of the practical operations of local banks make use of social mechanisms that rely essentially on vertical relationships. The growing need for a local guarantor to provide bail for poorer clients potentially reintroduces dependencies of the patron–client type. Also a situation such as in one local bank division in isolated Wiwilí, where a large part of the loan volume was provided to an influential peasant coffee-trader in order to channel it further to smaller coffee producers, point to dangers for repayment. Some of the local bank directors initially even considered the newly-created function of the local manager as an excellent opportunity to restore their previous discretionary powers.

Another important problem is that clients are not much interested in being involved in the bank affairs. A study by a Nitlapán evaluation team in 1996 revealed that more than half of the clients still lacked full information and knowledge about the 'rules of the game'. Neither did they seem to be worried about this situation. This probably reveals that the attitudes of clients concerning their roles and positions in the system and local society have not yet been sufficiently transformed. In the perception of some of them, the imposition of the co-management system simply meant the substitution of old patrons by new ones. The idea of being a shareholder with full rights of a local member organization is not as self-evident as one might hope. Neither should it be surprising that the participation of clients in the general assembly and their 'horizontal' relations with staff and local directors were also found to be relatively weak. In this respect, however, one should avoid making the mistake of expecting maximum client participation in the operations of the bank itself. Clients must not become bankers, but rather collaborative local citizens and more competitive peasants, artisans and traders. The primary interest must therefore be what the bank contributes to their development opportunities.

Finance alone is not enough

Concerning this contribution, it has been found that credit alone will not do the job. Largely in line with the general conclusion of Hulme and Mosley (1996), the Nitlapán evaluation team found evidence of only a limited positive impact of credit on the income of the poorer clients in particular. This moderate impact often operates through improvements in the secondary conditions of petty-commercial activities – often by the substitution of the bank's credit for usury loans – and much less through substantial improvements in the income-generating agricultural, processing or commercial activities as such (Nitlapán, 1997a). Other improvements in the access to resources, knowledge and markets are needed to generate a more substantial improvement in development prospects, especially of the poorer clients. In order for these to take place, a more profound change in the nature and capacity of local collective action is required. The disarticulated vertical governance structures that hampered the organization of a viable financial system also obstruct the dynamism of other market configurations and contribute to the exclusion of a significant layer of the local society (or sometimes the entirety of the local society) from the viable and dynamic segments of the national economy. As we have stressed, a more inclusive and dynamic rural development requires a broader institutional transition towards a more cooperative, transparent and reliable local environment.

Perspectives for broader institutional change

There is still a long way to go, however, before the local banks are articulated within such vibrant civic local communities. Nevertheless, not only do the local banks themselves constitute an innovative organizational layer, there are also signs that they provide an impetus for broader rural cooperation. The local development plan that is drawn up annually by the general assemblies and included in the guidelines for banking policies, deliberately tries to foster such externalities. This has led to financing activities in the sphere of rural commerce and transportation receiving much more attention. In many regions, access to markets constitutes a major constraint on development perspectives. Finance for coffee and cattle trade therefore comprises a substantial share of loans in the interior regions. Since this finance is provided in the framework of a kind of local development plan, it often triggers better coordination and cooperation between shareholder traders, transportation enterprises and producers. In another area, bank organization put the need for a better access road firmly on the local political agenda. They organized repair and maintenance activities by the community, pressurized the municipality to improve the road, and demanded a collective long-term loan from Nitlapán in order to contribute to financing road construction. Even though these positive externalities are clearly beginning to be realized, the process still falls short of achieving its full potential. Substantial differences in the socio-cultural 'soil conditions' (Klitgaard, 1995, p. 190) between different villages and even hamlets can also be observed. As witnessed by the continuing weak horizontal participation of clients in many general assemblies as well as in the surrounding organizational networks, attitudes of dependency and voluntary isolation are not changed overnight. For this reason, Nitlapán plans to direct more energy towards the fostering of the participatory local development debates around the definition of the local development plan. In this process, synergy with other local or supra-local initiatives in the field of technological innovation, definition of property rights regimes and commercialization will be sought. In the process, the bank official will also dedicate more time to personalized information-spreading and exchange of ideas with individual clients. The growing professionalization of routine banking is therefore not to be seen as a substitute, but rather as a precondition for promoting more active participation in innovative organization around the bank.

Institutional entrepreneurship, a promising avenue for development policy

We believe Nitlapán's experience contains lessons on the way to proceed in order to realize an institutional transition towards more inclusive and dynamic governance structures, also beyond the realm of finance. Possibly the most important is that the pervasive influence of vertical governance structures requires a strong constraining, facilitating and even structuring external intervention. The initial mistakes under the assisted self-management approach proves that an option for local participation should not be equated with non-intervention or romantic optimism about endogenous organizational capacity. An external development-promoting agent, with power over crucial resources for local development, can impose more civic, transparent and rule-based governance procedures as a condition for local participation in its activities. Such a top-down approach can create a mutually supportive synergy between local dynamics of transformation and supra-local initiatives.[9]

For this to succeed, however, an appropriate balance between local participation and external intervention must be maintained. Some analysts of Nitlapán's experiences in self-management concluded erroneously that local participation was redundant and that a sufficiently professional financial organization could do the job. It is, however, clear that a substantial degree of local participation is critical for the functioning of the financial system, even more so if a broader development impact is expected. Besides the continuing participation of clients in the local assemblies, it should not be forgotten that the present-day legitimacy of the more professionalized system was to a large extent forged during previous participatory experiences involving enormous investment of voluntary effort. Without the mutual learning and trust-building experiences of those days, the local banks would not enjoy the reputation and legitimacy they have in the late 1990s. It would be a dangerous illusion to take this gradually-crafted local environment for granted. It must also be clear that such processes take time and are therefore costly at the start, but the prospect of dynamic and inclusive rural development also promises a substantial reward.

Notes

1. Nitlapán is a research and development institute of the Universidad Centroaméricana in Managua, Nicaragua.
2. The *güegüense* is a literary figure of one of the oldest known written plays from Latin America. It tells the story of the ambiguous relationship between the Spanish *gobernador* and the colonized indigenous people from the latter's viewpoint. It cherishes the inventivity and bravery with which the *güegüense*, as the symbol of the colonized, seduces and circumvents the oppressor without ever confronting him directly. Today, the term *güegüense* is commonly used to denote similar behaviour towards any authority.
3. This factor might explain why a minority of poor people chose freely to devolve their agrarian reform land to the previous owner in order to return to the minimal protection of the patron–client relationship.
4. A more detailed analysis of the recent context of financial configurations in Nicaragua can be found in Bastiaensen (1997).
5. A good case for a subsidy policy can be made. First, there is the 'infant financial institutions' argument which justifies a subsidy because of positive information externalities for other lenders (Hulme and Mosley, 1996, p. 5). Our analysis will indicate that additional externalities might exist because of a beneficial effect on broader local institutions.
6. For this reason, Nitlapán participated in talks with the Nicaraguan government and multilateral institutions on the subject of new financial legislation.
7. They usually forget to mention that it is not in general the poorest who fail to repay.

8. In the pilot experiences, women of both Sandinista and (anti-Sandinista) Catholic-charismatic families showed a strong interest in participating in a revolving village chicken fund. Talking with others in their network and thinking that they would be joining a system alongside the Sandinista women, the charismatic women at the last moment decided not to show up at the first round of distribution of the chickens. The concept of a politically neutral project was difficult to imagine (Mendoza, 1991, pp. 4–5).

9. The argument is somewhat similar to Tendler and Alves's plea in favour of a demand-driven approach in the case of the organization of technological–commercial links between government procurement agencies and small artisan villages, although they do not seem to emphasize very much the need to facilitate local civic organization (Tendler and Alves Amorim, 1996).

Bibliography

Bastiaensen, J. (1997) 'Non-Conventional Rural Finance and the Crisis of Economic Institutions in Nicaragua', in J. P. De Groot and R. Ruben (eds), *Sustainable Agriculture in Central America*, London: Macmillan, pp. 191–209.

Evans, P. (1996) 'Government Action, Social Capital and Development: Reviewing the Evidence on Synergy', *World Development*, vol. 24, no. 6, pp. 1119–32.

Hoff, K., Braverman, A. and Stiglitz, J. (1993) 'Introduction' in *The Economics of Rural Organization. Theory, Practice, and Policy*, Oxford University Press.

Houtart, F. and Lemercinier, G. (1992) *El Campesino como actor. Sociología de una comarca de Nicaragua*, Ed. Nicarao, El Comejen, Managua.

Hulme, D. and Mosley, P. (1996) *Finance Against Poverty*, London: Routledge.

Klitgaard, R. (1995) 'Including Culture in Evaluation Research', R. Piocciotto and R. Rist (eds), *Evaluation and Development*, Proceedings of the 1994 World Bank Conference, Washington DC: World Bank.

Lipton, M. (1993) 'Land Reform as Commenced Business: The Evidence Against Stopping', *World Development*, vol. 21, no. 4, pp. 641–57.

Marchetti, P. (1994) *Experimentación con Nuevas Modalidades de la Educación Popular para el Desarrollo Local*, Managua: Nitlapán-Universidad Centroaméricana.

Mendoza, R. (1991) *El Rostro Femenino del Campesinado: hacia un nuevo estilo de organización y liderazgo comarcal*, Evaluación del proyecto pollos financiado por USOS y Broederlijk Delen, Managua: Instituto Nitlapán, UCA.

Mendoza, R. (1993) *Las Garantías en el Crédito Agricola/Rural: Una propuesta metodológica a partir de estudios especificos*, Nitlapán-UCA.

Narayan, D. and Pritchett, L. (1997) *Cents and Sociability: Household Income and Social Capital in Rural Tanzania*, World Bank Policy Research Working Paper No. 1796, Washington DC: World Bank.

Nitlapán (1994) *Financial Services Program*, Managua, Nitlapán-UCA.

Nitlapán (1997a) *Evaluación de Impacto Económico del Crédito en las Unidades Económicas Rurales*. Instituto Nitlapán–Universidad Centroamericana, Managua.

Nitlapán (1997b) *Informe Anual 1996. Programa de Desarrollo Local*, Managua, Instituto Nitlapán, Universidad Centroamericana.

North, D. C. (1990) *Institutions, Institutional Change and Economic Performance*. Cambridge: Cambridge University Press.

Putnam, R. D. with Leonardi, R. and Nanetti, R. Y. (1993) *Making Democracy Work: Civic Traditions in Modern Italy*, Princeton NJ: Princeton University Press.

Tendler, J. and Alves Amorim, M. (1996) 'Small Firms and Their Helpers: Lessons on Demand', *World Development*, vol. 24, no. 3, pp. 407–26.

Uphoff, N. (1993) 'Grassroots Organizations and NGOs in Rural Development: Opportunities with Diminishing States and Expanding Markets', *World Development*, vol. 21, no. 4, pp. 607–22.

Yaron, J. (1992) *Successful Rural Finance Institutions*, World Bank Discussion Paper No. 150, Washington DC, World Bank.

10
Credit and Rural Income: Biases in Credit Supply by Semi-Formal Financial Institutions in Nueva Guinea, Nicaragua

Arie Sanders, Harry Clemens and Eelco Mol

Introduction

The access to credit by small-scale farmers' households in developing countries has become an important research and policy question. Technological changes and incorporation into commodity markets lead to a greater need for external capital by the farm households. The argument states that increased productive credit is fundamental to generate adequate growth of production. Since the late 1980s many efforts have been made, and numerous credit programmes have been established to improve the access of peasant households to credit in low-income countries. However, relatively few peasant households are integrated into credit markets, and many do not use credit at all. According to the previous hypothesis, limited access affects production growth directly through lack of sufficient capital for investment, resulting in low farm incomes (Lipton in Sarap, 1990). As will be explained in the next section, there are several reasons why households do not borrow, and continue to work in suboptimal economic conditions.

At the beginning of the 1990s more than ten national and international organizations started activities in Nueva Guinea and have made an effort to increase the use of credit among rural households through special credit programmes (Sanders and Wattel, 1996). Our survey of small farm households in 1997 shows that 26 per cent had used credit during the previous year, mainly supplied by these semi-formal institutes.

The objective of this chapter is to provide some insights into the quantitative importance of the various factors affecting income and use of credit among farm households in the context of Nueva Guinea. To this end, a conceptual framework of household use of credit is presented, and estimations are made about the relative importance of the various variables that may influence use of credit.

The chapter starts with a brief description of Nueva Guinea in which emphasis is given to the agricultural production systems in the area. We then outline a conceptual framework to explain the demand for credit by farm households. Demand for and supply of capital in the farm households are analyzed in a model, and the data and methodology of the research is explained. A description is given of the data used in the analysis of the peasant household income function and its relation to credit use. The results of using ordinary least squares models (OLS) to estimate the determinants of the dependent income variable are presented. On the basis of these results, the relative share of subsistence crops within agricultural activities is calculated. We conclude with some observations on the influence of farm household income in relation to credit use.

The setting

Nueva Guinea is located in south-eastern Nicaragua, some 270 kilometres from Managua – about eight hours' travel by public transport. It is a settlement area on the agricultural frontier of Nicaragua's humid tropics. It absorbed a large number of immigrants following the 1965 settlement policies of the Nicaraguan government. The government provided legal titles to plots of land of up to 35 hectares for each family. At the end of the 1960s, about 1400 families had settled in the area and seven settlements (*colonias*) had been founded. During the 1970s, more than 5000 new families were settled by the government. However, unplanned colonization also increased. In 1981, Nueva Guinea obtained the status of municipality, covering an area of 2774 km². During the 1980s, migration to Nueva Guinea declined substantially, mainly because of the intensity of the military conflict in this area. By 1990, more than 12 600 families were living in the area, with a population of about 76 000. Since 1990, immigration has been on the rise again. About 58 per cent of the families are peasants, with about 24 per cent being landless. Only 18 per cent are active in non-agrarian activities (de Groot, 1996).

Nueva Guinea can be classified as an older agrarian frontier, compared to the new frontier, which is characterized by its geographical isolation and abundant availability of free or cheap land, and the maturing frontier, which is characterized by its incorporation into the market economy. The older frontier differs from the maturing frontier not so much in age, but because of its incomplete market incorporation. The economy relies mainly on agriculture; accessible roads and communication facilities are scarce. Only a few households are engaged in non-farm activities; more than 80 per cent of the households are active in the agrarian sector. Nevertheless, increasing commercial activities in the main village can be observed. Many new small enterprises, such as small retail shops, prepared foods, and furniture workshops, have been established.

The agrarian development process in Nueva Guinea shares many of the features of other agrarian frontiers in Central America. Settlers, mostly poor, coming to the frontier, start cutting trees and planting maize or other annual crops in the virgin soil. In the first years, high yields are obtained using very few external inputs. However, nutrient depletion leads to decreasing yields in subsequent years. Settlers get locked into a low-level productivity trap, as it is not attractive to invest in soil conservation or external inputs when cheap land is still available, and labour and capital are expensive (Bakker, 1993; de Groot, 1996).

The solution for many poor peasants is to sell their land to cattle ranchers and move on to the new frontier. Others try to acquire some cattle for themselves. As a result there is a strong tendency to transform agricultural land into pasture. In addition, animal husbandry presents relatively few marketing problems and relatively low risks, and it functions as a savings mechanism that can be transformed easily into cash. Therefore, the first thing that almost any small farmer in Central America does when he or she accumulates a little land or money is to purchase cattle (Kaimowitz, 1996). The main tendency in the economy of Nueva Guinea is to expand cattle raising. However, this expansion has been limited by the scarcity of capital for long-term investments and through decapitalization during the military conflict of the 1980s (Ambrogi, 1996).

Cattle-raising requires only a fraction of the amount of labour needed for crop production. It allows peasants to have up to 50 hectares and still cover more than 50 per cent of their labour requirements by using household labour (Kaimowitz, 1996). Most small peasants have dual-purpose systems, producing calves and small quantities of milk, allowing for a regular income, and sometimes selling a steer. In Nueva Guinea, cheese processed from milk is becoming increasingly important as a small-scale export product, mainly for the market in El Salvador.

Medium-sized, and relatively large-scale peasant farmers have more single-purpose systems, aimed at beef production for the national or export market. Compared with the small-scale sector, these producers have relatively high incomes. However, beef production has been affected by a declining profitability because of decreasing world market prices.

Besides cattle-raising, in recent years there has been an increase in the production of small-scale export crops, especially cocoyam and ginger, which are bought by traders from Costa Rica. The area in which these crops are cultivated was estimated by local sources to be between 1200 and 1600 hectares in 1996, involving some 1300 producers.

Most of the staple crops (maize and beans) are cultivated for local consumption, although beans are also a commercial crop. In recent years beans have also been exported to El Salvador; Salvadoran traders buy directly from peasants in the zone. Strong price fluctuations occur, as well as yield fluctuations; the 1996–7 harvest (when the survey was held) was very poor because of late rains.

The conceptual framework

There are several explanations why households do not use credit for their production systems. For example: (i) peasants do not borrow because of the uncertainty of the amount of returns affected by, for example, natural hazards or market fluctuations; (ii) peasants have sufficient liquidity to cover their planned expenditure; and (iii) peasants are confronted by high direct and indirect transaction costs (interest rates, red tape, and/or collateral requirements) of credit loans charged by lenders as result of asymmetric access to information.

Peasant households combine characteristics of both producers and consumers. Peasants make borrowing decisions not just on the basis of the market conditions defining their production, but also on the basis of their own savings or self-financing capacity (Iqbal, 1986). By using a model which includes production and the demand for and supply of credit we can estimate the circumstances in which a farmer household may borrow. The current model, shown in Figure 10.1, is based on the work of Colman and Young (1989).

The *production response* curve (OP) represents the production activities of a peasant household (Figure 10.1a). This curve depicts the relationship between the value of farm output (or income) and capital usage, and its slope indicates the *marginal productivity of the variable input capital* (*VMPc* in Figure 10.1b). A diminishing return to capital is assumed. The household will seek to choose the combination of output and investment that will maximize utility, given the constraints of the production response curve of the household.

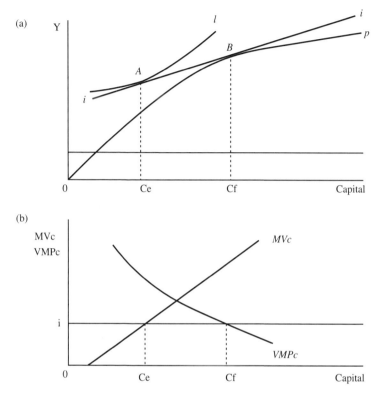

Figure 10.1   Agricultural production and the supply and demand of credit

It is assumed that the household is not only using its own capital but also has access to external funds at a determined *broad interest rate* (this broad interest rate is represented by the interest rate charged by the lending institute, transaction costs and risks for a specific household; and therefore it will vary in accordance with household characteristics). The broad interest rate, i, is the slope of the interest ii in Figure 10.1. The amount of capital invested in the farm (OCf) is determined by the equality of its *value of marginal product of capital* with the interest rate ($VMPc = i$).

In this model, the household has access to credit and will choose to borrow. A household, as a production and consumption unit, obtains utility from the income generated by production and from consumption. The utility obtained from any amount of income is offset by the loss of utility from consumption forgone in production activities. The slope of the indifference curve of the household measures that amount of income needed to just compensate the household for a small increase in household investment utilized. The slope represents the valuation of a marginal unit of the capital utilized, and is called the marginal valuation of capital by the household. The amount that will be used by the household is *OCf*, and the household itself invests *OCe*, with the remainder being borrowed on the credit market. The subjective equilibrium is found where the *marginal valuation of capital*, (the subjective discount rate of the household) reflected by the slope of the indifference curve is equal to the interest rate reflected by the slope of the interest line: or $MVc = i$.

The amount of credit borrowed decreases when the broad interest rate increases (including transaction costs). Households want to borrow until the value of marginal product and marginal value of capital have crossed each other. The cost of borrowing for the household is at this point equal to the benefits. At a higher level of i the cost of borrowing is greater than the expected return, and as a result the credit market is not used for the transaction.[1]

The outcome of the model is determined by the particular characteristics and constraints of a specific household and influence the household's demand for (and access to) credit. There are several basic factors which influence this demand (Barry and Baker, 1971; Feder *et al.*, 1993; Sadoulet and de Janvry, 1995 and Deaton, 1997). Farm size is a primary factor: the demand for credit by peasants for working capital purposes will be less than that of large-scale peasants. Second, there are the factors which influence the productivity of the resources acquired with credit. These include the adoption of new technologies, management skills and incorporation into the market. A higher level of these factors leads, in general, to a higher credit demand. Third, the risk-averse behaviour of households must be considered. Risk-averse households do not use all the credit available (credit reserve): this behaviour is in response to uncertainty. Households which are more risk-averse will have a greater credit reserve and will borrow less than the households that are more risk-taking. The fourth factor is the availability of liquidity, determined by cash flow and the total asset value of the household. This includes the degree of non-farm activities (whether permanent or not), and the household's saving capacity. A higher level of both factors will lead to an increase in self-investment in the farm. The level of asset accumulation can be partly explained by the life-cycle model: older people have accumulated over a longer period of time than younger ones, but are highly influenced by the income path of the specific household (for example, external shocks over time).

Combining household characteristics with the internal household supply of and demand for capital, allows us to estimate whether or not the household will want to borrow, and if the household does, the quantity of credit demanded. A lower broad interest rate and a household with characteristics that allow a high expected return of the loan, results in an increase of the credit demand by the peasant household. However, most peasant households experience problems in gaining access to external capital through the existence of imperfect markets, and are thus confronted with a supply restriction. Supply restriction refers to a situation where the borrower has exhausted all sources of loanable funds but still finds that the value of the marginal product of capital exceed the marginal costs of capital (Barry and Baker, 1971). In the case of capital constraint, investment is below the optimal level that a non-constrained household would have chosen.

Data and method of analysis

Nearly 300 farm households were surveyed in January and February 1997. The stratified and randomly drawn sample covered the municipality of Nueva Guinea. The 300 peasants in the survey include only small and medium peasants with between approximately 50 and 100 *manzanas* of land (1 *manzana* is 0.7 hectares).

The method of analysis used consists of estimating income functions using demographic and education variables, production features and access to institutional services as explanatory variables. Total gross household income includes income from agricultural production (animal husbandry and crops) and off-farm income (including remittances). Gross income from crops is calculated as the value of total production at market prices obtained by the specific farmer. Basic cereals include maize and beans, and export crops are cocoyam and ginger. Income from other crops is included in other on-farm income. The income from livestock is calculated as the value sold in the previous year. Some specific questions were included in the questionnaire related to off-farm income. Livestock possession at the time of the survey is a main determinant of assets, and is considered as one of the production feature variables. The use of credit by the household is included as one of the institutional variables. Credit sources include both formal and informal suppliers. The influence of the credit variable on household income will be the central issue in our analysis.

Variables and expected relationships between income and household characteristics

With regard to the relationship between credit and income, an important issue in the analysis is the causality of the relation between both variables. As we shall see, in Nueva Guinea, small-scale peasants use credit more often than the better-off. This may be explained by demand factors (for example, better-off peasants have enough resources to finance their production themselves) or by supply factors (for example, various development organizations with credit programmes prefer to loan to small peasants). To test this question, the regression function will be estimated both with and without household-specific variables. If the credit variable is not significant when no other variables are used, while a negative and significant correlation is found if household specific variables are included, this will shed light on the question of which types of household are more likely to use credit. On the basis of this information we shall try to determine which demand factors or supply factors may explain the limited use of credit by better-off peasants.

Table 10.1 shows the average income composition for all 286 households for which sufficient data on income generation has been obtained. On average, gross income was 46 061 córdobas (about US$4953), with livestock contributing 57 per cent of total income. Total on-farm income constitutes 90 per cent of total household income. Gross income will be specified as a function of demographic and educational variables (D), production features (P) and access to institutional services (I). The natural logarithm of gross income (Yg) was chosen because of non-normal distribution of residues. Furthermore, this makes the interpretation of the dummy variables for some explanatory

Table 10.1 Average gross household income composition (in córdobas)

Activity	Average income	Percentage
Basic cereals	7712 (11 134)	16.7
Export crops	5477 (19 360)	11.9
Livestock	26 274 (54 516)	57.0
Other on-farm income	1948 (4999)	4.3
Off-farm income (including remittances)	4649 (26 604)	10.1
Total gross household income	46 061 (69 721)	100.0
Sample size	286	

Notes: Standard deviation in parentheses.
US$ 1 = 9.30 córdobas (as at December 1996).

variables easier, such as referring to the growth of income. This income analysis is built around the function:

$$\ln Yg = \alpha_0 + \beta_1 D_i + \beta_2 P_i + \beta_3 I_i \tag{10.1}$$

Demographic variables include family size and the age of the head of the household. Production features include the area cultivated, possession of livestock, and types of crop cultivated. All these household-specific features are important, for two reasons: first, because they will influence the household's demand for credit; and second, because financial institutions are likely to base their decision to lend on such features, either for financial reasons (using these variables as proxies for the credit-worthiness of the household), or for administrative-political reasons, in the case of target credit. Table 10.2 shows the independent variables used in our analyses.

A positive correlation is expected between the *age of the household head* and income based on the life-cycle models. Nevertheless, it will also be influenced by the income path of the household, as mentioned above in the section on the conceptual framework. The education variable is defined as the *ability to read and write*, and described by one

Table 10.2 Definition of variables and descriptive statistics

	Mean	**Standard deviation**
Total gross household income in 1996 (Y_g)	46061	69720
Demographic features and education (D)		
Age of household head, 1996	48	13
Number of family members 12 years of age or older, 1996	4.71	2.25
Ability to read and write (dummy)	0.57	0.50
Production features (P)		
Livestock possession as at 31 December 1996	41826	64767
Area land cultivated (*manzanas*)	9.06	9.54
Area cultivated with export crops (dummy)	0.46	0.50
Total costs of external inputs in 1996 (whole farm)	866	1485
Subsistence ratio	0.21	0.21
Use of external labour in 1996 (dummy)	0.65	0.48
Hire out own labour (dummy)	0.37	0.48
Use of institutional services (I)		
Technical assistance in 1996 (dummy)	0.35	0.48
Credit in 1996 (dummy)	0.27	0.44
Sample Size	286	

dummy variable, uneducated (0) and educated (1). It is expected to influence income positively because of its contribution to the management capacity of the farmer. A final demographic variable is defined as the *number of family members of 12 years or older*: that is, members with a high labour power contribution. An increase in the labour supply within the household will affect income positively, because of the availability of labour power, which can be used either to cultivate more land (or to cultivate land more intensively), or to generate off-farm income.

Land-ownership and livestock possession are key variables for measuring asset accumulation and the savings capacity of households. However, because of the relative abundance of land in Nueva Guinea, we use *livestock possession* as the most reliable indicator of the degree of asset accumulation. The variable estimates the value of livestock in cordobas on 31 December 1996.

Most peasants have an integrated production system involving cultivation of more than one crop and active livestock breeding. *Total area cultivated* is defined as the total area of annual or perennial crops. The expected sign in the income function is positive. The dummy for *export crops* (with a value of 1 if the household grows an export crop, and 0 otherwise) is expected to be related positively to income. Compared to basic cereals and livestock, economic returns for this activity are relatively high (although risks may also be high). The *total use of external inputs*, defined by the total cost of fertilizers, herbicides and pesticides in cordobas, will depend on the availability of financial resources, and so this variable is expected to be correlated positively to income.

Most of the farm households in Nicaragua grow basic cereals for home consumption, providing a subsistence livelihood basis. The variable *subsistence ratio* is defined as the proportion of farm output directly consumed by the household. To calculate the value of this proportion consumed we use the average sales price for that particular product of the whole sample. This value is divided by the whole farm output (including consumption of milk and cheese). This may be an underestimate because of the limited inclusion of products and the use of average sales prices. However, for an approximation, main products will suffice. The subsistence ratio indicates the degree of integration into the commodity market for outputs and is expected to be correlated negatively with income.

Labour is relatively expensive in extensive farming systems in agrarian frontier areas. Small-scale peasant farmers mostly work only with their own labour force, as hiring external labour means direct financial costs. A dummy variable *use of external labour* is defined, taking the value 1 if the household hires external labour, and 0 if it does not. The function also includes a dummy for households that *hire out their own labour power* to generate off-farm income. It is not clear if off-farm employment generates less or more income for a household, because of the trade-off between the use of labour power for farm production and to generate off-farm income. It will depend, in the first place, on the number of days involved and the type of off-farm work (skilled or unskilled). To examine the effects of off-farm income we introduce this variable in the income function. Off-farm income is defined as a dummy variable, taking the value 1 if the household is active in the labour market as a supplier, and 0 otherwise.

It is expected that external institutional services, represented by the variable *use of technical assistance*, will have a positive effect on farm income. Technical support provides knowledge about production technology and management; it will improve production and marketing skills. The variable is defined as a dummy variable, 1 for technical support received last year and 0 if none was received.

Similarly, the variable *use of credit* is expected to have a positive influence on farm income. Use of credit facilitates more working capital and new investments, both necessary to improve the production system. As mentioned above, this variable will be the main focus of our analysis.

Econometric results

Income function

Table 10.3 shows the results of the estimation of the household income function. The OLS test is satisfactory; the equation explains approximately 56 per cent of the variability of income per household. From the eleven anticipated signs, six are correct and significant and three are correct but not significant, while two variables show unanticipated signs.

The most important factors associated with household income are livestock possession (assets); use of chemical inputs and external labour; family labour availability; and the degree of market incorporation (negative sign of subsistence ratio). Total crop area is also significant and related positively to income. However, the dummy for the cultivation of export crops is not significant. The other variables that show no significance are education and the use of technical support. That the latter is not significant is a somewhat surprising finding: more than 37 per cent of the peasant households used technical assistance without there being a significant impact on gross income. This does

Table 10.3   OLS estimates of household income function

	B	**Standard Error**
Intercept (α)	4.120	0.110
Demographic features and education (D)		
Age of household head, 1996	−0.003*	0.002
Number of family members 12 years of age or older, 1996	0.051***	0.051
Ability to read and write (1 if able to read and write, 0 otherwise)	0.032	0.042
Production characteristics (P)		
Livestock possession as at 31 December 1996	0.003***	0.000
Total crop area (*manzanas*)	0.005**	0.002
Cultivation of export crops (dummy)	0.041	0.040
Costs of external inputs in 1996	0.049***	0.016
Subsistence ratio	−0.593***	0.098
Use of external labour in 1996 (dummy)	0.139***	0.044
Hire out own labour (dummy)	0.070*	0.042
Use of institutional services (I)		
Technical assistance in 1996 (dummy)	0.099	0.042
Credit in 1996 (dummy)	−0.104**	0.044
R^2	0.56	
R^2 adjusted	0.55	
F-value***	29.47	
Sample size	286	

Notes: *$P<0.1$; **$P<0.05$; ***$P<0.01$.

not mean that participation in technical support programmes has no production effect, but rather that whatever positive production effect exists, it is in the direction of crops that are less profitable: the basic cereals.

Among the social variables, the labour force and the age of the household are both significant. However, a negative sign is shown for the age of the household. The off-farm employment coefficient is positively related to income and significant, albeit at the 10 per cent level. Even though only few households are active in this market, earnings are higher than those generated on their own farms. Also, the use of external labour is positively correlated and significant. Households with higher incomes use external labour for sowing and harvesting crops, and more importantly, to clear their pastures.

The use of credit shows a negative correlation: that is, higher income households use less credit. The causality of the credit factor is an important issue. We therefore investigated how the credit variable is processed when it is first used in an income regression function without controlling for other variables, and then sequentially adding more explanatory variables. At first, the credit variable is not significant, but it becomes stronger as other variables (social and production related) are included. It is concluded that household-specific and productive features influence the use of credit, as well as income levels. Higher-income households have less of a demand for, or less access to, credit. But specific features determine that some low-income households have a higher demand or better access than other low-income households.

This is consistent with the discussion above in the conceptual framework about the demand side. Peasant households with higher incomes depend mainly on cattle-raising, and are endowed with relatively more resources. Livestock assets illustrate the savings capacity of a household. It seems that the liquidity constraint, or better, the demand for short-term working capital by livestock-orientated peasants, is less than that of crop-orientated households. Livestock-orientated households have a greater demand for longer-term investment capital – for example, to invest in cattle, improvement of pasture, dairy-processing equipment, and so on. On the other hand, livestock assets are easy to capitalize, and investments are distributed throughout the year, but in the case of crop production there is a concentrated liquidity demand during the sowing and harvesting seasons.

Composition of production

One of the interesting results of the income function estimate was the negative correlation of the credit variable. One of the reasons could be that credit has a positive effect on production, but that such an effect is not translated into significantly higher total income: possibly a bias toward basic cereals that semi-formal credit institutions may induce. In this part we try to gain some insights into the relationship between credit use and the composition of agricultural production. Table 10.4 provides variable estimates of the share of basic cereals. We set the share of gross income of basic cereals (Ybc) to the whole farm income (Yf) as the independent variable. We use the same dependent variables as in the income function:

$$\ln (Ybc/Yf) = \alpha_0 + \beta_1 \ln D_i + \beta_2 \ln P_i + \beta_3 \ln I_i \qquad (10.2)$$

The credit dummy is highly significant and correlated positively with an increasing share of income from basic cereals. Basic-cereals-orientated peasants belong to the lowest income group. The negatively

Table 10.4   OLS estimates of basic grains income share

	Coefficient	Standard error
Intercept (α)	-1.792***	0.749
Demographic features and education (D)		
Age of household head, 1996	-0.054	0.004
Number of family members 12 years of age or older, 1996	-0.017	0.020
Ability to read and write (1 if able to read and write, 0 otherwise)	-0.075	0.092
Production characteristics (P)		
Livestock possession as at 31 December 1996	-0.322***	0.032
Area land cultivated (*manzanas*)	0.452***	0.076
Area cultivated with export crops (1 if cultivated, 0 otherwise)	-0.366***	0.101
Costs of external inputs in 1996	0.020	0.025
Subsistence ratio	-0.007	0.054
Costs of external labour 1996	-0.017	0.015
Use of institutional services (I)		
Technical assistance in 1996 (1 if received, 0 otherwise)	0.107	0.101
Credit in 1996 (1 if received, 0 otherwise)	0.231**	0.108
R^2	0.39	
R^2 adjusted-value	0.36	
F-value***	15.12	
Sample size	271	

Notes: The sample size is reduced by households because the dependent variable for this group is zero.
$*P<0.1$; $**P<0.05$; $***P<0.01$.

significant sign of livestock assets suggests a low savings capacity. This is a group with strong liquidity problems in the agricultural peak seasons (sowing and harvesting). From this perspective it is logical that this group displays a credit demand. Nevertheless, the correlation with the export crop dummy is negative, so basic-cereal-orientated peasants are not active in export-orientated crops. Reasons may be high investments, a longer vegetative cycle and high risks compared with basic cereals.

Households which depend mainly on basic cereals have the lowest income levels and have less collateral than the livestock-orientated households. The low savings capacity and the concentration on a relatively low productive crop make them very vulnerable to external shocks, and in the case of credit use, to defaulting. The fact that we found a positively significant correlation of the credit dummy with an increasing income share of basic cereals using the same household variables sustains our hypothesis that semi-formal institutions prefer to finance basic cereals, thus reaching the lower social class of the agricultural sector in Nueva Guinea. The broad interest rate costs for this group of borrowers are low enough to make the use of credit in basic cereals attractive. Referring to our model, especially where the risk premiums for the borrowers are low, we argue that the entire risk for the cereal production is diverted and assumed by the semi-formal credit institutions. If a disaster occurs, the borrowers probably do not pay.

The policy of financing mainly basic cereals provokes thought, because basic cereals are crops with a high risk and low productivity. The risk of default is substantial, and can affect the sustainability of the semi-financial institutions.

Conclusions

Only few farm households in Nueva Guinea use credit. As shown in the conceptual framework, there are several possible reasons why a household may decide not to use credit, including sufficient liquidity, low expected returns on production, and high borrowing and transaction costs.

The income function analysis shows that higher-income households use less credit than low-income households. The high importance of livestock production for the income of the former may explain why their demand for credit is low, as liquidity constraints are less for this kind of production than for crop production. However, supply restrictions, especially for long-term investment credit, also apply.

The function for basic cereal output shows a positive effect of the use of credit, as opposed to the income function. It is concluded that credit supply is less restricted for basic-cereals-orientated households than for other households. This can be explained by a bias created by semi-formal institutions, which prefer to lend to basic-cereals-orientated households, and strong restrictions for credit supply to other types of household. The low broad interest rate for the basic-cereals-orientated households, in this case where production risks, as we postulated, are diverted and assumed by the semi-formal credit institutions, make borrowing attractive. However, this affects the financial sustainability of these institutions and access to credit.

Note

1. Not using credit when the cost of a transaction through market exchange creates disutility greater than the utility gain that it produces is, according to de Janvry *et al.*, (1991), an extreme case of market failure. As will be argued below, this failure is household-specific. In general, credit markets exist, but they fail selectively for particular households, because of the high broad interest rate.

Bibliography

Ambrogi, R. (1996) *La Frontera Agrícola en Nicaragua*, Managua: ESECA-UNAN.

Bakker, M. L. (1993) *Colonization and Land Use in the Humid Tropics of Latin America*, Wageningen: BOS.

Barry, P. J. and Baker, C. B. (1971) 'Reservation Prices on Credit Use: A Measure of Response to Uncertainty', *American Journal of Applied Economics*, no. 53, pp. 222–8.

Colman, D. and Young, T. (1989) *Principles of Agricultural Economics: Markets and Prices in Less Developed Countries*, Cambridge University Press.

Deaton, A. (1997) *The Analysis of Household Surveys: A Microeconometric Approach to Development Policy*, Baltimore and London: Johns Hopkins University Press.

de Janvry, A., Fafchamps, M. and Sadoulet, E. (1991) 'Peasant Household Behaviour with Missing Markets: Some Paradoxes Explained', *Economic Journal*, vol. 101, pp. 1400–17.

Feder, G., Lau, L. J., Lin, J. Y. and Luo, X. (1993) 'The Nascent Rural Credit Market in China', in K. Hoff, A. Braverman and J. E. Stiglitz (eds), *The Economics of Rural Organization: Theory, Practice and Policy*, Washington: World Bank.

de Groot, J. P. (1996) *Towards Sustainable Land Use in the Humid Tropics: A Case Study of a Nueva Guinea Settlement, Nicaragua*, Amsterdam: Vrije Universiteit Amsterdam.

Iqbal, F. (1986) 'The Demand and Supply of Funds Among Agricultural Households in India', in I. Singh, L. Squire and J. Strauss (eds), *Agricultural Household Models*, Baltimore: Johns Hopkins University Press.

Kaimowitz, D. (1996) *Livestock and Deforestation in Central America in the 1980s and 1990s: A Policy Perspective*. Djakarta: CIFOR.

Sadoulet, E. and de Janvry, A. (1995) *Quantitative Development Policy Analysis*, Baltimore: Johns Hopkins University Press.

Sanders, A. and Wattel, C. J. (1996) *La Estrategia de Reactivación de la Economía Campesina en Nueva Guinea, Nicaragua: Algunos planteamientos y temas de debate*, Costa Rica: Centro de Estudios para el Desarrollo Rural/Vrije Universiteit Amsterdam, San José.

Sarap, K. (1990) 'Factors Affecting Small Farmers' Access to Institutional Credit in Rural Orissa, India', *Development and Change*, vol. 21, pp. 281–307.

Part 4

Labour Markets and Technological Change

11
Farmers' Selective Participation in Rural Markets: Off-Farm Employment in Honduras

Ruerd Ruben and Marrit van den Berg

Introduction

Honduras is one of the few Latin American countries where more than half of the economically active population is still engaged in agricultural activities. Primary farm production, however, represents only a minor share of small peasants' household income, since their livelihood strategies have become increasingly dependent on income generated through engagement in the rural labour market. The agricultural labour force comprises about 75 per cent of self-employed workers and family labour, while rural wage labour represents the remaining 25 per cent of the labour force (DGEC, 1988). However, most statistics do not reveal the simultaneous relationships that small farm households tend to maintain with land, labour and commodity markets, giving rise to multiple income sources. The 1993 national socio-economic household survey revealed that farm households of up to 5 *manzanas* in size only derive 30 per cent of their family income from farm activities, with the remaining part coming from off-farm wages and non-agricultural self-employment activities (Swindale, 1994).

In this chapter we analyze the importance of the off-farm employment component of family income, and discuss the relevant farm and household characteristics that give rise to engagement in the rural labour market. While considering off-farm employment as a compensating device for limited access to rural financial and land markets, linkages between off-farm income, the use of credit and the mobilization of savings are highlighted. Moreover, expenditure effects are addressed through the discussion of the implications of off-farm income for household food security. Instead of looking at off-farm employment of small peasant households as only a secondary component, we focus attention on wage income as a major element of the rural livelihood strategy that permits the maintenance of a survival strategy based on the combination of a number of complementary activities. This enables small farmers better to overcome limitations in the access to markets and favours the adoption of risk-sharing strategies that are considered typical for resource-poor households operating under conditions of selective market failure.

We begin with a brief historical review of the structure of agricultural employment and the development of the rural factor and commodity markets in Honduras. The contribution of off-farm employment to household income is then assessed, paying special attention to the possibilities for substitution between labour and capital. Under conditions of selective market failure, off-farm employment might become a feasible substitute to overcome constrained access to land or financial markets. Empirical evidence is presented, focusing on the internal farm and household characteristics that explain the relative importance of off-farm income in the process of household income formation. The relationships between off-farm employment, reliance on credit, and adequacy of food consumption are also reviewed. Finally, some policy implications for enhancing agricultural productivity and food security are derived, based on the linkages between off-farm income and farm-level expenditure.

Peasant producers and rural markets in Honduras

The agrarian structure in Honduras is generally characterized by a high level of fragmentation and the limited access of peasant households to local factor and commodity markets. In his review of the land reform and rural development policies in Honduras, Brockett (1988) affirms the limitations of reformism while referring to the growing number of landless families and the high level of rural unemployment and underemployment. Compared to other Central-American countries, basic grain yields and agricultural labour productivity remain extremely low (PREALC, 1986) and thus rural incomes and purchasing power fail to meet minimum requirements for food security.

Livelihood strategies of small peasant households are strongly related to their relationship with local factor and commodity markets, and the occurrence of selective market failures (see below). Rural labour markets are important to guarantee additional off-farm income, while access to the land market will be important to enhance food self-sufficiency. Access to the rural financial market may enable improved input use and land productivity. Finally, the prevailing conditions on input and output markets determine the pattern of land use and the level of factor productivity that can be reached.

Rural labour market

The structure of rural employment in the Honduran countryside can be derived from a number of key facts (Baumeister *et al.*, 1996). Supply of labour is mainly dependent on farm size and the related household income level. Rural farms with less than 5 hectares of land – considered as the minimum land area for a viable family farm – represented almost half of the total rural population in 1993. The rural landless who depend exclusively on renting land and wage labour contracts account for 125 000 families, or a further 27 per cent of the rural economically-active population. Both categories require permanent or temporary wage employment in order to complement their family income. Roughly half of the family labour force of *minifundio* farms (0–1 ha) and about a quarter of the family labour in *subfamily* farms between 1 and 5 ha is engaged in off-farm employment (Salgado *et al.*, 1994, p. 109).

Demand for agricultural labour is strongly related to farm size and cropping pattern. Wage employment is more commonly found among medium-sized producers and entrepreneurial enterprises, although labour intensity of production decreases sharply with farm size. However, even on smaller, (sub)family farms, permanent and temporary wage labour represents between 35 and 47 per cent of the labour force (Baumeister *et al.*, 1996, p. 38). Non-agricultural rural employment is usually underestimated in income surveys. In Honduras, 28 per cent of the rural economically active population is engaged in non-farm employment (DGEC, 1988). Income derived from rural non-agricultural activities in small peasant households represents about 17 per cent of income (CADESCA, 1989).

Welfare effects of off-farm employment may include both income and substitution effects. The engagement of farm household members in the rural labour market can be understood either as a strategy to supplement deficient levels of household income or as a device for risk management through activity diversification. In both cases, farm production has to be maintained with less labour or by sacrificing leisure. Off-farm income can be used again for consumptive expenditures, or be invested in the purchase of yield-enhancing inputs (for example, fertilizers). In the latter case, income from off-farm employment can be considered as a substitute for lending.

Land market

Access to land has always been fairly restricted in Honduras. According to the 1993 agricultural census, only 40 per cent of the established farms possess a full legal title (SECPLAN-SRN, 1994). Frequent transactions take place in the land market, but they are mainly registered as private buying and selling operations. Land prices for leasehold tend to maintain a more-or-less direct relationship with the evolution of net (expected) returns to major annual cropping activities (Salgado *et al.*, 1994). Similarly, Fadiño *et al.* (1986) demonstrate that land transactions in the hillside regions are mainly dependent on the developments in the coffee market.

Interlinkages between the land market and other factor markets are quite loosely developed in the Honduran countryside. The collateral function of land ownership for rural lending operations is not generally recognized. Agricultural credit from public or private banks meets quantitative constraints, while informal lenders evaluate clients' creditworthiness with other criteria. Purchase of land is usually financed with farmers' own savings or personal credit; bank credit for land transactions is not available for the smaller farm strata (Salgado *et al.*, 1994, p. 120). Off-farm income represents one of the most important sources for financing land acquisitions.

Credit and technical assistance

The fragmentation of rural factor markets and the restricted access of small producers to credit services and technical assistance also becomes apparent from data derived from the 1993 agricultural census (SECPLAN-SRN, 1994). Only 6.7 per cent of all producers have access to formal credit, and 7.3 per cent receive technical assistance from public or private sources. For farm households with less than 5 hectares, these figures are even worse: 4.6 per cent receive credit and 5.4 per cent benefit from technical assistance. Consequently, the use of equipment and the level of external input use are severely restricted for the Honduran small-farm sector.

Small farmers' access to rural financial markets in Honduras is severely constrained by high transaction costs and the risks associated with rainfed production. The small amount of available credit can only be used to finance current production costs. Moreover, pre-harvest selling occurs frequently in order to maintain consumption expenditure. Additional income from off-farm employment tends to be highly important for reducing these compulsory sales, as well as to enable the maintenance or purchase of fixed assets.

Commodity markets

Until the 1970s, peasant production systems in Honduras were characterized by a limited use of market-purchased inputs and a low level of *commoditization* of production. Land reform, agrarian colonization and subsidized credit programmes strongly enhanced the incorporation of small farm households into market production (Boyer, 1986; Brockett, 1987). In the ten years between 1978 and 1988, the share of producers making use of chemical fertilizers increased from 5 per cent to 25 per cent (Baumeister *et al.*, 1996, p. 26). Similarly, the proportion of maize production devoted to market exchange increased from 34 per cent during the 1970s to almost 60 per cent at the end of the 1980s (Ibid., p. 28). Both tendencies confirm the strong linkages of peasant production with the market system.

Available empirical evidence on the welfare effects of the enhanced level of commoditization is, however, less conclusive. For peasant farms in Southern Honduras during the 1970s, Boyer (1986) registers a shift from a food surplus to a deficit related to the declining per capita availability of basic grains. Recent studies on changes of internal terms of trade for peasant producers during the 1980s reveal that real output prices and wage rates changed more than material input costs, thus yielding a potential positive result for small farmers (Díaz and Cruz, 1992; World Bank, 1994). In practice, however, local traders appropriated a major part of this surplus, and farmers received only a minor share. Otherwise, strong price fluctuations on basic grains markets may have led to higher risks, making producers reluctant to make farm investments. Taking into account rising prices for consumer goods, pressure to increase the rural wage rate became effective, and income from off-farm employment represents an increasingly important share of the household income.

The role of off-farm employment under selective market failures

Most research on the impact of market linkages on household income and farm resource use has been based on a separate analysis of the linkages with factor markets for labour or credit. Within this framework, engagement in off-farm employment is mainly considered to be provoked by low opportunity costs of labour within the farm household compared to occupational opportunities offered outside the farm (off-farm labour) or the region (migration). Limited use of credit by small-farm households is explained by constraints in the rural financial market related to high risk and the inability to satisfy collateral requirements.

Institutional approaches to farm household relations with factor markets devote more attention to the specific subjective motivations for (not) attracting external resources and the linkages between farm and non-farm allocation of resources. In case of absent or deficient finance or insurance markets, off-farm employment can then be considered as an important device for income diversification and risk management (Rosenzweig and Wolpin, 1993). Feder *et al.* (1990) explain that a clear difference should be made between households that do not borrow because they have sufficient liquidity from their own reserves, and credit-constrained households that cannot borrow. For the latter case, Maitra (1996) demonstrates that small farmers in rural India are able to compensate for income changes through adjustment of their labour market participation. Similar evidence on the opportunities for increasing engagement in off-farm employment in case of credit market failures can be found in Reardon *et al.* (1994) for sub-Saharan Africa, and in Jacoby (1993) for the Peruvian Sierra region.

The importance of off-farm employment has also been neglected in empirical studies on the expenditure of agricultural households. While attention is focused on income derived from land use and agricultural production, options to improve household food security or to intensify cropping systems financed with off-farm income have received little attention. Recently, the potential role of rural off-farm and non-farm employment has been emphasized again, looking for options to enhance household income and investment opportunities through selective engagement in the rural labour market (Lanjouw and Lanjouw, 1995; Reardon, 1997).

Members of rural households can use their labour force for a broad range of different activities. Besides working on their own farm or engaging in home work within the household, family labour can be allocated to *off-farm* employment and *non-farm* activities. In the latter case, family labour is mainly used for self-employment in commerce or small-scale manufacturing. These self-employed activities belong mainly to the domain of the non-agricultural sector. The concept of off-farm employment is reserved for permanent or temporary wage labour contracts that are arranged through the local labour market, with other farmers (for example, assistance in peak agricultural activities such as weeding and harvesting), in related processing activities, or in non-agricultural activities. Wage employment in the agricultural sector is subject to seasonality, while non-agricultural activities may permit a more stable contract. Migration is excluded from the analysis of labour allocation decisions and is only taken into account as far as remittances are received.

The implications of engagement in off-farm employment can be considered at two different levels. First, the individual choice of household members for wage labour contracts can be analyzed, paying attention to personal characteristics (that is, age, gender and education) that determine competitiveness on the labour market. Second, pooling of income sources at the household level is supposed,[1] enabling an appraisal of the impact of off-farm employment on household expenditure and consumption.

Analytical framework

The analytical framework for this chapter is based on farm household models (Sadoulet and de Janvry, 1995). Hence, we consider the household as a complex of the farm firm (combining inputs to produce agricultural outputs), the consumer household (spending money to maximize utility), and the worker household (supplying labour and earning wage income). We are especially interested in the impact of off-farm labour allocation on input-intensity of the farming system and the contribution of off-farm income to basic food security requirements. Moreover, we intend to verify whether off-farm (wage) income can function as a compensating device for credit.

Small farm households often face imperfect factor and commodity markets. In combination with high transaction costs, this implies limited tradability or high oppportunity costs for some production factors. Under these conditions of production and consumption, decisions cannot be kept separate. We focus our analysis on a situation of *selective* market failures: for example, limited access to the rural financial market while opportunities to participate in the rural labour market do exist. This implies that failures on the financial market may be partly or wholly compensated through engagement in the labour market. Limited use of credit resources does not necessarily imply, however, that credit is also constrained on the supply side. Households can *choose* not to take credit (because of high wealth or risk-averse behaviour), or can be *unable* to secure credit funds (access constraints). The latter case is more likely to occur in the segment of small-farm households. In order to distinguish between these situations, separate analyses are made for all households, and for those households with a component of wage-labour income.

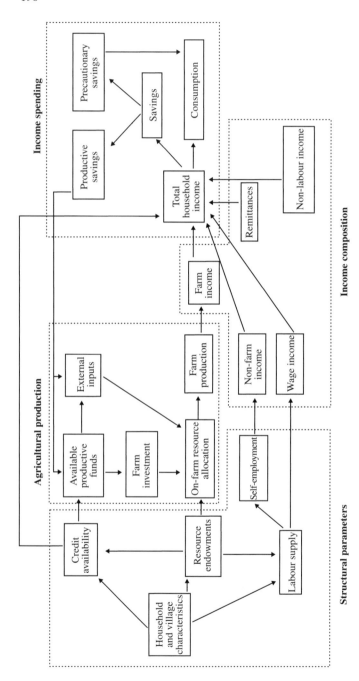

Figure 11.1 Analytical framework for the analysis of off-farm income

Figure 11.1 shows that risk and credit market imperfections influence both income-generation and consumption decisions. Agricultural production requires the use of external inputs, which must be financed from savings and credit. The availability of these funds will influence the capital intensity of agricultural production and the allocation of household resources between agricultural production and off-farm employment. As income fluctuates, liquid assets and credit are also important to guarantee a reasonable consumption level in low-income years. Credit market constraints and a limited savings capacity induce households to opt for income stabilization. Off-farm income is less volatile than income from agricultural production. Households may therefore choose a high level of labour market participation relative to agricultural production.

This leads us to the following hypotheses regarding the role of off-farm employment for small farm households:

1 *Probability of off-farm employment.* We hypothesize that specific individual and household characteristics will influence the possibilities for being engaged in off-farm employment. At the individual level, family members who are younger and better-educated are assumed to be more competitive. For certain activities (for example, coffee harvesting) female labourers are preferred, while in other activities (for example, land preparation, weeding) mainly male labour is used. At the household level, we hypothesize that the supply of labour for wage employment is higher on small farms facing less favourable resource endowments for agricultural production (for example, inferior soils, low dependency rate).

2 *Credit use and other income sources.* Engagement of household members in wage employment may be related to limitations in access to other factor markets. We hypothesize that small farms lacking collateral for borrowing or maintaining risk-averse behaviour *vis-à-vis* the rural financial market prefer wage labour in order to obtain access to necessary capital funds. Off-farm income can thus serve as a substitute for borrowing. We also hypothesize that wage income is lower when other income is higher.

3 *Production (input substitution) effects.* Since wage income can be used for the purchase of inputs, we hypothesize that there is a positive relationship between the value of wage income and the amount of external capital used in production. This effect may be reinforced by the decrease in labour availability because of the engagement in the labour market of the most productive members.

4   *Expenditure effects*. We hypothesize that, given the level of income, a higher share of wage income in total income means a higher food security. First, wage income is less volatile than crop income, and we therefore expect a higher consumption coefficient. Second, wage income that is not directly consumed can be used for the purchase of material inputs or for hiring contract labour, and can therefore increase farm income in the same period.

Empirical evidence

For the empirical analysis, we used the Encuesta Nacional de Consumo, Ingreso, Gasto y Nutrición 1993–94, an extensive database collected by the Agriculture and Resource Office (ARDO)/USAID/Honduras. The database covers a total of 2727 farm households located in all parts of Honduras. For our analysis, we only used data from rural farm households. After elimination of outliers, our sample consists of 1528 economically active family members and 629 farm households. We first present some descriptive statistics regarding the importance of different economic activities for the sample households and the extent to which they participate in the financial (credit) and labour markets. Then we test our basic hypotheses.

Descriptive analysis

Preliminary examination of the data indicates that farming is by far the main activity of Honduran farm households. Sixty per cent of all economically active adults[2] work on the family farm, 37 per cent engage in wage employment, and 33 per cent undertake self-employed non-agricultural activities. Most people do not restrict themselves to a single activity (see Table 11.1). At the household level, labour market participation is even higher than at the individual level: 56 per cent of all farm households have some wage income (see Table 11.2). Especially for smaller farms, non-agricultural income is important (see Figure 11.2).

In order to form a first impression of the relationship between farm and household characteristics and market participation, we classified the households according to their engagement in the labour or credit markets (Table 11.2). Credit-market participation is much lower than labour-market participation: only 7 per cent of all households reported a change in their debt position or the receiving of a loan during the 1993/4 agricultural cycle. Moreover, credit use seems not to be strongly

Table 11.1 Economic activities of farm household members

Activities	Economically active adults
Farming only	491 (32.1%)
Farming and wage employment	328 (21.5%)
Farming and own account, non-agriculture	82 (5.4%)
Wage employment only	211 (13.8%)
Own account, non-agriculture only	391 (25.6%)
Wage employment and own account, non-agriculture	15 (1.0%)
All three activities	10 (0.7%)
Total	**1528 (100%)**

Table 11.2 Market participation and farm and household characteristics

	No credit, no wage labour 246 (39.1%)	No credit, wage labour 338 (53.7%)	Credit, no wage labour 24 (3.8%)	Credit and wage labour 21 (3.3%)
Farm characteristics				
Farm area (*manzana*)	6.2	3.0	13.9	5.4
Level area (*manzana*)	2.0	0.7	3.2	2.2
Household characteristics				
Age household head	49	47	47	43
No. of household members	6	7	6	6
Percentage male household heads	87	88	88	100
Family income (lempiras)				
Real annual income	5761	5814	10746	4084
Real agricultural income	4060	2076	8013	1097
Wage income	0	2683	0	2365
Remittances	162	77	100	158
Food security				
Nutritional adequacy >0.99	0.15	0.09	0.46	0.14
Nutritional adequacy >0.80	0.35	0.26	0.63	0.24

Note: 1 US$ = 10 lempiras (1994).

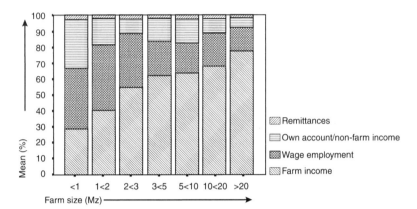

Figure 11.2 Farm size and income composition in rural Honduras, 1993/4

related to farm size. This confirms our observation in the previous section that land is generally not accepted as collateral.

There seems to be an inverse relationship between wage income and farm income. Nutritional status as calculated by ARDO/USAID/Honduras is low for all groups. Food adequacy is computed by assigning a daily calorie and protein requirement to all household members, summing it over the household and dividing it by the actual household consumption. The result is two ratios: nutritional adequacy is more than 0.99 if both ratios are higher than 0.99. The high frequency of values as low as 0.20 may indicate that the actual needs are lower than the computed requirements.

Labour market participation

Using probit analysis, we estimated the probability that an individual engages in wage employment as a function of individual and household characteristics. The results are presented in Table 11.3. As expected, individuals from small-farm households with poor quality soils are most likely to be engaged in wage labour. The effect of soil quality is substantially larger than that of soil quantity. Moreover, the smaller the amount of produce marketed, the higher the chance that an individual has a wage income. Members of households with non-farm commercial activities are somewhat less inclined to sell their labour, indicating that substitution possibilities are relatively limited. With respect to individual characteristics, gender and education have the

Table 11.3 Probability of labour market participation by economically active adults

Variable	Coefficient	Significance	Marginal effect at mean
Regional dummies			
Rural West	−0.28208	0.00100	−0.10130
Rural South	−0.02614	0.77705	−0.00939
Farm characteristics			
Farm area	−0.04293	0.00000	−0.01542
Percentage of flat land	−0.30309	0.00007	−0.10884
Technical assistance (yes = 1)	−0.08429	0.55308	−0.03027
Tenancy dummy (owned = 1)	−0.07361	0.32363	−0.02643
Production costs/mz	0.00002	0.90905	0.00001
Household characteristics			
No. of adults	0.00541	0.81048	0.00194
Share self-consumption	0.35305	0.00138	0.12678
Credit dummy (yes = 1)[1]	−0.08740	0.58223	−0.03139
Remittances	−0.00016	0.15693	−0.00006
Non-farm income	−0.00009	0.00000	−0.00003
Individual characteristics			
Age	0.04749	0.00025	0.01705
Age squared	−0.00069	0.00004	−0.00025
Sex dummy (male = 1)	−1.09570	0.00000	−0.39347
Education (primary school = 1)	0.95100	0.00000	0.34151
Constant	0.72657	0.02595	0.26091

Notes: [1]Loan taken and/or a change in debt position.
Pseudo R^2: 0.54.
Predicted correctly: 71%.

largest influence on participation in the labour market. Economically active women participate much more often in the labour market than men. Since we excluded housewives from the sample, this means that women who are engaged in productive activities are very likely to sell their labour on the market. This can be explained by the importance of coffee harvesting for rural employment. Contrary to our expectations, older people are more likely to work off-farm. This indicates that experience is an important factor for wage labourers. The positive effect of age is, nevertheless, very small and strongest for young people.

Off-farm income, other income sources and the use of credit

We analyzed the relationship between wage income, other income and credit use by directly regressing wage income on all other sources of

Table 11.4 Relationships between wage income and other income sources, dependent variable = log(wage income)

Variable	Coefficient	Significance	Marginal effect at mean
log(remittances)	−0.18614	0.06762	−0.17249
log(change in debt position)	−0.67580	0.02132	−0.62626
log(farm income)	−0.78926	0.00000	−0.73140
log(non-farm income)	−0.18827	0.01236	−0.17447
Constant	8.57150	0.00000	7.94310
s^2	5.90490	0.00000	

income, including credit (see Table 11.4). As wage income is censored at zero, we used tobit regression. The coefficients can be interpreted as elasticities, as we used a double logarithmic specification of the wage function.

The results confirm our hypothesis of substitution between wage income and other sources of income. The effects are particularly large for farm and credit income. The negative sign for all other income categories indicates the inverse relationship. Households with a farm income that is 10 per cent lower than that of the mean household have a wage income that is more than 7 per cent higher. A similar (10 per cent) change in debt position means a difference in wage income of over 6 per cent. The effects for remittances and non-farm income are somewhat smaller (almost 2 per cent for a difference of 10 per cent).

The relatively high substitution effect between wage income and farm income is easily explained. As long as the marginal product of family labour is higher than the effective off-farm wage and the shadow value of leisure, labour will be used for farm production. If the off-farm wage is higher, household members will prefer working off-farm. A rise in productive capacity of the family farm therefore implies an increase in the amount of labour used in farm production and a higher farm income. Both result in a lower off-farm income (the latter because the shadow value of leisure is determined not only by the number of hours worked, but also by income). A similar effect was expected for self-employed non-farm income, but the coefficient is much smaller. This indicates that non-farm operations are relatively isolated activities. This has already been indicated by Table 11.1, demonstrating that few individuals combine non-farm activities and wage labour (or even farm work). Also, the coefficient for remittances is relatively low. This is not surprising, since remittances are exogenous and do not compete for labour. Hence, there is only an income effect. Seen in this light, the high coefficient for credit income is surprising, even more so because it is a 'temporary' source of income: at some time in the future these loans must be repaid. Apparently, the role of credit – stabilization of income over the years and generating funds for investment – is in many cases overtaken by wage income.

Production effects of off-farm employment

As discussed in the previous section, the presence of credit constraints causes interdependence of agricultural production and other income sources of the household. Tables 11.5 and 11.6 show that this interdependence is indeed important for the sample households. We regressed the monetary value of external inputs per *manzana* on the values of income from different sources. Because the level of inputs is often zero, we used tobit regression. We correct for differences in relative prices and fixed factor availability. By using inputs per *manzana* as a dependent variable, we implicitly take the most important fixed factor – land – into account. The availability of family labour could also be considered as a fixed factor. However, its coefficient is not significant, which indicates the possibility of substitution with hired labour. Since price data were not available, we used regional dummies to account for possible price differences. However, the low significance implies that the dummies are not very adequate.

When we consider the income variables, we see that for the entire sample only the coefficient for the change in debt position is significant (see Table 11.5). Apparently, credit plays a pivotal role in the finance of

Table 11.5 Income sources and capital intensity of agricultural production (all households), dependent variable = log(production costs/mz)

Variable	Coefficient	Significance	Marginal effect at mean
Regional dummies			
Rural West	0.33752	0.09827	0.32044
Rural South	0.15822	0.47182	0.15021
Fixed inputs			
log(adults/mz)	−0.09556	0.27630	−0.09073
Income effects			
log(wage income)	−0.00352	0.88202	−0.00334
log(remittances)	0.01624	0.64172	0.01542
log(non-farm income)	−0.00201	0.93730	−0.00192
log(change in debt position)	0.14245	0.06978	0.13524
Constant	3.52580	0.00000	3.34740
s^2	2.15110	0.00000	

Table 11.6 Wage income and capital intensity of agricultural production (households with wage income), dependent variable = ln(production costs/mz)

Variable	Coefficient	Significance	Marginal effect at mean
Regional dummies			
Rural West	0.21677	0.42737	0.14477
Rural South	0.03746	0.89591	0.02502
Fixed inputs			
ln(adults/mz)	−0.09302	0.43305	−0.06212
Income effects			
ln(wage income)	0.35602	0.00354	0.23775
ln(remittances)	0.03030	0.54577	0.02023
ln(non-farm income)	−0.03620	0.32541	−0.02418
ln(change in debt position)	0.05381	0.79484	0.03594
Constant	0.92672	0.33334	0.61887
s^2	2.13590	0.00000	

input purchase for agricultural production: a household with a change in debt position that is 10 per cent higher than the mean has an input use that is about 1 per cent higher. When we restrict our analysis, however, to those households with labour income (see Table 11.6), credit stops being important.[3] Wage income seems to take over its role as source of funds for agricultural input purchase. The effect is almost twice as high as the effect of credit for all households. Interestingly, remittances and income from non-farm self-employment do not play this role. We therefore suppose that savings from non-farm income are mainly invested in non-farm activities and not so much in agriculture. Similarly, remittances may be used mainly for consumptive purposes.

Off-farm employment and food security

In order to analyze the expenditure effects of off-farm employment, we regressed a proxy for food security with the different income categories of the sample households. Again, we included regional dummies to account for price differences. As a food security proxy we use the calorie adequacy described in the previous paragraph. We chose calorie adequacy and not protein adequacy because, in general, the former is lower. A squatter plot of (the log of) calorie adequacy on (the log of) income shows that the correlation is low. As a result, the explanatory power of the regression is limited.[4] Nevertheless, the regression renders some interesting insights (see Table 11.7).

Table 11.7 Income sources and food security (all households), dependent variable = ln(calorie consumption/calorie needs)

Variable	Coefficient	Standard error	*t*-statistic	Significance
Regional dummies				
Rural West	−0.168300	0.043549	−3.864639	0.0001
Rural South	−0.033082	0.042230	−0.783364	0.4338
Income effects				
ln(farm income per capita)	0.087047	0.015786	5.514068	0.0000
ln(remittances per capita)	0.032762	0.010232	3.201757	0.0014
ln(non-farm income per capita)	0.006566	0.007828	0.838741	0.4020
ln(change in debt position per capita)	−0.007891	0.028122	−0.280603	0.7791
ln(wage income per capita)	−0.005466	0.006631	−0.824341	0.4101
Smoothing				
Credit dummy	0.357324	0.105709	3.380253	0.0008
Constant	3.728230	0.102636	36.324630	0.0000

Notes: White Heteroscedasticity-Consistent Standard Errors & Covariance Adjusted R^2: 0.13.

Agricultural income is most important for food security: a 10 per cent rise in farm income implies an improvement of 0.9 per cent in nutritional adequacy. This is not surprising, since it includes consumption of own produce. Also, the effect of remittances is significant: an improvement of 0.2 in food adequacy as a result of an increase of 10 per cent in remittances. The effects of the other sources of income are not significant. This seems to imply that these are not used directly for food consumption.

For households with access to wage income, however, all income sources but credit are important for food security (see Table 11.8). Wage income is becoming more important: a rise of 10 per cent of wage income causes a rise of 1.1 per cent in food security, while the same rise in agricultural income increases food security by only 0.4 per cent. The influence of remittances and non-agricultural income is even smaller. The fact that the change in debt position is not significant in either equation is not caused by collinearity with the credit use dummy. Inclusion of this dummy hardly changes the coefficients of the other variables. However, it shows that – despite the insignificance of the coefficient for the change in debt position – credit is very important for food security. *Ceteris paribus*, a change from not participating to participating in the credit market implies an improvement in food security

Table 11.8   Income sources and food security (households with wage income), dependent variable = ln(calorie consumption/calorie needs)

Variable	Coefficient	Standard error	*t*-statistic	Significance
Regional dummies				
Rural West	−0.194018	0.058005	−3.344816	0.0009
Rural South	−0.097460	0.053067	−1.836554	0.0673
Income effects				
ln(farm income per capita)	0.043151	0.020135	2.143123	0.0330
ln(remittances per capita)	0.023123	0.013500	1.712736	0.0879
ln(non-farm income per capita)	0.015384	0.010127	1.519151	0.1298
ln(change in debt position per capita)	−0.038441	0.062600	−0.614074	0.5397
ln(wage income per capita)	0.096367	0.028349	3.399338	0.0008
Smoothing				
Credit dummy	0.352699	0.172939	2.039445	0.0423
Constant	3.383105	0.174656	19.370050	0.0000

of a factor $e^{0.35} = 1.4$ for all households. The effect is the same for households with and without wage income.

Policy implications

Rural households in the Honduran countryside are becoming increasingly involved in market exchange, but face highly imperfect exchange conditions on local factor and commodity markets. While access to rural land and financial markets is severely restricted, options for participation in the labour market are becoming more important. Consequently, peasant livelihood strategies are not only related to farm production, but also depend to a large extent on engagement with the rural labour market. Off-farm employment contributes an important share to household income, and is especially important for those families possessing smaller farms and poor soil quality who maintain a low level of commoditization. Female household members and members with a higher educational level are more likely to be engaged in off-farm employment.

Taking into account multiple income sources at household level – farming, wage labour and non-agricultural self-employed activities – we registered that more than half of all households receive (at least part of their) income from wage labour, while most families combine two or three activities in order to diversify their income composition. The latter tendency can be explained by the preference for income diversification under conditions of high risk and/or by the occurrence of (selective) market failures. We focused our attention on the latter aspect, since small-farm households may prefer engagement in off-farm employment in order to compensate for the limited use of rural credit. In fact, a significant and inverse relationship between wage income and change in the debt position was confirmed, revealing that income derived from off-farm employment can partly replace credit. Similarly, between farm and off-farm income substitution is also large. Off-farm income proved to be less a substitute for income derived from remittances and from non-farm activities, indicating that these income sources are most likely to be used for the purchase of durables and less for financing current consumption or variable input purchase.

The empirical analysis allows us to draw a number of policy conclusions with respect to the potential contribution of off-farm employment to improve farm household food security and farming systems intensification. Positive production and expenditure effects of wage income from off-farm employment were confirmed. Farming systems intensification based on increased use of externally purchased inputs is strongly influenced by the availability of wage labour. Income derived from remittances or non-farm activities does not have a significant effect on input purchase and seems mainly to be used for consumptive purposes. Compared with credit, wage income has a stronger impact on input purchase (for those households participating in the labour market).

Food security objectives can be enhanced effectively through off-farm employment, since an important part of wage income is used for consumptive expenditure. The high and strongly significant coefficient for the use of credit also confirms the importance of rural finance for consumption-smoothing. Increase of wage income contributes far more to food security than an equivalent increase in the amount of remittances, as the latter will be used for the purchase of durables. In particular for small-farm households, marginal income from off-farm employment contributes even more to the level of calorie adequacy than does farm production.

Targeted rural development policies and programmes whose objective is to contribute to improvement of food security objectives through a higher participation of certain members of peasant households in the labour market can be expected to yield favourable income and expenditure effects and tend to be far more cost-effective compared to credit-orientated interventions. Engagement in rural off-farm employment also contributes more to food security than does income from non-farm activities and remittances. Resources available from the Honduran Social Investment Fund (FHIS) at the time of writing could therefore better be made available to enhance non-agricultural employment instead of the actual focus of this programme on capital-intensive rural physical infrastructure.

Demand for off-farm employment opportunities is most important for small farm households located in marginal (hillside) regions characterized by a high degree of home production. As can be expected, credit and technical assistance are of limited importance to these households. Improving individual chances to be engaged in the rural labour market requires targeting in favour of female household members and a strong emphasis on education, since these variables demonstrate the strongest effects on labour market participation.

Notes

The empirical analyses presented in this chapter are based on data derived from the Encuesta Nacional de Consumo, Ingreso, Gasto y Nutrición 1993–94 (CIENS94) database that was made available by the Agricultural and Natural Resource Office (ARDO) of the USAID mission in Honduras (ARDO/USAID contract no. 522-8103-C-3315-00). We owe thanks to Dr Mike Wise for permission to use this database for research purposes. Ir. Eelco Mol (currently working with FAO Honduras) helped with preliminary processing of the database. The authors are responsible for the analysis and the conclusions presented.

1. Differences in intra-household income distribution are thus neglected in this analysis.
2. Defined as farm household members over fifteen years of age, working in at least one of the three activities (total number of 1864 household members).
3. If we run the estimation for those households without wage income, the results are similar to the results for the entire sample.
4. We tried to improve the regression by taking calorie consumption per capita as dependent, but this hardly changed the results.

Bibliography

Baumeister, E., Wattel, C. J., Salgado, R., Posas, M., Kaimowitz, D. and Clarex, L. (1996) *El agro Hondureño y su futuro*, Tegucigalpa: Editorial Guaymuras.

Boyer, J. C. (1986) 'Capitalism, Campesinos and Calories in Southern Honduras', *Urban Anthropology*, vol. 15, nos 1/2, pp. 3–24.

Brockett, C. D. (1987) 'The Commercialization of Agriculture and Rural Development in Honduras', *Studies in Comparative International Development*, vol. 22, no. 1, pp. 82–102.

Brockett, C. D. (1988) *Land, Power and Poverty: Agrarian Transformation and Political Conflict in Central America*, Boston, Mass.: Unwin Hyman.

CADESCA (1989) *Encuesta de caracterización de los productores de granos básicos*, Tegucigalpa: CEE-PFSA.

DGEC (1988) *Encuesta Permanente de Hogares de Propósitos Múltiples – Area Rural*, Tegucigalpa: Secretaría de Planificación, Coordinación y Presupuesto, Dirección General de Estadistica y Censos.

Díaz, E. and Cruz, D. (1992) *Ajuste estructural, términos de intercambio interno y la pequeña producción de granos básicos en Honduras*, San José: CDR-ULA/ PRIAG-IICA-ALA.

Fadiño, J. M., Coles, A., Caballero, L. and Stanfield, D. (1986) *La titulación de tierras y la estructura social rural en Honduras*, Wisconsin: Land Tenure Centre.

Feder, G., Lau, L. J., Lin, Y. and Luo, X. (1990) 'The Relationship between Credit and Productivity in Chinese Agriculture: A Microeconomic Model of Disequilibrium', *American Journal of Agricultural Economics*, vol. 72, pp. 1151–7.

Jacoby, H. H. (1993) 'Shadow Wages and Peasant Family Labour Supply: An Econometric Application to the Peruvian Sierra', *Review of Economic Studies*, vol. 60, pp. 903–21.

Lanjouw, J. O. and Lanjouw, P. (1995) *Rural non-farm Employment: A Survey*, World Bank Policy Research Working Paper No. 1463, Washington DC.

Maitra, P. (1996) *Is Consumption Smooth at the Cost of Volatile Leisure? An Investigation of Rural India*, Los Angeles: University of Southern California, Department of Economics.

PREALC (Programa Regional del Empleo para América Latina y el Caribe) (1986) *Cambio y polarización ocupacional en Centroamérica*, Costa Rica: EDUCA.

Reardon, T., Crawford, E. and Kelly, V. (1994) 'Links Between Nonfarm Income and Farm Investment in African Households: Adding the Capital Market Perspective', *American Journal of Agricultural Economics*, vol. 76, pp. 1172–6.

Reardon, T. (1997) 'Using Evidence of Household Income Diversification to Inform Study of the Rural Nonfarm Labour Market in Africa', *World Development*, vol. 25, no. 5, pp. 735–747.

Rosenzweig, M. R. and Wolpin, K. I. (1993) 'Credit Market Constraints, Consumption Smoothing, and the Accumulation of Durable Production Assets in Low-income Countries: Investment in Bullocks in India', *Journal of Political Economy*, vol. 101, no. 2, pp. 223–44.

Sadoulet, E. and de Janvry, A. (1995) *Quantitative Development Policy Analysis*, Baltimore, MD and London: Johns Hopkins University Press.

Salgado, R. (ed.) (1994) *El mercado de tierras en Honduras*, Tegucigalpa: CEDOH for POSCAE and LTC Wisconsin.

SECPLAN-SRN (1994) *IV Censo nacional agropecuario 1993*, Tegucigalpa: Secretaría de Planificación, Coordinación y Presupuesto/Secretaria de Recursos Naturales.

Swindale, A. J. (1994) *La seguridad alimentaria en Honduras: resultados de la Encuesta Nacional de Indicadores Socioeconómicos de 1993–94*, Tegucigalpa: USAID.

World Bank (1994) *Honduras: Country Economic Memorandum and Poverty Assessment*, World Bank Report No. 13317-HO, Washington DC.

12
Seasonal Migration and Peasant Livelihood Strategies: Migration of Nicaraguan Smallholders to Costa Rica

Giel Ton

Introduction

The classical debate in migration studies has long been about whether rural outmigration should be considered to bring about relief from demographic pressures that challenge the reproduction of rural social life, or whether it should be considered a way in which rural social structures are changed by diffusion of new ideas that have 'uprooting effects' and accelerate social change (Goldschneider, 1984). Both positions concentrated on the cultural impact of migration. When economic consequences were mentioned, emphasis was laid on transfer mechanisms between the urban and the rural, and between industrial capitalism and rural peasant production. Analysis of the changes as a result of migration in access to and control over crucial resources necessary for peasant production and reproduction (Wood, 1980; Sen, 1981) and the 'array' of adaptive strategies of the individual peasant to cope with opportunities and constraints in the household production system (Long and van der Ploeg, 1989), challenged simplistic thinking about 'the' peasant and 'the' rural social structure. Not only the complex social composition of rural societies, but also the dynamics of peasant livelihood strategies and 'real' markets are now focal points for social research. Stonich analyzes for Honduras:

> The participation of rural families in diverse economic activities is essential, in part, because of the failure of any single activity to provide an adequate living. This inadequacy is a product of the environmental constraints encountered in highland areas, the growing population and the low level of returns to labor and its products. Participation in multiple economic activities allows the maintenance

and reproduction of the household under adverse circumstances... The fact that integration into a poorly paid seasonal labor force can be functional for peasants explains in part their compliance with an exploitative system. When the ability to meet subsistence needs through agriculture is limited by forces beyond their control, families welcome direct participation in the cash economy as a way to make ends meet. (Stonich, 1991, pp. 158–9)

She concludes that agricultural development policies should evaluate their impact on the possibilities that family members have to participate in seasonal labour markets and that households' decisions to migrate affect agricultural practices and limit farmers' flexibility in adopting new agricultural technologies: 'Development efforts should endeavor to augment access to productive resources through effective land reform and improved land rental agreements or, if these are not forthcoming, through enhanced opportunities for off-farm employment' (Stonich, 1991, pp. 160–1).

We shall try to take the argument a step further by emphasizing that seasonal migration can be beneficial for poor peasants even without strong government interference. We shall present material that supports the hypothesis that seasonal migration could provide an incentive for endogenous agricultural development, conceptualizing it as a mechanism for saving and investment for even the poorest sections of the peasantry.

Migration from Nicaragua to Costa Rica

Migration from Nicaragua to Costa Rica is not a recent phenomenon, but form and extent changed a lot during the 1990s. Political or war-related push factors have disappeared and towards the end of the decade migrant motivations are essentially economic (ILO, 1995, p. 9). Migration increased rapidly from 50 000 at the end of the 1970s, to 150 000 in the early 1990s and to at least 350 000 in 1997. Numbers are only estimates, as no reliable data exist on illegal migration between the two countries, and recent figures on employment for Nicaraguan migrants in Costa Rica are absent.

Demand for cheap labour comes principally from agro-export plantations in Costa Rica. To a lesser extent, employment can be found in construction and for women as domestic workers. Most Nicaraguan migrant workers are peasants who lack attractive employment opportunities in Nicaragua. Some of them stay permanently in Costa Rica, bring in their families and act as brokers for other relatives who want to migrate. In this way they become permanent residents and rely on public services provided by taxpayers' money (for education, health and so on). While no precise data exist on the proportion of migrants that 'settle down', Costa Rican public opinion assumes it to be the majority, and presses for restrictive policies (Wiley, 1995, p. 425). This characteristic image of the Nicaraguan migrant is also reflected in policy documents:

> Generally, once his first temporary job in the fields has finished, the migrant, considering the situation of unemployment that awaits him in his home country, decides to search for new employment ... When the migrant attains a certain level of stability ... he brings in his family and they will try to establish themselves in a more permanent way in Costa Rica. (ILO, 1995, p. 10)

We believe this image should be reconsidered. The supply of Nicaraguan labour is concentrated in the dry season (December–May), when thousands of peasants migrate temporally to Costa Rica. They return to Nicaragua to work their fields when the wet season begins. This category of migrants, not aiming to stay for a longer period in Costa Rica, is absent from most policy documents, and has therefore been underestimated and undervalued as an economic productive activity. Costa Rican migration policies have long been based on the dichotomy of political refugees and illegal migrants (Wiley, 1995). International cooperation has focused on political refugees and cannot cope with diffuse categories. As identity and status was difficult to determine for large groups of immigrants, seasonal migrants could easily be stigmatized as being illegal and parasitic on Costa Rican society. However, this attitude has changed somewhat over time. Special regulations now exist for seasonal work at harvest-time ('the seasonal work card'), but these do not regulate international migration, as the card gives permission only to work, but not to enter or leave the country. We believe that special migration policies for seasonal migrants are of utmost importance to regularize demand and supply of labour. At the same time, they would strengthen survival strategies and rural development in the Nicaraguan smallholder areas.

Many development projects aim to establish conditions for a sustainable peasant economy, increasingly based on a comprehensive approach to productive activities carried out within the farm unit, but rarely paying attention to off-farm activities. Many field workers consider seasonal migration of peasants to be an obstacle to development: they are not on their farm for several months of the year, they participate less in extension activities, and they have difficulty in implementing soil conservation techniques, establishing plant nurseries and so on. Many projects concentrate on the people who stay more permanently in the villages. In this way, the seasonal migrants 'disappear' as important actors for rural development. Even when temporary absence is accepted, beneficial effects of seasonal migration on agricultural production are ignored. This article attempts to present some arguments that indicate the importance of income from activities 'outside' the farm for the development of the production system 'inside' it. We use the terms 'outside' and 'inside' as we want to stress that seasonal migration is an integral part of the production system: seasonal migration is made possible because of the subsistence base provided by farm production, and farm production is facilitated to a large extent by migrant income.

In this chapter we shall highlight the expenditure effects of migrant income and relate these to livelihood strategies, agricultural development and social mobility in a relatively homogeneous semi-arid region in north Nicaragua. The research took place in Condega, a small agricultural village in the north of Nicaragua, 35 km north of Estelí.[1] The municipality has 27000 inhabitants, of which 18000 live in the rural area, and 2352 families are registered as agricultural producers (Alcaldía Condega, 1996, p. 73). The Pire Area, a watershed area around the Rio Pire, comprises 34 per cent of total producers, settled in seventeen hamlets. The survey sample was taken from five hamlets in the Pire Area, which form part of the nine villages participating in the ACCP (Condega Peasant Association 'Conociéndonos y Produciendo'). These hamlets are Chagüite Grande (56 households); La Laguna de los Hernández (69 households); El Algodonal (30 households); El Espino (40 households); and La Labranza No. 2 (140 households), totalling almost 2000 habitants.

A list of peasant producers (Alcaldía Condega, 1995) was used to select respondents. Sample size was 109 out of a total household population of 335 (33 per cent). Additional information was gathered through six detailed budget studies of seasonal migrants working in Costa Rica. Other data are derived from a general demographic census by key informants in each hamlet (UNAN-ESECA/UNAG-COOPIBO, 1995a) and from a detailed description of farming systems in the region (TLOD-UNAG, 1990).

Migration in the Pire Area

The Pire Area consists of volcanic terraces eroded by rivers and rainfall, resulting in a mountainous topography with steep slopes (Zelaya, 1995). Some relatively flat highland areas exist (*mesas*), but most agriculture is on slopes with a gradient between 15 per cent and 40 per cent at an altitude of 750–1000 m. Table 12.1 indicates the small average plot size and homogeneous crop pattern.

The peasant households depend almost completely on agriculture and migration. Main crops are maize and beans, and 62 per cent of all families have some cattle. Cash income comes from migration, red beans, eggs and, incidentally, from cattle. There is no non-agricultural employment in the area, except a few jobs in construction, petty retailing and teaching.

The survey provided data from which gross average income of peasant families from the most important subsystems could be estimated: basic grains (cereals and beans), meat and migration. No data was gathered on other subsystems: milk processing (cheese and fresh milk), irregular paid labour inside the area (*al día*), or petty retailing. When we compare these gross values of production, migration appears to be only slightly less important than basic grain production in the 1994/5 season (with low agricultural prices).[2] If we compare the cash income from each subsystem the picture shows even more contrast. Only part of the agricultural production is sold; most of it is used for direct household consumption. Migration proves to be by far the most important cash generator in the area.[3]

Table 12.1   Farm size and land use in the Pire area (in *manzana* = 0.7 hectare)

Crops	Primera		Postrera	Total
Maize	1.92		0.29	2.21
Red Beans	0.78		1.32	2.10
Sorghum	0.17		0.28	0.45
Coffee		0.20		0.20
Other	0.19		0.13	0.32
Cultivated area	3.26		2.22	5.28
Arable land		2.82		2.82
Pasture and bush		2.78		2.78
Crop intensity				±150%

Source: Siles and Ramos, 1996.

Table 12.2 Average gross value of production for the major subsystems, 1995/6, in córdobas (1 US\$ = 7 C\$)

Subsystem	Average gross value
Basic grains	2863
Cattle	429
Yard production	857
Migration to Costa Rica	2152
Total	**6301**

Source: UNAN-ESECA/UNAG-COOPIBO, 1995b; Cáceres *et al.*, 1996.

The agricultural calendar shows two clearly defined seasons: a wet season (May–November) and a dry season (December–April). The wet season is divided by a month with relatively little rainfall (August): *la primera* from May to July, and *la postrera* from September to November. These seasons determine to a large extent the possibilities for male (self-)employment on the farm.

Yard production (small-scale husbandry, fruit trees, etc.) and housework, culturally defined as work for women, are less affected by climate. Migration of women is basically constrained by their domestic position. The number of women migrating is much lower compared with men and concentrated in the period when they do not have large families. Most female migrants find employment as domestic workers in urban areas within Nicaragua, some of them work in coffee picking and a few look for work in Costa Rica (usually as domestic workers too). Women with migrant husbands or sons show contradictory emotions concerning temporary male absence. On the one hand, the workload increases and feelings of insecurity are stronger. But, on the other hand, they have more responsibilities, more self-esteem and enjoy more freedom and mobility. The situation of women in Pire is very similar to that of women in Guanacaste in Northern Costa Rica:

migrant women tend to move in accordance with their traditional gender-assigned reproductive roles in the context of male-headed households. However, ... as members of households with migrant partners, women do enjoy certain freedoms and authority denied to their counterparts whose domestic space is constantly occupied by men. (Chant, 1992, p. 68)

Staple food production, culturally defined as work for men, is related directly to climatic conditions. The dry season is the period when most

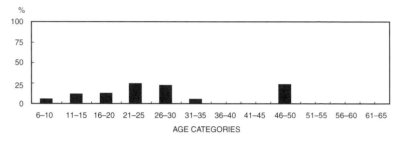

Figure 12.1   Migration of women by age category
Source: ESECA-UNAN/UNAG-COOPIBO, 1995b.

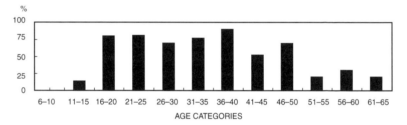

Figure 12.2   Migration of men by age category
Source: ESECA-UNAN/UNAG-COOPIBO, 1995b.

men work outside the area. In this period there is structural sub-employment of male labour in rain-fed farming systems. Migration is constrained mainly by age: the elderly do not migrate as much as younger people. Average age of the migrating heads of households is 37 years, while the average age of heads of households who stay in the area is 48 years.

Historically, men migrate to the coffee-picking areas and to the sugar plantations in Nicaragua (Jinotega and Chinandega). After 1990, opportunities to enter Costa Rica improved as the civil war ended. Neo-liberal monetary policies tempered real salaries inside Nicaragua and made Costa Rican wages very attractive. Most people interviewed did not experience difficulties in finding employment. The *zafra*, the sugar-cane harvest in the Guanacaste area, in particular, provides ample employment. Other migrants from Pire work for banana companies in the Limón area, and a few in the coffee areas around San José and cattle ranches in Guanacaste.

A census by local leaders indicates that migration is a generalized phenomenon, as 91 per cent of all households experience migration of one or more members to outside the Pire area. Migration to Costa Rica occurs from 87 per cent of all households. Sixty-seven per cent of all males older than 16 years of age migrate outside the area during the dry season. If we assume that 80 per cent of them go to Costa Rica, this means that 770 people leave the Pire Area and cross the border each year.

To understand the motivation of these migrants it is important to know that the 1994 maize harvest was very bad (10 cwt/household), while red bean production was excellent (26 cwt/household). Many migrants needed cash to complement basic consumption needs during 1995. Some did sell beans in order to generate cash, but bean prices reached an all-time low that year (US$15–20/100 lb). Many peasants decided to sell only part of the crop just to cover travel expenses and generate cash in Costa Rica. Table 12.3 shows the 'expenditure basket' for migrant income produced from budget studies.

The 1995 harvest showed a different picture: a very good maize harvest (24 cwt/household) but a very low bean yield (6 cwt/household). Though most families had enough food to match family consumption (an estimated 20 cwt maize and 5 cwt beans for the year), cash needs could not be covered by selling agricultural products. For many households, migration income was the prime cash generator, not only for consumer goods, but especially for agricultural inputs and debts.

Migration proves to be a very effective resource for solving cash needs related to agricultural production in high-risk conditions (for example, weather and prices). Migration revenues are used to buy agricultural inputs or other means of production. These revenues also stabilize consumption capacity as they are independent of weather conditions and regional price fluctuations (Ruben and Clemens, 1996).

Table 12.3 Expenditure from migratory income (1994/5)

Expenditure	Amount	Percentage
Food	210	10
Clothes	740	34
Herbicides	150	7
Fertilizers	550	26
Debts	350	16
Other	150	7
Total	**2150**	**100**

Source: UNAN-ESECA/UNAG-COOPIBO, 1995b.

The Pire Area provides a strong case for this argument on the interrelationship between migration and agricultural production. A significant proportion of migrant income is invested in farm-based productive activities. Food security improves, as migration income both reduces the need to sell agricultural products and improves the access to food by enlarging the peasants' purchasing power. More importantly, migrant income seems to form the basis for accumulation for most Pire families: they use migration revenues to improve their homes, buy cattle and buy land.[4]

At the same time, travelling to and staying in Costa Rica enlarge the cultural horizon and probably the aspirations for personal well-being. For many young people, working in Costa Rica provides them with a means of independence from their parents. In the situation of acute poverty from which they come, it is very unlikely that they would be able to generate resources in another way.

Different patterns of migration

In the relatively homogeneous Pire Area we identified two different patterns of migration: organized migration to sugar estates; and individual migration to banana plantations. Analysis of variance shows that the villages differ significantly from each other when one looks at the proportion of migrants going to the banana plantations or sugar estates. In Chagüite Grande, and La Laguna de los Hernández at least 50 per cent of all migrants work in the banana plantations, while in La Labranza No. 2 and El Algodonal this is less than 5 per cent, and in El Espino 16 per cent. Most migrants from these villages work in the sugar-cane harvest. We assume that an important reason for this difference is the presence of an 'organizer' in La Labranza. The organizer is an intermediary between the labour contractor in Costa Rica and the interested peasants. The Costa Rican labour contractor plans the number of labourers s/he needs to harvest a particular area and 'orders' that number of migrants from the organizer. On a fixed date, the organizer delivers the migrants at a fixed spot in Costa Rica. After smuggling several groups of migrants over the border, the organizer works as a supervisor during the harvest. S/he serves as both an employee of the contractor and a spokesperson for the migrants in labour disputes (Ton, 1996).

In most hamlets, migration to Costa Rica is a recent phenomenon: few peasants have migrated more than twice to Costa Rica. But particularly in La Labranza No. 2, migration to Costa Rica seems to be

Table 12.4 Migration patterns of villages

Village	Sugar estates	Banana plantations	No data	Total	Migration experience (times/ migrant)	Incidence (percentage of total households)
Labranza No. 2	13	1	5	19	3.1	42
El Espino	3	1	2	6	1.3	46
Algodonal	2	0	3	5	1.0	45
La Laguna	2	3	1	6	1.0	32
Chagüite	2	5	3	10	1.4	48

Source: UNAN-ESECA/UNAG-COOPIBO, 1995b.

establishing itself as a regular custom. It is important to stress that peasants from both El Espino and La Labranza No. 2 have had experience of sugar-cane harvesting, as they worked previously in the sugar estates in Chinandega, and cane-cutting has always been part of survival strategies in these hamlets. What is new is the geographical location and the extent to which peasants participate in migration. In both hamlets, 39 per cent of all migrants to Costa Rica mention that they have worked previously in cane harvesting. Analyzing the working experience of all migrants in the Pire Area who work in cane harvesting, 73 per cent of them have had experience of this in Nicaragua. If we calculate the migrants with cane-cutting experience within the group of migrants working in banana plantations it turns out to be only 8 per cent. But 54 per cent of the banana migrants have had previous experience in coffee-picking. This difference is understandable, as salaries in cane harvesting are related to the amount of cane harvested. In banana plantations, pay is related to work time. Experienced cane-cutters therefore have advantages that result in higher average income compared to inexperienced workers.

Factors that influence the probability of migration

It is important to examine the social position of the seasonal migrants: are they the landless, the better-educated, or peasants who can mobilize sufficient cash for travel expenses? Following suggestions by Todaro (1976, pp. 60–3), we have opted for logistic regression as our statistical analysis method. This procedure estimates the coefficients of a probabilistic model, involving a set of independent variables that best predict the value of a dichotomous dependent variable. For all cases, the probability of migration is calculated. If the probability is less than 0.50 the case is ranked as non-migrant, and if over 0.50 as migrant. The factors are selected that best predict observed values. One of the main advantages of this procedure is the possibility of including a variety of categorical variables where linearity cannot be assumed, for example age categories, types of land tenure arrangement, or different geographical locations.

If we analyze the output of the logistic regression we see that some factors prove to be significantly related to the propensity to migrate. The logistic regression model can ascertain fairly accurately if a peasant did or did not migrate to Costa Rica in 1994 and/or 1995. The results of our analysis regarding individual and farm-household characteristics explain almost 80 per cent of migration decisions. As explanatory factors we included:

- the amount of staple food produced during 1994 (beans, maize and sorghum);
- the number of cattle as an important indicator of peasant wealth;
- the size of the household (number of family members);
- the age of the peasant (in age categories of 10 years);
- schooling defined as a categorical variable (no formal education; one to three years; more than three years);
- the access to arable land as the amount of land cultivated in 1995;
- the specific land tenure arrangements as a categorical variable (no sharecropping; additional sharecropping; totally sharecropping);
- village dummies as a categorical variable to check whether local specificity would prove to be a determining factor; and
- a constant term reflecting the exogenous tendency of peasants of that area to migrate. This factor can be considered as an indicator of local cultural customs.

The results of our analysis regarding the individual and farm-household characteristics that influence engagement in migration indicate that the variables related to the production system (income from cropping activities and livestock), farm and family size, age, education and tenure together explain almost 80 per cent of migration decisions.

Considering only those variables significant at a 90 per cent level and making use of the formal notation of the logistic model:

$$\text{Prob(event)} = \frac{(e^{b_0 + b_1 X_1 + b_2 X_2 + \cdots + b_p X_p})}{(1 + e^{b_0 + b_1 X_1 + b_2 X_2 + \cdots + b_p X_p})} = \frac{1}{1 + e^{-z}}$$

Table 12.5   Factors determining the probability of seasonal migration

Variable	Coefficient	Sign
Beans production (1994)	0.0025	0.8573
Maize production (1994)	0.0045	0.8378
Sorghum production (1994)	0.0250	0.3109
Livestock (herd size)	−0.2692	0.0318
Household size (members)	0.1190	0.3035
Age (<25 years)		0.0195
Age (26–35 years)	1.4296	0.6937
Age (36–45 years)	3.0773	0.3831
Age (46–55 years)	1.0961	0.7536
Age (56–65 years)	−0.6689	0.8495
Age (>65 years)	0.5011	0.8871
No formal education		0.9560
1–3 years of education	0.1135	0.7642
>3 years of education	−0.0604	0.8817
Arable land	−0.0662	0.7405
Ownership		0.6327
Additional sharecropping	−0.3164	0.4237
Complete sharecropping	−0.0789	0.8747
Labranza No. 2 Village		0.9664
El Espino Village	0.1536	0.7144
Algodonal Village	−0.4156	0.5190
La Laguna Village	0.1810	0.7572
Chagüite Village	−0.0583	0.9158
Constant	−1.5455	0.6646

where z is the logistic regression equation, we get the following final equation.

$Z = -0.1365*$ (number of cows) $+ 0.1572*$ (number of years, when younger than 25) ... etc.

This implies that when someone is under 25 years of age, the probability of seasonal migration becomes extremely high. For example, for a 20-year-old male without cattle, the probability is 95.9 per cent. Even if he has five head of cattle, he still has a propensity to migrate of 92.1 per cent. Peasants in this age category almost always migrate to Costa Rica. For all other categories the probability is 50 per cent for those who do not possess cattle, and 34 per cent for those who have five cows. The latter means this farmer will most probably be non-migrant.

The autonomous probability that a peasant will engage in seasonal migration is quite high. As we have already stated, we consider this to be a reflection of 'cultural practices' in the area. Migration has always been part of the livelihood strategies in the area, so households are 'used to it'. If we assume that the variables used in the simulation give a good picture of the factors that influence peasant rationality, the fact that most factors do not influence significantly the propensity to migrate, is very revealing. It indicates that the reason will lie outside the socio-economic realm and outside the productive realm that influences peasant rationality!

Several other factors show tendencies, but are not significant. Hypotheses that clearly have to be rejected are those related to production levels of basic grains (maize and beans), and to formal education levels. There seems to be no relationship between production levels and migration in the dry area: relatively low individual yields do not induce migration, nor does migration affect production levels negatively. However, these conclusions are based on inter-household comparisons in a single year. An historical comparison of migration and average household yields in each year may possibly indicate a relationship. Peasants themselves indicate that increasing migration from the Pire Area has been accelerated by low yields in previous years. However, as we only collected data over a two-year period, we could not test that hypothesis and we assume that cultural and political factors will also be influential.

Age and the number of cattle a peasant owns prove to be strong explanatory variables. The more cattle a peasant owns, the less is the propensity to migrate. That herd size is negatively related to the propensity to migrate seems obvious. Cattle needs labour in the dry season, especially when herd size increases and grazing from nearby farm remnants is insufficient as a primary feeding source. Both migration and cattle can be considered as effective ways to mobilize cash within the household economy.

Migrant income and the peasant economy

As herd size increases, the need for off-farm income decreases. Peasants with no herd, or with only one cow, migrate massively to Costa Rica, while peasants with more animals migrate far less. Salaries for seasonal work do not motivate them any more: farm work has become more 'profitable' for them. Peasants seem to act 'rationally' as far as economic calculations of on-farm and off-farm employment are concerned. It is therefore interesting to calculate the net income that migrants manage to send home or bring back to their farms.

Average net income per working day of responding migrants is C$28. This is far higher than the wage for unskilled labour in Nicaragua

Table 12.6 Net migrant income from work in Costa Rica, 1995, in Cordobas (1 US$ = 7 C$)

Sector	No. of respondents	Net average migrant income (C$)	Average working period (days)	Average daily wage (C$)
Bananas	8	1544	71	22.04
Sugar cane	29	2169	71	30.70
Coffee	2	2150	52	41.46
Domestic work	2	2500	78	32.05

Source: UNAN-ESECA/UNAG-COOPIBO, 1995b.

(C$10 with one meal). Considering some social costs of migration, we argue that a wage of C$20–25 with permanent employment during the dry season could motivate peasants to stay in their home country. It is clear that these employment opportunities do not exist in the Pire Area. In the Condega tobacco area, after the reactivation from 1995 onwards, the daily wage rose to C$20 in 1996 and a significant reduction was observed in migration to Costa Rica from that area. Average net migrant income in Costa Rica can vary greatly, principally according to the number of weeks that peasants manage to work there. Net incomes can vary a lot, even within the same sector and during the same time span. Daily income depends on ability (experience), capacity to work extra hours (*fanagear*), and personal health. When someone cannot work as expected, net income shrinks sharply because accommodation and meals take up 35–50 per cent of gross income. The high cost of accommodation in Costa Rica is an obstacle to staying there when unemployed: one has to return to Nicaragua or search for new employment in another sector. This situation clearly discourages the influx of accompanying migrants (that is, spouses and young children): it is cheaper to leave them on the farm.

Conclusion

Although the Pire Area is a geographically small area with specific characteristics, we believe that our research allows some conclusions and suggestions that are of broader relevance. The study indicates that the phenomenon of seasonal migration of peasants to Costa Rica is not limited to the border zones (as is argued by Samandú and Pereira, 1996, p. 12). Nicaragua is small enough to consider the whole country as 'bordering' with Costa Rica. It seems to be a phenomenon that occurs particularly in semi-arid smallholder areas where agricultural production and off-farm employment are limited during the dry season. Not all poor peasants migrate to Costa Rica, though many of them have experience in crossing the border and working in Costa Rica. The decision to migrate seems to be based on an economic calculation considering other components of the peasant economy, especially animal husbandry and wage labour. It seems plausible that migration will slow down or decrease if Nicaraguan wages rise and employment opportunities increase. This Nicaraguan wage level could be much lower than the Costa Rican average, as migrants incur high economic and social costs while abroad.

The research also indicates that a large proportion of migrant income is being spent on agricultural inputs and other means of production on the farm. Agricultural production and rural development are affected positively by seasonal migration: seasonal migration is an intrinsic part of the local production system and livelihood strategies. Many families intend to increase reproduction levels by acquiring land or investing in their housing. The investments indicate that they do not intend to stay and settle in Costa Rica. They do not want to live in Costa Rica, but just earn enough money to satisfy household needs. These seasonal workers go to Costa Rica to work. They do not introduce dependent family members and they do not use schools or housing. They work for relatively low wages as they supplement their household needs with farm production, and if they lose their jobs, or when the rainy period starts, they return to their home country. These semi-proletarians can work for lower wages than full-time labourers and are thus very functional as a source of labour power in seasonal activities in the Costa Rican agro-export sector, which is becoming internationally less competitive because of relatively high wages.

Considering that migration forms a vital part of survival strategies, and is one of the only means of social mobility for peasant households in the poorest areas of Nicaragua, it seems obvious that the government should try to regulate migration problems in a way that will benefit these peasant families. Regulatory measures between Nicaragua and Costa Rica could take advantage of the specific characteristics of these migrants:

- They live in smallholder districts in semi-arid areas. Whereas organizing seasonal migrants who are already within Costa Rica seems difficult (Samandú and Pereira, 1996, p. 12), organizing Nicaraguans in their home areas can be relatively easy, as many of them already travel in an organized way to Costa Rica with local subcontractors.[5]

- They produce grain crops and therefore go to Costa Rica after the harvest and return to Nicaragua when rain permits cultivation. Though young people without land may attempt to stay longer, peasants with families and farms in the home area will most probably have a very limited time period of staying as an illegal worker in Costa Rica.

- Every area has its specific agricultural calendar, but for most semi-arid areas in Nicaragua the period between January and May is the period when plenty of peasants are willing to work in Costa Rica.

It is important that Costa Rica and Nicaragua work on the suggestion of the International Labour Organization (ILO) to give these Nicaraguan migrants a labour permit that can be used to enter and leave the country and to work during a previously determined period and in specific sectors of the Costa Rican economy. This permit could be valid for several years, limiting the resources needed to set up the system, while reducing insecurity for migrating peasants and their employers.

From an economic point of view, and considering the process of Central-American integration, both countries benefit from seasonal migration. There are clear indications that a situation exists in which Costa Rican citizens have permanent employment and do relatively clean work, leaving the dirty and seasonal employment to Nicaraguans. These migrants earn miserable salaries from the Costa Rican point of view, but they earn more than they would at home, as there are still not enough employment opportunities during the dry season in Nicaragua.

Notes

1. The author is research fellow of the TLOD Foundation in Wageningen, The Netherlands. He worked between 1992 and 1997 in Condega (Nicaragua) for COOPIBO, a Belgian NGO, and UNAG, the Nicaraguan peasant union. The survey was carried out by students of UNAN-ESECA, supervised by Dr Gustavo Siles. He is grateful to Ligia Monge, Gerda Zijm and the peasant leaders of the Asociación Campesina de Condega 'Conociéndonos y Produciendo' (ACCP) for their information and encouragement during the research.
2. Prices influence these figures a lot. We used 1995 average prices: maize C$50 cwt; beans C$150 cwt; sorghum C$40 cwt. Prices almost doubled in 1996 and 1997, but production levels were very low.

3. The Talavera Calderón family (El Espino) estimated gross production value, cash needs and cash generation of farm production and off-farm employment. For the 1995/6 period this family used 74 per cent of gross agricultural production for household consumption. Migration added a further 21 per cent of total gross household production. However, comparing the cash generated in each subsystem, migration proves to be very important, accounting for 63 per cent of total household cash income (Ton, 1997).
4. The ACCP provides loans to landless sharecroppers to buy land, which are paid back with migrant income (Ton, 1997).
5. The ACCP in Condega helped peasants to submit documents to the migration office and to humanize migration, offering an alternative to the illegal border crossing. In a few months nearly seventy peasants used and paid for these facilities.

Bibliography

Alcaldia Condega (1995) *Censo Municipal Agropecuario, hojas por comunidad,* Equipo Técnico Alcaldía, Condega.

Alcaldia Condega (1996) *Caracterización del Municipio de Condega,* Equipo Técnico Alcaldía, Condega.

Beneker, T. (1997) 'Buscar mejor Ambiente: migratie naar, uit en langs een kleine stad in Costa Rica', *Nederlandse Geografische Studies,* vol. 216, Utrecht.

Cáceres, L., Gonzales, M., Calderón, A. M. and Zijm, G. M. (1996) *Informe Final Estudio de Patio en San Andrés y La Labranza No. 2, Condega,* PDA 'Conociéndonos y Produciendo', Condega: UNAG-COOPIBO.

Chant, S. (1992) 'Migration at the Margins: Gender, Poverty and Population Movements on the Costa Rican Periphery, in S. Chant (ed.), *Gender and Migration,* pp. 49–72.

Chant, S. (ed.) (1992) *Gender and Migration in Developing Countries,* London and New York: Belhaven Press.

Goldschneider, C. (ed.) (1984) *Rural Migration in Developing Countries: Comparative Studies of Korea, Sri Lanka, and Mali,* Boulder, Col. and London: Westview Press.

ILO (1995) *La Situación Migratoria de los Trabajadores Nicaragüenses en Costa Rica,* Servicio de Migraciones para el Empleo-Equipo Técnico Multidisciplinario, Geneva: ILO.

Long, N. and van der Ploeg, J. D. (1989) 'Demythologizing Planned Intervention: An Actor Perspective', *Sociologia Ruralis,* vol. 29, nos. 3/4, pp. 226–49.

Ruben, R. and Clemens, H. (1996) *Rural Off-Farm Employment and Food Security in Honduras,* Working paper for Primer Congreso Europeo para Americanistas, Salamanca, June 29–30.

Samandú, L. and Pereira, R. (1996) *Los Nicaragüenses en Costa Rica: enfoques de una problemática,* San José: Consejeria en Proyectos para Refugiados Latinoamericanos.

Sen, A. (1981) *Poverty and Famines. An Essay on Entitlement and Deprivation.* Oxford: Clarendon Press.

Siles, G. and Ramos, M. (1996) *La Migración Campesina en la Zona de Pire, Municipio de Condega,* Managua: Departmento de Estelí, ESECA-UNAN.

Stonich, S. C. (1991) 'Rural Families and Income from Migration: Honduran Households in the World Economy', *Latin American Studies*, vol. 23, pp. 131–61.

TLOD-UNAG (1990) *Conociéndonos y Produciendo: programa de desarrollo agrícola Condega*, UNAG.

Todaro, M. P. (1976) *Internal Migration in Developing Countries*, Geneva, ILO.

Ton, G. (1997) 'El Banco de Tierra en Condega', *Seminario: Tenencia de Tierra y el Acceso de las Mujeres a la tierra*, Managua: SNV, pp. 101–8.

Ton, G. (1996) ' "Cuando está la Temporada, Todos se Van ... "': la importancia de la migración a Costa Rica para las familias campesinas en la Zona de Pire (Condega)', *Cuaderno de Libre Opinión: special issue*, Managua: SIMAS.

UNAN-ESECA/UNAG-COOPIBO (1995a) *Perspectivas de la Agricultura en la Zona de Pire: entrevistas a lideres*, Condega: PDA 'Conociéndonos y Produciendo'.

UNAN-ESECA/UNAG-COOPIBO (1995b) *Perspectivas de la Agricultura en la Zona de Pire: encuestas a productores*, Condega: PDA 'Conociéndonos y Produciendo'.

Wiley, J. (1995) 'Undocumented Aliens and Recognized Refugees: The Right to Work in Costa Rica', *International Migration Review*, New York, vol. 29, no. 2, pp. 423–40.

Wood, C. H. (1980) 'Structural Changes and Household Strategies: A Conceptual Framework for the Study of Rural Migration', *Human Organization*, vol. 40, pp. 338–43.

Zelaya, C. (ed.) (1995) *Estudio de Reconocimiento y Caracterización de los Recursos Hídricos, Edáficos y Forestales del Municipio de Condega, Departamento de Estelí, Nicaragua*, Managua: UNA-FARENA-Redes para el Desarrollo Local.

13

Low and High-External Input Agriculture in the Agrarian Frontier

Michiel Bourgondiën

Introduction

Soil degradation is a major threat to the sustainability of agricultural production systems in Central America. Estimates indicate that 25 per cent of land with vegetation is moderately to extremely degraded, mainly as a result of agricultural activities (Oldeman *et al.*, 1990). Agricultural production generally involves a flow of nutrients out of the area where the crops are cultivated. When no nutrients are added to the soil, land productivity declines after a few years of cultivation because of the decreased availability of plant nutrients in the soil. This may result in a temporary abandonment of the land (as in shifting cultivation and fallow systems) to restore the content of organic matter and thereby the production capacity of the soil. However, as pressure on the land is growing, the duration of fallow periods have been shortened with the risk of irreversible loss of soil and reduction in agricultural productivity (Lutz *et al.*, 1994; García Espinoza *et al.*, 1994; Ruthenberg, 1980).

The conventional scientific approach to improving low-productivity agriculture is to increase the use of external inputs such as inorganic fertilizer, adding nutrients to the soil that have been withdrawn during the crop harvest. However, it is questionable whether these high-external-input agriculture (HEIA) technologies are appropriate ways for small farmers to increase production and to reverse the process of soil degradation. Various development and research communities have put forward low-external-input agriculture (LEIA) as a viable option for many small-scale farmers seeking an alternative to traditional low-productivity and environmentally harmful production systems. LEIA techniques seek to optimize the use of locally available resources, and use external inputs only to the extent that they are needed to provide elements that are deficient in the system, or they enhance the efficiency of internal inputs (Reijntjes *et al.*, 1992). This approach is based on the assumptions that small farmers generally lack resources to invest in high-external-input agriculture, that this type of intensification is not desirable because of its harmful effects to the environment, and that high-external-input agriculture is not sustainable. An important question is whether, and under what circumstances, farm households are willing to adopt these ecological farming techniques. A changeover to LEIA generally involves a fundamental shift in resource requirements. Often labour is substituted for capital through reliance on more labour-intensive cultivation methods, which will lead to changes in production and factor productivity. These changes in production and factor productivity might explain why certain households choose a particular technology according to its resource endowments.

Against this background, this chapter analyses the economic aspects of three maize production systems in the colonization area of Nueva Guinea, Nicaragua. Most of the farm households cultivate their maize without any form of fertilization and rely on fallow to restore nutrients, but a small proportion of farm households applies inorganic fertilizers. Since the end of the 1980s, low-external-input maize production, based on the use of the velvet bean as a substitute for inorganic fertilizer, has been promoted by farmers and non-governmental organizations as a low-cost, ecologically sustainable technology to increase yield and restore the soil fertility of degraded land. Although this technique gives good results in terms of these aims (Sanclemente, 1994), adoption so far has been limited, estimated to be only 2–3 per cent (PRODES Nueva Guinea, 1997). Analyzing the economic aspects of these technologies within the regional economic context is of special importance to colonization areas such as Nueva Guinea where often 'agricultural expansion at the extensive margin' can be found, a pattern of agricultural development also observed in the Brazilian Amazon (Kyle and Cunha, 1994). This type of development is a consequence of economic conditions resulting from an abundance of land and scarcity of almost every other factor of production, and is characterized by extensive and careless use of land. In such a situation, ecological technologies that are relatively labour intensive are not likely to be adopted by farm households.

The main objectives of this chapter are to analyze the economic aspects of the three maize production systems mentioned above and to identify factors that are likely to influence the pattern of adoption.

We begin by focusing on the arguments put forward by advocates of LEIA, who argue that this is a viable alternative for small farmers. This is followed by a description of the study area and the maize production systems are analyzed. In the fourth section, the core of the chapter, three maize production systems are compared with respect to differences in the use of internal and external inputs, production and factor productivity. The results are discussed within the socio-economic context of the study area. Household, farm and institutional characteristics relevant for adoption are identified. Finally, we conclude with a discussion of the results and indicate their implications for policy and further research.

Low-external-input agriculture as a viable alternative?

The validation of LEIA as a development approach for the intensification of agricultural production systems enabling small–scale farmers to escape low-productive and environmentally harmful traditional production systems is not widely accepted. We discuss this issue by focusing on three arguments put forward by advocates of LEIA: (1) high-external-input is not accessible for small farmers; (2) high-external-input agriculture is harmful to the environment; and (3) sustainability can only be achieved by pursuing low-external-input agriculture.

HEIA is not accessible for small farmers

Several authors argue that HEIA (that is, increasing the production of land already under cultivation by increasing the use of inputs) is not an accessible intensification path for small farmers as they lack sufficient funds to cover the high cash outlays associated with the use of these high-external-input technologies. (Pretty, 1995; Reijntjes *et al.*, 1992). It is indeed true that adoption of innovations such as tractors and irrigation equipment involves high initial investment. For large farms, average costs associated with innovation are lower, making adoption more attractive than for small farmers. However, this is not the case for divisible inputs such as seeds, fertilizer, herbicides and pesticides which can often be bought in small amounts. For these types of input, cost economies are not relevant, and adoption is possible for both small and large farms (Ellis, 1988). However differences are found in timing and the extent of adoption. Large farmers are often early adopters, whereas small farmers are often the reverse. Moreover, large farmers are more likely to adopt the whole technological package at once, whereas small farmers adopt only a few components at a time

(CIMMYT, 1993; Herdt and Capule, 1983). Empirical evidence indicates that the adoption of green revolution technologies in Asia was not monopolized by larger farmers. This indicates that farm size is not always a constraint in adopting green-revolution technologies, although some cases can be found where small farmers lagged behind larger farmers. However, this was not because of the technology but rather a consequence of initial extremely skewed farm-size distribution (Hayami and Ruttan, 1985, pp. 336–40).

HEIA is harmful to the environment

Arguments against HEIA are that the excessive use of inputs such as fertilizers, herbicides and pesticides in this kind of agriculture is harmful to humans and the environment[1] and depletes stocks of non-renewable resources such as phosphates and oil (Pretty, 1995; Lee, 1992; Reijntjes *et al.*, 1992). However, LEIA can also be harmful to the environment. Reardon (1997), considering the African context, argues that LEIA techniques will be unable to increase production to the levels required to meet the needs of an ever-increasing population. As a result, farmers are likely to start cultivating hillsides and fragile soils, causing more damage than the use of inorganic fertilizer. In his opinion, a combination of HEIA and LEIA techniques is the most appropriate intensification path for farmers in many parts of Africa. Pinstrup-Andersen and Pandya-Loch (1994) take a more extreme stand. They argue that agricultural intensification based on irrigation, pesticides and fertilizers is the only way to avoid the exploitation of the natural resource base. According to them, the problem in most developing countries farms is insufficient, rather than excessive, fertilizer use. Furthermore, attempts to reduce the use of pesticides, irrigation and fertilizers might decrease food supplies when appropriate alternatives are not available to farmers at reasonable prices. However, they acknowledge that, in some cases, this type of agricultural intensification has led to environmental degradation because of inappropriate price policies, externalities, and lack of knowledge application and available alternatives (Pinstrup-Andersen and Pandya-Lorch, 1994, pp. 11–15).

Sustainability can only be achieved by pursuing LEIA techniques

Advocates of LEIA often equate this type of agriculture with *sustainable* agriculture, and argue that other forms of agriculture are not sustainable. Although we do not discuss the concept of sustainability itself here, we shall discuss below what Reardon (1997) calls the cat-and-mouse game between farmers and environmentalists. There often appears to be a conflict between ecological sustainability and economic viability at the household level when LEIA techniques are being pursued. However, this is not always apparent in the literature or policy prescriptions, as technical perspectives tend to dominate, thereby ignoring the importance of socio-economic aspects in the acceptance of measures to conserve the environment from the perspective of the farm household (Low, 1994). This can be illustrated by evidence from Zimbabwe, where attempts were made to introduce a new tillage technology that required less draught power and had clear advantages for the soil as it conserved moisture, but required extra manual weeding. The increased labour requirements made the new technology unattractive to farmers in a situation of labour scarcity. Adoption would reduce returns to labour and smaller-farm household income, which would ultimately result in less economically sustainable livelihoods (Low, 1994, p. 220). Thus the feasibility of this new technique at the household level depended on the socio-economic environment in which the households were operating. Farm households facing relative labour abundance and land scarcity would opt for techniques that optimize returns to land, whereas farm households facing relative labour scarcity and land abundance would opt for techniques that optimize returns to labour.

LEIA as a viable alternative?

The above illustrates that the arguments put forward by LEIA advocates are not all that convincing. This does not mean that LEIA cannot be a good strategy to intensify agriculture, but the merits of technology should not be judged on their ecological aspects only. Promoters of sustainable agriculture should keep in mind the role of economics in the decisions of households. According to Low (1994, p. 223), a problem with the promotion of LEIA techniques is that they often seem to be based more on ecological considerations than on a sound economic evaluation from the perspective of the farm household. Perhaps, as stated by Triomphe (1996), NGOs promoting low-external-input agriculture are lured by the success of others, and forget that a major challenge is not only to promote alternatives that are ecologically sound, but also ones that are economically profitable. Without the latter, no system can ever be sustained (Altieri and Masera, 1993).

Description of the study area

The colonization area of Nueva Guinea, located in the south-east of Nicaragua, covers 2850 km². The area can be characterized as humid tropical lowland, with an average annual rainfall of 2300 to 3100 mm, increasing from the west to the east. There is a long rainy season (called *invierno*) of 8–9 months from May to January (with a peak in June), and a short 'drier' season from February to April (called *verano*). Annual average temperature is about 24°C (Tapia, 1990). Official colonization started in 1965 with the settlement of farmers who were granted legal land titles of 50 or 70 *manzanas* (one *manzana* = 0.7 hectare) (Clerx, 1990). It is estimated that more than 100000 people currently live in the area, spread over thirty villages.

Some general tendencies in land use can be observed. First, rapid and complete deforestation is taking place, which is in large part caused by humans, although hurricane Juana also devastated a large area in 1988. Second, the production of basic grains for subsistence needs is characterized by low physical productivity. Once the standing forest has been cut, and the plot cultivated for two or three years, subsistence crop yields decline rapidly, leaving farmers no other option than to clear another part of the forest. The low productivity is related directly to the poor quality of the soil. Most of the soil is acid and lacks both organic matter and phosphorus. The high acidity and the low cation exchange capacity of the soil means that nutrients leach easily. Therefore, in order for chemical fertilizers to work, their application has to be well timed. Much of the degraded land has been converted into pasture of low quality and productivity, representing the third, and dominant, form of land use (Gómez *et al.*, 1991). However, as most of the colonists lack their own funds and do not have access to credit, there are hardly any opportunities for them to invest in cattle. According to de Groot *et al.* (1997), many colonists get locked into a low equilibrium trap, having degraded land with pasture, but no cattle. As other farmers do have cattle or access to credit for livestock, and eventually expand their holdings by buying degraded pastures of other farmers, a process of social differentiation occurs.

Based on a survey of 340 farm households, PRODES Nueva Guinea[2] distinguishes five different types of agricultural producers: (1) sharecroppers, owning less than 10 mz, without livestock of any significance, and representing 10 per cent of the producers; (2) subsistence crop producers, owing about 50 mz, with six head of cattle being the largest group, with 53 per cent; (3) subsistence livestock-crop producers, owning on average 57 mz, with thirteen head of cattle, representing 20 per cent of the producers; (4) peasant livestock producers, owning about 103 mz, with about thirty-nine head of cattle, representing 12 per cent of the producers; and (5) farmer livestock producers, owning an average of 170 mz, with ninety head of cattle, representing about 5 per cent of the population (Pijnenburg and Martínez, 1992; for translation of terms, terminology used by de Groot *et al.* (1997) has been followed).

Maize is cultivated by most of the households in Nueva Guinea partly for subsistence and partly for commercial purposes. Maize can be cultivated twice a year, during the rainy season (*maíz de primera*, cultivated in the period June–October) and the drier season (*maíz de postrera*, cultivated in the period October–April). *Maíz de postrera* is considered the most important harvest by local farmers. Three different maize production systems can be distinguished, based on the form of fertilizer application. The first system is based on fallow. The standing vegetation, consisting of weeds, shrubs and regenerating trees is cleared, and maize sown for one or two seasons, after which the plot is left fallow. As land is not a limiting factor in production for most of the farmers, a new plot of land will be cleared for subsequent years. The second system is based on inorganic fertilizers. In principle, maize can be cultivated twice a year continuously for many years when using this type of fertilization. The third system is based on organic fertilizers, called *frijol abono* (fertilizer bean) or *frijol terciopelo* (velvet bean) by local farmers. Maize can be cultivated only once a year as the field is occupied with the standing velvet bean vegetation during the *primera*. The maize–velvet bean is a rotation between the velvet bean sown in the *primera* and the *maíz de postrera* and forms a double-cropping system. This system was introduced to Nueva Guinea in the late 1980s by farmers and non-governmental organizations. A well-known feature of the velvet bean is its capacity to fix nitrogen from the air, which is released upon decomposition, thereby acting as a (partial) substitute for nitrogen fertilizer (Yost and Evans, 1988). Although local data are scarce, studies in other parts of Central America estimated that a standing velvet bean vegetation can accumulate 10–12 tons/ha of dry matter and 250–350 kg/ha of nitrogen in its above-ground biomass. However, it should be noted that part of this comes from nutrient cycling (soil–plant–soil), but it appears to be reasonable to assume that velvet bean can fix anywhere between 70 and 130 kg/ha of N per cycle (Triomphe, 1996). Moreover, velvet bean seems very effective in controlling weeds in the subsequent maize field (Eijk-Bos *et al.*, 1987), which reduces the amount of labour required for weeding (Buckles *et al.*, 1992), and it maintains the structure and texture of the soil (CIDICCO, 1991; Triomphe, 1996). Despite extension efforts, adoption of maize–velvet bean rotation in Nueva Guinea is still relatively low: at the time of writing it is estimated at

2 or 3 per cent. The traditional system is the most common in the area, probably practised by 75 per cent of the farmers, whereas inorganic fertilizer is used by approximately 20 per cent of the farmers (PRODES, Nueva, Guinea, 1997).

Empirical evidence

Data used in the empirical analysis were collected during April and May 1997 from 106 farmers in thirteen different villages. The sample was stratified *ex post* into three groups, based on the types of fertilization used in maize production: chemical fertilizer, velvet bean, or no form of fertilization. In the empirical analysis we shall refer to these forms as: (i) chemical: maize production based on inorganic fertilizer; (ii) ecological: maize–velvet bean rotation; and (iii) traditional: maize production based on fallow, with no use of inorganic fertilizer. In total, the farmers cultivated 131 different plots,[3] of which thirty-eight were classified as chemical, thirty-three as ecological, and sixty as traditional. In the analysis, fifteen cases were left out of the analysis because of missing data and statistical considerations.

Use of agricultural inputs

Land

Table 13.1 shows the average plot size and the tenancy status of 116 plots. The ecological plots are, on average, the smallest. The traditional plots are the largest, differing significantly from ecological plots. Chemical plot size does not differ significantly from either traditional or ecological plots. However, no hard conclusions can be drawn from

Table 13.1 Plot size and tenancy status

	Chemical (*n* = 33)	Ecological (*n* = 28)	Traditional (*n* = 55)	Average (*N* = 116)	Sign*
Plot size (*manzana*)	2.3 (1.8)	1.5 (0.8)	3.1 (3.3)	(2.5) (2.6)	E–T
Plot ownership (%)	85	100	90	91	

Notes: Standard deviations are in parentheses.
*Results of multiple comparison tests. using the Games-Howell procedure.
(C–E) = differ significantly between chemical and ecological.
(C–T) = differ significantly between chemical and traditional.
(E–T) = differ significantly between ecological and traditional.
(ns) = do not differ significantly.
(nr) = not relevant.

this. Of the twenty-eight farmers who cultivated the ecological plots, twenty-one mentioned that they also cultivated another plot. The main reason for not cultivating all their maize in rotation with velvet bean was the lack of sufficient velvet bean seeds, but other farmers mentioned that they were comparing the performance of the ecological plot with a traditional plot and had therefore limited the area of the ecological plot.

All the ecological plots are cultivator-owned, compared to 85 per cent and 90 per cent of the chemical and traditional plots, respectively (indicated with plot ownership in Table 13.1). All farmers who rented a plot mentioned that the contract was only for a single harvest. Although no information was available about tenancy contracts in general, it might give an indication that the use of velvet bean is considered to be an investment that improves the quality of the soil, and is therefore used only on plots owned by the farmer.

Labour

Fourteen different labour activities were distinguished in the survey. Activities are grouped into five major categories, according to whether they are related to: (i) planting; (ii) fertilization; (iii) weed control; (iv) control of pests and diseases; or (v) harvesting. It should be noted that this is not a chronological sequence. For example, fertilization activities on the ecological plots take place in between the various activities of planting. Table 13.2 gives a breakdown of the labour requirements per *manzana* for the five categories.

Labour requirements are highest for ecological plots, followed by chemical and traditional plots. A large part of the difference can be explained by the labour requirements for fertilization, which accounts

Table 13.2   Labour requirements (in man days per *manzana*)

Category	**Chemical** **(*n* = 33)**	**Ecological** **(*n* = 28)**	**Traditional** **(*n* = 55)**	**Average** **(*N* = 116)**	**Sign***
Planting	12.1 (5.0)	9.3 (3.3)	10.6 (2.8)	10.7 (3.8)	C–E
Fertilization	2.4 (1.4)	10.6 (3.7)	– –	3.2 (4.7)	C–E
Weed control	4.3 (2.5)	4.8 (2.7)	3.3 (2.3)	3.9 (2.5)	E–T
Pests and diseases	0.3 (0.6)	0 –	0 –	0.1 (0.4)	C–T
Harvesting	3.6 (1.9)	4.4 (2.1)	3.4 (1.8)	3.7 (1.9)	ns
Total	**22.7 (6.9)**	**29.1 (7.9)**	**17.3 (4.6)**	**21.7 (7.8)**	**ALL**

Notes: Standard deviations are in parentheses.
*See notes, Table 13.1.

for 36 per cent of the labour use on ecological plots, compared to only 11 per cent on the chemical plots. Surprisingly, labour use for weed control is highest on ecological plots, which is contrary to what we expected, as velvet bean is known for its weed-reducing capacity. This can be explained by the fact that weed control on ecological plots is mainly done manually, whereas herbicides are generally used to control weeds on the other plot types.

Non-labour inputs

Table 13.3 gives a summary of non-labour input costs for cultivating one *manzana*. Use of maize seeds is spread more or less equally between the three different systems. On almost 90 per cent of the plots, between 20 and 30 lb was used, with an average of 24.9 lb per *manzana*. Means do not differ among the three systems. A price of C$2/lb has been used for conversion into monetary terms. In order to give a cost estimation of material inputs for fertilization, the following procedure was used. For the ecological plots, a shadow price of C$3/lb was used.[4] Farmers used on average 52.4 lb of velvet bean seeds per *manzana*. It should be noted that on almost 70 per cent of the plots, less than the technical recommendation of 80 lb per *manzana* was used. A reason for this might be the problems many farmers had in obtaining seed. Costs for the chemical plots were calculated by multiplying the price by the amount used. Total costs for chemical plots were almost C$260 per *manzana*, compared to C$157 per *manzana* for ecological plots. Herbicides were used at two different times: farmers applied herbicide just before planting to give the young maize plants a weed-free environment; and/or a few weeks after planting, when new weeds had emerged between the growing maize plants. The use of herbicides was highest on the chemical plots (farmers spent almost C$98 per *manzana*

Table 13.3   Non-labour input costs (in C$ per *manzana*)

Input	Chemical (*n* = 38)	Ecological (*n* = 33)	Traditonal (*n* = 59)	Average (*N* = 130)	Sign*
Maize seeds	50.8 (15.5)	51.6 (20.6)	48.2 (9.2)	49.8 (14.5)	ns
Fertilization	259.6 (105.5)	157.2 (101.7)	– –	111.8 (135.2)	C–E
Herbicides	97.5 (79.8)	20.8 (34.1)	39.0 (51.9)	51.2 (65.0)	C–E, C–T
Biocides	16.2 (36.8)	5.8 (28.4)	0.3 (1.8)	6.2 (24.8)	nc

Notes: Standard deviations are in parentheses.
*See notes Table 13.1.

on herbicides) and is significantly higher than herbicide use on both traditional (C$39) and ecological plots (C$21). Pesticides or fungicides were used on only 11 per cent of the plots (mostly chemical). On the chemical plots, farmers spent an average of C$16 per *manzana*, compared to almost zero for the traditional and ecological plots. Significant differences cannot be computed because of the small number of observations for the traditional and ecological plots.

Production costs, production, productivity and returns to factors of production

Table 13.4 provides an overview of total production costs, production, productivity and returns to the factors of production. As can be seen, total input costs on the traditional plots are the lowest, amounting to about half of the costs made on chemical and ecological plots, and the cost structure differs significantly from both the ecological and chemical plots. Total input costs for the chemical and ecological plots do not differ significantly. However, when we compare the structure of total costs between ecological and chemical plots, we see that labour costs account for 72 per cent of the total input costs on the ecological plots, compared to 52 per cent on the chemical plots.

With respect to the physical productivity of the land, it can be observed that yields on the chemical plots are superior to yields on the ecological and traditional plots, reaching almost 14 cwt/mz, closely followed by the chemical plots with 13 cwt/mz. Traditional plots yield only 8 cwt/mz, significantly lower than the yields from either the ecological or the chemical plots. However, when productivity is measured as the average amount of production per worked day (thus, labour productivity), no significant differences are found between the three systems. This can be explained by the fact that labour use on the ecological and chemical plots is higher than on the traditional plots. Thus, although land productivity on the ecological and chemical plots is higher than on the traditional plots, it is equal among the three systems, because of the higher labour requirements on the ecological and chemical plots. Table 13.4 shows returns to land, labour and capital. Returns are calculated using maize price of C$80 per cwt.[5] The net return to land is on average C$215 per *manzana*, and does not differ significantly between chemical, ecological and traditional plots. Net returns to labour and capital are highest on traditional plots. However, none of the net returns differs significantly between the three systems.

Table 13.4 Production costs, productivity and returns to factors of production

Indicator	Chemical (n = 33)	Ecological (n = 28)	Traditional (n = 55)	Average (N = 116)	Sign*
Production costs					
Total (C$/mz)	878.4 (189.8)	816.5 (188.6)	433.5 (106.9)	652.5 (260.5)	C–T, E–T
Ratio (labour/total)	0.52 (0.12)	0.72 (0.11)	0.80 (0.10)	0.70 (0.16)	All
Productivity					
Land (cwt/mz)	13.8 (7.1)	13.0 (8.3)	8.0 (4.8)	10.8 (7.0)	C–T, E–T
Labour (cwt/day)	0.63 (0.33)	0.45 (0.25)	0.49 (0.34)	0.52 (0.32)	ns
Returns					
Gross returns (C$/mz)	1100 (565)	1038 (664)	641 (389)	868 (557)	C–T, E–T
Net returns (C$/mz)	222 (487)	221 (607)	208 (377)	215 (468)	ns
Net returns					
Land (C$/mz)	222 (487)	221 (607)	208 (377)	215 (468)	ns
Labour (C$/day)	8.7 (24.1)	7.5 (19.5)	13.7 (25.7)	10.8 (23.8)	ns
Capital (C$/c$)	0.23 (0.56)	0.26 (0.67)	0.52 (0.96)	0.37 (0.80)	ns

Note: Standard deviations are in parentheses.
*See notes Table 13.1.

Estimation of production function

A Cobb–Douglas production function was estimated with total maize production as a dependent variable, and with land, labour and non-labour inputs (the aggregate of seeds, fertilizers, herbicides, and biocides) as independent variables. Estimated coefficients should be interpreted as partial elasticities of production, indicating the percentage change of output resulting from a given percentage change in the variable input, *ceteris paribus* (Pindyck and Rubinfeld, 1991).

From Table 13.5, it can be observed that, for the total sample, all three estimated coefficients are positive and significantly different from zero (at a 10 per cent significance level). Thus increases in the area under cultivation, in labour and in non-labour inputs increase production. For the three sub-samples, the estimated coefficients for labour and non-labour are positive and significantly different from zero (at a 10 per cent significance level). The coefficient for land is positive for the ecological and traditional plots, and negative for the chemical plots. However, none of the estimated land coefficients is significant. The negative land coefficient for the chemical plots can be explained by multicollinearity.[6] Economies of scale are not present in maize production.

Table 13.5 Regression results of three systems of maize production

Independent	Chemical	Ecological	Traditional	Total sample
Intercept	−3.788**	−2.036	−1.070	−1.122**
	(1.962)	(1.917)	(0.968)	(0.534)
Land	−0.488	0.065	0.318	0.202*
	(0.380)	(0.488)	(0.300)	(0.139)
Labour	0.718**	0.762*	0.507**	0.588***
	(0.304)	(0.479)	(0.259)	(0.163)
Non-labour	0.683***	0.345*	0.328**	0.293***
	(0.266)	(0.205)	(0.149)	(0.063)
N	33	28	55	116
R^2_{adj}	0.567	0.526	0.678	0.633
F-ratio	14.969	11.004	38.872	67.203
Significance	0.000	0.000	0.000	0.000
Chow-test	–	–	–	1.022
Economies of scale	0.913	1.172	1.153	1.080

Notes: Standard errors of the estimated coefficients are in parentheses.
 *Significant at $P<0.10$.
 **Significant at $P<0.05$.
 ***Significant at $P<0.01$.

Although the sum of the three coeffcicients is 1.084, indicating increasing returns to scale, this result does not differ significantly from 1, so constant economies of scale are present in maize production.

In order to see whether structural differences exist between the responsiveness to factors of production, the Chow-statistic was calculated. This tests whether the three individual regression models are identical, or if three separate regressions have to be estimated. The value of the Chow-statistic shows that the null-hypothesis of identical regressions is not rejected, indicating that the responsiveness of production to land, labour and non-labour inputs is identical for the three technologies under study.

Factors relevant for adoption

In the analysis of adoption patterns, our focus is on household, farm and institutional characteristics. Three different multinomial logit functions have been estimated, taking chemical, ecological and traditional systems as points of departure. The models estimate the probability that an individual with known characteristics chooses one of the alternatives relative to the technology taken as point of departure. Estimated coefficients indicate in what way the relative probability changes as a result of a change in one of the independent variables (Dijkstra, 1997; Maddala, 1983). The results of the estimation procedures are summarized in Table 13.6 (only the direction of the significant variables is shown).

Of the five household characteristics considered, only gender and family size are relevant in explaining the adoption of technology. Age, literacy and expertise are not significant, which implies that these three factors are not important in the decision to adopt one of the technologies. The probability of traditional relative to chemical increases when the farmer is male, and decreases when the farmer is female.[7] This variable is not significant when we compare ecological versus chemical, and traditional versus ecological. The probability of ecological and traditional relative to chemical increases when family size increases. This variable is not significant when we compare the probability of ecological versus traditional. These results indicate that smaller households are more likely to adopt chemical fertilizers. A logical explanation for this is that these households face a relative labour scarcity, which is offset by the use of external inputs. Households using chemical fertilizers have an average land/person ratio of 12.5, compared to 6.0 and 6.7 for households using velvet bean or no forms of fertilizer, respectively.

Table 13.6 Factors influencing the choice of chemical, ecological or traditional maize production systems (multinomial logit analysis)

Factors	Chemical as reference		Ecological as reference		Traditional as reference	
	Ecological	Traditional	Chemical	Traditional	Chemical	Ecological
Household						
Age (years)						
Gender (male)		Positive			Negative	
Literacy (yes)						
Expertise (years)						
Family size (persons)	Positive	Positive	Negative		Negative	
Farm						
Area (*manzana*)						
Livestock (units)						
Export crops (yes)						
Chemical fertilizer (yes)	Negative	Negative	Positive		Positive	
Hired labour (yes)						
Off-farm I (yes)						
Off-farm II (yes)				Positive		Negative
Environment						
Credit (yes)						
Extension (yes)	Positive		Negative			
Tenancy (yes)						
Total number of cases	116					
Model Chi-square	77.43					
Significance	0.000					
Percentage correctly predicted	63.8%					

With respect to farm characteristics, the use of chemical fertilizers only on crops other than maize and the involvement of family members in off-farm employment are relevant to explaining the adoption of methods. Farm size and the possession of livestock, considered to be important indicators of the process of social stratification, are not relevant to explaining the observed adoption pattern. Thus, adoption is spread equally among the various social groups encountered. The use of chemical fertilizers on crops other than maize is significant in explaining the observed adoption pattern. Chemical is more likely to be found on farms where fertilizer is used on crops other than maize, indicating that for ecological and traditional farmers, access to chemical fertilizers might be a problem. Involvement in off-farm employment by members of the household is only significant in distinguishing traditional from ecological. The probability of encountering traditional versus ecological increases when one of the members is involved in off-farm employment, indicating that off-farm employment is found to be more rewarding than investing labour in ecological maize production.

With respect to the institutional environment in which the households operate, only the extension variable is significant. Credit does not influence adoption decisions. Nor does tenancy status of the cultivated plot influence the decision of how to fertilize. This is contrary to expectations, as it is often stated that farmers are only willing to invest in soil fertility measures when they are sure that they will reap benefits in the future. The extension variable is only significant in distinguishing ecological from chemical. The probability of encountering ecological versus chemical increases when farmers receive extension. Thus ecological is more likely to be found on farms where farmers receive technical extension. For extension services promoting the incorporation of velvet bean into maize production, this indicates that less is to be expected of increased efforts to promote this technology. Extension is only relevant where changes from chemical to ecological are being sought, which is a minority group. Extension seems to be a weak instrument to induce farmers to change from traditional to ecological.

Conclusions

LEIA has been proposed by various development and research communities as a viable option for many small farmers in the tropics to escape low productivity and environmentally harmful traditional agricultural production systems. This approach is based on the assumption that small farmers lack resources to invest in HEIA, and that this type of agricultural intensification is not desirable because of its harmful environmental effects. However, the question is whether farmers are willing to adopt these ecologically-based technologies.

The results of the empirical analysis indicate that ecological maize production is a good option for farmers to increase yields, which can reach similar levels to those achieved by farmers using inorganic fertilizers, and is much higher than yields on plots where no form of fertilizer is used. However, a change towards ecological maize production is not without cost. Farmers using velvet bean have to invest much more labour, which is not totally offset by the increased production. As a result, labour productivity does not change. Moreover, net returns to land, labour and capital do not differ significantly in the three systems. This indicates that ecological maize production is most suitable for farm households with very small land holdings and a large amount of labour available, whose main interest is to increase production. But for most of the households in Nueva Guinea, where land is the most abundant factor of production, there is no economic motivation for farmers to turn to ecological maize production.

In the future, pressure on the land will grow as the population increases and farmers reach the limits of opening up new land. In this situation, labour will become a relatively abundant resource for farm households. We have seen that, in such a situation, farmers are more likely to use velvet bean or no form of fertilizer rather than use chemical fertilizers. However, when this pressure on the land comes together with increased and rewarding opportunities for off-farm employment, households will be more likely to invest their efforts in traditional rather than ecological maize production. Where these two factors coincide in the future, the prospects for ecological maize production are likely to be small.

However, this does not mean that there is no future for this technology in Nueva Guinea. Policy and intervention efforts should be made to increase the productivity (both land and labour) of the maize–velvet bean system: for example, through the introduction of animal traction to incorporate the slashed velvet-bean vegetation into the soil. This will increase the nitrogen efficiency and enhance the productivity of the system, making it a more attractive alternative to farmers. Non-governmental organisations (NGOs) working in Nueva Guinea should put more efforts in making this complementary technology available to farmers instead of focusing on more extension activities.

Notes

This chapter has been based largely on fieldwork carried out by the author for his MSc thesis research. I owe many thanks to the following people, who provided suggestions and support during that period: Dr Ruerd Ruben (Wageningen Agricultural University, the Netherlands) for all his support and encouragement. Ing. Oscar Sanclemente (PRODES Nueva Guinea) for supervising the fieldwork and making all the arrangements that made it possible. PRODES Nueva Guinea for providing me with an office and logistical support, and Carlos Flores Acuña, Alexis Calero Sequiera and Augustín Benavides Gómez for all their efforts during the fieldwork.

1. For example, the use of pesticides is still growing in developing countries, at high human and environmental costs. A large amount of the pesticides applied does not reach the target organism; instead they damage wildlife, plant life, and soil and water organisms. Humans are directly exposed during application or indirectly due to water or air pollution (WRI, 1992, pp. 111–5).
2. PRODES Nueva Guinea Proyecto de desarrallo rural en la zona de Nueva Guinea is a development project initiated in 1991 by the governments of the Netherlands and Nicaragua. The main objective is to strengthen local production systems by introducing sustainable technologies for farm households (PRODES, 1997).
3. The word 'plot' is used here *not* to differentiate between maize sown in different geographical areas, but to distinguish between the various forms of specific land use: that is, the various forms of fertilizer use.
4. The price is used by PRODES Nueva Guinea. Farmers who have received velvet bean seeds, have to pay back in kind, or have to pay a price of C$3/lb obtained from PRODES (personal communication, O. Sanclemente, Coordinator of PRODES Nueva Guinea, June 1997).
5. This price is thought to be a good approximation of the average seasonal price of this harvest (personal communication, R. Arguello, PRODES Nueva Guinea, June 1997).
6. The cultivated maize area is highly correlated with both the labour and capital variables. When the land variable is omitted from the analysis, or included with either labour or capital, the coefficient becomes positive. However, in none of the three alternative formulations is the land coefficient significant.
7. This is shown as being *positive* in Table 13.6 when 'chemical' is used as reference, and *negative* when 'traditional' is used as reference. If the probability of traditional relative to chemical increases (positive), then the probability of chemical relative to traditional is exactly the opposite and thus decreases (negative).

Bibliography

Altieri, M. and Masera, O. (1993) 'Sustainable Rural Development in Latin America: Building from the Bottom Up', *Ecological Economics*, vol. 7, pp. 93–121.

Buckles, D., Ponce, I., Sain, G. and Medina, G. (1992) *Tierra cobarde se vuelve valiente. Uso y difusión del frijol abono (Mucuna deeringianum) en las laderas del Litoral Atlántico de Honduras*, México, Distrito Federal (DF): CIMMYT.

CIDICCO (1991) *Noticias sobre el uso de los cultivos de cobertura*, Brief no. 1, Tegucigalpa: Centro Internacional de Información sobre Cultivos de Cobertura.

CIMMYT Economics Program (1993) *The Adoption of Agricultural Technology: A Guide for Survey Design*, Mexico, Distrito Federal (DF): CIMMYT.

Clerx, L. (1990) *Historia de la colonización de Nueva Guinea y la formación de la estuctura social*, Estudios de base del Programa de Desarrollo Rural para la zona de Nueva Guinea, Informe no. 5, San José: CDR/ULA.

Dijkstra, T. (1997) *Horticultural Marketing Channels in Kenya: Structure and Development*, PhD thesis, Wageningen Agricultural University.

van Eijk-Bos, C., Moreno, L. A. and Vega Gonzalez, V. (1987) *Recuperación de Tierras Invadidas por el Imperata contracta (H.B.K.) Hitchc. A partir de la Incorporación de la Leguminosa Mucuna deeringiana (Bort.) Small en Uraba – Colombia*, CONIF Informe No. 8, Bogota: CONIF-Holanda-CORPOURABA.

Ellis, F. (1988) *Peasant Economics: Farm Households and Agrarian Development*, Wye studies in agricultural and rural development, Cambridge University Press.

García Espinosa, R., Madrigal, R. Q. and Alvarez, N. G. (1994) 'Agroecosistemas de Productividad Sostenida de Maíz, en las Regiones Cálido Húmedas de México', in H. D. Thurston, M. Smith, G. Abawi and S. Kearl (eds), *TAPADO, los sistemas de siembra con cobertura*, Turrialba and New York: CATIA and CIIFAF.

Gomez, D., Smits, H. and Waaijenberg, H. (1991) *Perspectivas para cultivos agrícolas del trópico humedo de Nueva Guinea*, Estudio de base del Programa de desarollo rural para la zona de Nueva Guinea, San José: CDR/ULA.

de Groot, J. P., Ambrogui, R. and Jiménez, M. L. (1997) 'Production Systems in the Humid Tropics of Nicaragua: A Comparison of Two Colonization Areas', in J. P. de Groot and R. Ruben (eds), *Sustainable Agriculture in Central America*, London: Macmillan.

Hayami, Y. and Ruttan, V. W. (1985) *Agricultural Development: An International Perspective*, revised and expanded edn, Baltimore, MD: Johns Hopkins University Press.

Herdt, R. W. and Capule, C. (1983) *Adoption, Spread, and Production Impact of Modern Rice Varieties in Asia*, Los Baños: International Rice Research Institute.

Kyle, S. C. and Cunha, A. S. (1992) 'National Factor Markets and the Macroeconomic context for Environmental destruction in the Brazilian Amazon', *Development and Change*, vol. 23, no. 1, pp. 7–33.

Lee, L. K. (1992) 'A Perspective on the Economic Impacts of Reducing Agricultural Chemical Use', *American Journal of Alternative Agriculture*, vol. 7, pp. 82–8.

Low, A. R. C. (1994) 'Environmental and Economic Dilemmas for Farmhouseholds in Africa: When "Low-input Sustainable Agriculture" Translates to "High-cost Unsustainable Livelihoods"', *Environmental Conservation*, vol. 21, no. 3, Autumn.

Lutz, E., Pagiola, S. and Reiche, C. (1994) 'Lessons from Economic and Institutional Analyses of Soil Conservation Projects in Central America and the Caribbean', in E. Lutz, S. Pagiola and C. Reiche (eds), *Economic and Institutional*

Analyses of Soil Conservation Projects in Central America and the Caribbean, World Bank Environmental Paper No. 8, Washington DC: World Bank.

Maddala, G. S. (1983) *Limited-dependent and Qualitative Variables in Econometrics*, Econometric Society Publication No. 3, Cambridge University Press.

Oldeman, L. R., van Engelen, V. W. P. and Jules, J. H. M. (1990) *World Map of the Status of Human-Induced Soil Degradation*, Wageningen: International Soil Reference and Information Centre.

Pijnenburg, T. and Martinez, P. (1992) *Diagnóstico Socio-Económico*, Document No. 1, Nueva Guinea: PRODES Nueva Guinea.

Pindyck, R. S. and Rubinfeld, D. L. (1991) *Econometric Models and Economic Forecasts*, 3rd edn, New York: McGraw Hill.

Pinstrup-Andersen, P. and Pandya-Lorch, R. (1994) *Alleviating Poverty, Intensifying Agriculture, and Effectively Managing Natural Resources*, Food, Agriculture and the Environment Discussion Paper No. 1, Washington DC: International Food Policy Research Institute (IFPRI).

Pretty, J. N. (1995) *Regenerating Agriculture. Policies and Practice for Sustainability and Self-reliance*, London: Earthscan.

PRODES Nueva Guinea (1997) *Informe de la misión de seguimiento y apoyo 1997*, Internal memorandum, Nueva Guinea: PRODES Nueva Guinea.

Reardon, T. (1997) 'African Agriculture: Productivity and Sustainability Issues', in C. Eicher and J. Staatz (eds), *Agricultural Development in the Third World*, Baltimore, MD: Johns Hopkins University Press.

Reijntjes, C., Haverkort, B. and Waters-Bayer, A. (1992) *Farming for the Future: An Introduction to Low External Input and Sustainable Agriculture*, London: Macmillan.

Ruthenberg, H. (1980) *Farming Systems in the Tropics*, 3rd edn, Oxford: Clarendon Press.

Sanclemente, O., Salas, L. M. and Molijn, B. (1994) *Resultados de los ensayos de la producción de maíz en rotación con frijol abono (ciclos 1992/1993 y 1993/1994)*, Document No. 8, Nueva Guinea: PRODES Nueva Guinea.

Tapia, A. (1990) *Datos básicos sobre la zona de Nueva Guinea*, Estudio de base del Programa de Desarrollo Rural para la zona de Nueva Guinea, Informe no. 2, San José: CDR/ULA.

Triomphe, B. L. (1996) *Seasonal Nitrogen Dynamics and Long-term Changes in Soil Properties Under the Mucuna/Maize Cropping System on the Hillsides of Northern Honduras*, PhD dissertation, Cornell University.

WRI (1992) *World Resources 1992–1993. Towards Sustainable Development*, Report by World Resource Institute in collaboration with United Nations Environmental Programme and United Nations Development Programme, New York: Oxford University Press.

Yost, R. and Evans, D. (1988) *Green Manure and Legume Covers in the Tropics*, Research Series 055, Manoa:University of Hawaii.

Index

Accountability, 53, 62–3, 67, 75, 163
Accumulation, 13, 103, 105, 113, 125,
    132–4, 148, 176, 180, 218
Actor, 5–6, 8–9, 21, 23–4, 42, 46, 51,
    54, 65, 69, 70–2, 75, 113, 153–4,
    157, 164, 213
Agent, 3, 17, 23, 35, 43, 47–8, 52–3,
    62, 68
Agrarian debt, 82, 89, 90
Agrarian frontier, 9, 16, 80, 172–3, 180
Agrarian reform, 10, 13, 75, 87,
    98–106, 108–13, 168
Agricultural production, 9–11, 53, 89,
    115, 116–19, 122, 130, 133–4, 172,
    177, 183, 194, 197, 203–4, 213–14,
    217–18, 224, 226, 228, 230
Agriculture, high-input, 228, 230–1
Agriculture, low-input, 228–32
Agroforestry, 103, 112–13
Agroindustry, 44, 47–8, 91–2

Banana, 2, 16, 110, 216, 218–19
Basic grains (cereals), 11, 16, 123, 126,
    131, 177–8, 180, 182–5, 184, 190,
    193, 214–15, 222, 233
Beans, 16, 27, 32–3, 59, 64, 91, 99,
    174, 177, 214, 217, 220–2, 225

Capital, social, 12, 17, 34, 148–9, 154,
    165
Capital, working, 14, 48, 65, 176, 181,
    183
Capital-intensive (-intensity), 120–1,
    197, 204, 208
Capitalization, 108, 111, 160
Central America, 1–2, 4–7, 12, 17,
    40–1, 80, 90–2, 94–5, 114, 141–8,
    173, 225, 228, 234
Chain, alternative, 8, 46, 58–9, 65–8,
    69, 70, 73
Chain, commodity, 7–9, 17, 45–7, 58,
    61, 70–1, 75
Chain, traditional, 58, 63, 65–8, 71

Civil society, 6, 34, 55, 83
Client, 153, 159–61, 165
Coffee, 2, 8–9, 26, 30, 42, 58–9, 60–1,
    63–75, 80–1, 91, 93, 165–6, 192,
    197, 201, 214–16, 219, 223
Collateral, 12, 30–2, 130, 144–5, 149,
    161, 174, 184, 192, 194, 197, 200
Commercialization, 1, 25, 75, 103,
    112–13, 152, 167
Commodity markets, 1, 2, 6, 8–9, 17,
    171, 180, 189, 190, 193, 195, 206
Competition, 43, 65, 70, 91, 119, 152
Consumption, 2, 15, 21, 27, 29, 31–3,
    48, 93, 102–3, 105, 112, 114, 142,
    174–6, 180, 190, 192, 195, 197–8,
    200, 205–8, 214, 217, 226
Contract, choice, 11, 116, 118–19,
    121, 123, 125, 128, 130–1, 133–4,
    136
Contract, enforcement, 5, 13, 151,
    154–5, 157, 160–1, 165
Cooperation, 5, 9, 51, 62–3, 70–1, 75,
    113, 144, 152, 154, 166, 212
Cooperative, 5, 8–12, 17, 34–5, 43,
    46–9, 52–5, 61, 66–70, 81–2, 95,
    99–102, 105–6, 108, 111, 115–28,
    130, 132–5, 166
Costa Rica, 15–16, 104, 174, 210–13,
    215–25
Cotton, 2, 26, 30, 39, 43–5, 91,
    99–100, 117, 123, 126, 128, 132–3
Credit, 1, 3, 8, 10, 12–15, 24, 28–34,
    45, 47–9, 52–3, 64, 66–7, 69, 72–3,
    75, 85–7, 92, 95, 100, 103–6,
    108–9, 112–13, 117, 120, 130–1,
    142–3, 145–9, 155–6, 159–64, 166,
    171–2, 174–9, 181–6, 189, 190,
    192–5, 197–9, 201–8, 233, 242–3
Crop, annual, 106, 173, 192
Crop, perennial, 11, 105–6, 108–9, 180
Crop, staple/food, 10, 21, 23, 25–7,
    29, 34, 79, 87–8, 91, 99–102, 104,
    106–8, 110–11, 174, 215, 220

Debt, 3, 22, 25, 27, 29, 31–3, 79, 82, 87, 89–90, 93, 100, 108, 111, 113, 127–30, 132, 136, 143, 155, 198, 201–7, 217

Decollectivization, 11, 101–2, 115–16, 121–3, 125, 127–8, 130, 134

Development, rural, 1, 2, 4, 10, 17, 32, 111, 152–4, 166, 168, 190, 207, 212–13, 224

Differentiation, 4, 22, 27, 36, 233

Diversification, 9–12, 90, 98, 104–5, 110–12, 115, 119, 133, 191, 194, 207

Ecological, 16, 42, 70, 229, 232, 235–44

Education, 5, 10, 15, 53, 86, 128–9, 136, 162, 177, 179, 181–2, 184, 195, 200–1, 208, 212, 220–2

Efficiency, 5, 8, 16, 35, 48–9, 51, 54, 58, 61, 69, 74–5, 85, 118, 153, 229, 244

El Salvador, 9, 40–2, 79–80, 83–4, 87–8, 90–4, 173–4

Employment, off-farm, 9, 15, 25, 119, 128, 181–2, 189–95, 197, 203–4, 206–8, 211, 222, 224, 226, 243–4

Enterprise, 9, 11, 39, 43, 46, 51, 58, 61, 64, 66–9, 71–2, 74–6, 81, 92, 95, 117, 122, 157, 161, 164, 166, 173, 191

Entitlement, 21, 24–6, 29, 33–4

Entrepreneur(ship), 99, 151, 155–6, 162, 167

Exchange, market, 1, 2, 9, 186, 193, 206

Exchange, non-market, 4–5, 7, 21–4, 26

Export, 7, 8, 22, 26, 39–47, 49, 51, 53–5, 58, 60, 75, 91, 95, 103, 173–4, 177–82, 184, 242

Extension, 3, 24, 45, 50, 146, 148, 213, 234, 242–4

Externalities, 166–8, 231

Fair trade, 8–9, 58–60

Farm size, 14, 28, 176, 191, 200, 214, 231, 243

Farmer (producer), commercial, 7, 26, 29–30

Farmer (producer), medium, 26, 32, 49, 663, 111, 117, 142, 151, 156, 173, 191

Farmer (producer), small, 7–9, 15, 21–7, 29–32, 34–5, 39, 45, 49–50, 52–3, 58, 61, 63, 65, 75, 79–80, 86, 88, 92, 94–5, 101, 103, 109, 111–12, 117, 135, 143, 148, 151, 155, 165, 171, 173, 177–8, 180, 189–95, 197–8, 200, 206–8, 212, 224, 228–31, 243–4

Fertilizer, 11, 16, 31–2, 101, 120, 180, 191, 193, 217, 228–9, 230–1, 233–5, 240–4

Finance, 10, 12–13, 23, 26, 28–30, 33–4, 49, 60, 100, 110, 141, 143–4, 148–9, 156, 161, 164, 166–7, 178, 185, 192, 194, 203, 207

Food (in)security, 6–7, 15, 21–6, 107, 189–90, 194–5, 198–9, 204–8, 218

Fragmentation, 17, 62, 80, 99, 103, 110–11, 190, 192

Gender, 15, 123, 142, 195, 200

Governance, 2, 5, 13, 17, 21, 34, 35, 46, 51–3, 71, 75, 151–6, 161–2, 164–7

Guatemala, 40–2, 47–52, 54

Herbicides, 180, 217, 230–1, 237–8, 240

Hierarchy, 2, 8, 17, 30, 51, 53–4, 58, 61–3, 65, 67, 68, 70–5

Honduras, 6–7, 15, 21–2, 25–6, 32, 34–5, 41, 148, 189, 190–3, 198, 200, 208, 210

Household, 2, 4, 11, 14–15, 24, 26–7, 29, 36, 104–5, 108, 118, 128, 171–86, 189–91, 193–5, 197–204, 206–8, 210–11, 213–14, 217, 220–2, 224, 226, 230, 232, 241–3

Import, 22, 60, 91

Income composition, 107, 178, 207

Income function, 14, 172, 177, 180–1, 183, 185

Income, off-farm/wage, 15, 110,
177–8, 180–1, 189, 190–2, 194–5,
197–208, 222
Income, source, 15, 104, 111, 189,
195, 197, 201–13, 205–7
Information, 1, 5, 8–9, 12–13, 16, 23,
42, 51, 53–5, 62, 64–5, 84–5, 115,
118–19, 144–5, 152–4, 157, 159,
163, 165, 167–8, 174, 178, 213,
225, 236
Infrastructure, 3, 5, 17, 44, 99, 102,
108–9, 113, 157, 208
Institution, financial/credit, 12, 14,
17, 69, 74, 106, 142–4, 147–8, 168,
179, 183, 185
Institutional arrangement, 21, 23–4,
26, 118
Institutional change, 6, 7, 13, 21,
23–4, 34, 67, 71, 141, 151–2, 166
Institutional environment, 4–6, 8, 11,
13, 61, 74, 120, 149, 151, 162, 243
Institutional failure, 2–3, 16
Institutional framework, 3–4, 7, 21,
34, 112
Institutional innovation, 154, 162,
164
Institutional linkage, 3, 133
Institutional structure, 61–3, 66,
68–70, 73, 86, 94
Integration, 2, 11, 45–6, 51, 54–5, 61,
72, 84, 89–90, 180, 211, 225
Intensification, 10, 11, 207, 229–31,
244
Investment, 9, 11, 14, 17, 44–5, 51,
86, 102–3, 105, 107–8, 110–13,
128, 154, 157, 160, 168, 171,
173–4, 176–7, 181, 183–5, 193–4,
203, 208, 211, 224, 230, 236

Knowledge, 1, 30, 43, 109–10, 136,
144–5, 148, 154, 159, 165–6, 181,
231

Land bank, 10, 34, 83–6, 92
Land market, 2, 9–10, 30, 79, 81, 83,
85–6, 88, 102, 108, 189–90, 192
Land reform, 1, 3, 9, 10, 26, 35–6,
79–88, 90, 99, 102–3, 115, 117,
153, 190, 193, 211

Land tenure, 28, 79, 87–8, 117, 220
Land titling, 9, 101, 117
Land transfer, 10, 81, 84–6
Landlord/owner, 7, 10, 24–6, 29–31,
33–5, 80–2, 84, 86, 98, 126, 153
Latin America, 74, 82, 86, 90, 115,
143–4, 149, 168, 189
Liberalization, 2–4, 7, 13, 17, 22, 40,
43, 54, 88, 92, 116–17, 144, 156
Livelihood, 2–4, 15–17, 22–3, 180,
189–90, 206, 210, 213, 221, 224,
232

Maize, 6–7, 21, 24–36, 88, 91,
99–100, 106, 108–10, 123, 173–4,
177, 193, 214, 217, 220–2, 225,
229–30, 234–8, 240–5
Management, 35, 85, 104–5, 110,
118, 127, 129, 135, 159–60, 163,
176, 180–1, 191, 194
Market, commodity/product, 1–2,
5–6, 8–9, 17, 103–4, 112, 171, 180,
189–90, 193, 195, 206
Market, factor/input, 192–4, 197
Market failure, 1, 15, 144, 186, 190,
193–5, 207
Market, (inter)national/world, 1, 3, 8,
40, 51, 53–4, 60, 73, 79, 91, 100,
174
Marketing, 1, 9–10, 22, 26, 32, 43,
46–7, 53, 60, 63–9, 72, 75, 115,
145, 173, 181
Migration, 14–16, 93, 104, 172, 193,
195, 210–26
Monitoring, 84, 157, 159, 161

Network, 1, 3–5, 8, 43, 46–7, 53, 64,
103, 105, 112–13, 133, 151–2,
154–7, 159, 161, 164–5, 167, 169
Nicaragua, 6–8, 10–11, 13, 15–16,
39–46, 50–2, 58, 61, 66, 71, 75, 98,
111, 115–16, 120–1, 134–6, 149,
151, 154–5, 162, 164, 168, 171–2,
180, 211–13, 215–16, 219, 222–5,
229, 232, 245

Opportunism, 54, 61–2, 71, 74–5,
153, 163

Organic, 16, 42, 53, 58–60, 68, 69–71, 73–5, 228, 233–4
Organization, local/grassroot, 66, 71, 162
Organization, peasant, 1–2, 90
Organization, social, 3, 61, 63, 71, 94, 112, 153, 155
Outreach, 12, 141–3, 145–6, 149, 160–1, 163

Parcellation, 11, 125, 128, 130, 133–4
Participation, 15, 17, 46, 50–1, 55, 58, 60–1, 79, 83, 85, 89, 113, 159, 163, 165, 167–8, 182, 189, 194, 197–201, 206, 208, 210–11
Pastures, 11, 26, 29–31, 125–6, 173, 182–3, 214, 233
Patron (-client), 5, 8, 13, 25, 62, 71, 151–3, 155, 163, 165, 168
Peasant, 1–3, 9–10, 15–17, 36, 39, 43, 49, 51, 55, 63–4, 80–2, 88, 90–1, 95, 99, 102–4, 106–7, 109, 111–14, 136, 155–6, 165, 171–4, 176–8, 180–1, 183–4, 189–91, 193, 206, 208, 210–14, 217–19, 220–6, 233
Pesticides, 180, 230–1, 238, 245
Poverty, 12, 34, 58, 61–3, 70–1, 73, 75, 93–4, 141–3, 146, 148, 151, 218
Price, market, 29–30, 32, 42, 174, 177
Price, producer, 50, 64
Privatization, 3, 43, 45, 80, 92, 143
Processing, 1, 7–8, 26, 41, 43, 45–9, 51–2, 55, 58, 59–60, 63, 66–7, 69–70, 72, 74–5, 89, 92, 144, 157, 166, 183, 194, 208, 214
Production system, 14–16, 99–100, 103, 105–6, 108–9, 111–13, 117, 123, 125–6, 130–1, 136, 172, 174, 180–1, 193, 210, 213, 220, 224, 228–30, 234, 242, 244–5
Production technology, 9, 16, 181
Property right, 1, 3, 9, 17, 34, 98, 101–2, 111, 167

Remittances, 15, 25, 91, 129, 131, 147, 177–8, 195, 199, 201–8
Risk, 9, 12, 14, 104–5, 110, 115, 119, 130, 133, 154, 176, 185, 190–1, 194–5, 197, 207, 217, 228

Savings, 5, 14, 142, 160–1, 174, 184, 189, 192, 197, 204
Seed, 11, 31–2, 36, 40–3, 45–9, 51–3, 55, 120, 162, 230, 236–7, 240, 245
Sesame, 7–8, 39–55, 99, 123
Sharecropping, 101, 220–1
Soil, fertility, 89, 99, 109, 117, 229, 243
Soil, nutrients, 101, 228–9, 233
Squatter, 83–7, 204
State, 3–7, 10, 17, 22, 25–6, 32, 34, 43, 45, 55, 63, 74–5, 81, 83–4, 91–2, 101, 105, 116, 136, 143, 149, 161
Storage, 1, 43, 47, 60, 89, 92, 157
Structural adjustment, 3, 10–11, 14, 17, 91, 95, 110, 116, 156
Subsidies, 3, 10, 13, 17, 39, 44, 67, 91, 100, 116, 118, 155–7, 168
Sustainability, 13, 71, 142–3, 145–6, 149, 157, 161, 185, 228, 230–2

Technical assistance, 49, 52–3, 69, 72–5, 86–7, 92, 158, 179, 181–2, 184, 192, 201, 208
Tenancy, 201, 235–6, 242–3
Tobacco, 26, 30, 91, 223
Transaction, 1, 4–5, 7, 12–13, 17, 22–3, 31, 33, 48–9, 51, 53–4, 60, 62, 65, 69, 75, 94, 106, 118, 120, 144, 148–9, 154–6, 165, 174–6, 185–6, 192, 195
Transaction cost, 1, 5, 12–13, 17, 49, 53–4, 60, 62, 65, 69, 106, 120, 144, 148–9, 154, 156, 165, 174–6, 185, 192, 195
Transport, 1, 60, 65, 89, 157, 166, 172
Trust, 9, 62, 68, 160–4

Velvet bean, 16, 229, 234–7, 241, 243–5
Village, 15, 26–33, 152, 157, 162, 167, 169, 173, 213, 218–21, 233, 235

Wage, 3, 14–16, 23, 26–30, 32–3, 36, 93, 101, 104–7, 134, 135, 156, 159, 189, 190–1, 193–5, 197–208, 222–4
Water, 89, 99, 109, 111, 245